Battle *of* Britain

Battle *of* Britain

JON LAKE

amber
BOOKS

ISBN: 978-1-78274-744-4

Published by
Amber Books Ltd
United House
North Road
London N7 9DP
United Kingdom
www.amberbooks.co.uk
Instagram: amberbooksltd
Facebook: www.facebook.com/amberbooks
Twitter: @amberbooks

Project Editor: Charles Catton
Editor: Chris McNab
Designer: Jeremy Williams
Picture Research: TRH Pictures

PICTURE CREDITS
Aerospace Publishing Ltd: 1, 9 (t), 37 (b), 42 (m), 69, 88 (b), 150 (b), 156, 172, 183 (t), 189, 191, 192 (b), 201 (m), 215. Hugh W. Cowin: 30, 34, 36 (t), 51 (b), 78 (m), 126 (t), 127, 133 (b), 136 (t), 160 (b), 168 (t), 204 (t), 231. The Robert Hunt Library: 6-7, 9 (b) (Imperial War Museum), 15 (b), 16 (t), 17, 19 (t), 24 (t), 36 (b), 40 (t), 42 (t), 43 (t), 43 (b), 44 (b), 46 (t), 47 (b), 53 (b), 55, 57 (Bundesarchiv), 59 (b) (Bundesarchiv), 60 (b) (Bundesarchiv), 63 (Bundesarchiv), 68, 75 (b) (M.O.D), 81, 90 (t), 94 (t), 103, 114, 116-117, 122 (b), 125 (Imperial War Museum), 131 (t), 132, 134 (b), 135, 137 (t), 140, 144 (b), 152, 165 (t), 169, 170 (m), 180 (b), 184 (t), 186-187, 188 (b), 190 (t), 194, 195 (t), 195 (b), 202 (b), 208 (t), 208 (b), 217 (b), 224 (t). TRH Pictures: 8, 10-11, 12 (b) (Imperial War Museum), 12-13 (Imperial War Museum), 13 (r) (Imperial War Museum), 14 (t), 14 (m) (Imperial War Museum), 15 (mr), 18 (m), 18 (t), 19 (b), 20, 21 (t) (Imperial War Museum), 22, 23 (b), 23 (t), 24 (b), 25 (b) (Imperial War Museum), 26 (t) (Imperial War Museum), 26 (b), 27 (t) (Imperial War Museum), 27 (b), 28 (t) (Imperial War Museum), 28 (b) (Imperial War Museum), 29 (t) (RAF), 32, 33 (t), 33 (b), 35, 37 (t), 38, 39, 40 (b), 41 (t), 41 (m), 44 (t), 46 (b), 47 (t), 47 (m), 48, 49, 50 (t), 53 (t), 54, 58, 59 (t) (Imperial War Museum), 60 (t), 61, 62, 64 (t), 64 (b), 65, 67, 70-71, 72 (t) (Imperial War Museum), 72 (b) (M.O.D), 73, 74 (Vickers), 75 (t&b) (M.O.D), 77, 78 (t), 78 (b) (Vickers), 79, 80 (b), 82, 83 (all), 84 (NASM), 85, 86, 87 (both), 88 (t) (Imperial War Museum), 90 (b), 91, 92, 93, 94 (b), 95 (t), 95 (b), 96 (both), 97 (t), 97 (b) (Imperial War Museum), 98 (Imperial War Museum), 99 (both), 100, 101, 102, 104, 105 (both), 106 (both), 107, 108 (t) (Imperial War Museum), 108 (b), 109, 110 (Imperial War Museum), 111 (both), 112 (t), 112 (m) (RAF Museum), 113, 115, 118 (b), 119, 120 (all), 121, 122 (t&m), 123, 124 (t), 124 (b), 126 (b), 129 (both), 130 (both), 131 (Imperial War Museum), 133 (t), 134 (t) (Imperial War Museum), 136 (m) (Imperial War Museum), 137 (b), 138 (both), 141, 142, 143 (RAF Museum), 144 (b) (Imperial War Museum), 146-147 (Imperial War Museum), 148, 149 (t) (Imperial War Museum), 149 (b), 150 (t), 151, 153 (both), 154-155, 155 (both) (Imperial War Museum), 158 (b), 159, 160 (t), 161, 162, 163 (m&t) (Imperial War Museum), 163 (b), 164 (t) (Imperial War Museum), 164 (b), 165 (b) (RAF Museum), 166, 167, 168 (b), 170 (t) (Imperial War Museum), 171 (both), 174 (Imperial War Museum), 175 (t) (Imperial War Museum), 175 (b), 176 (t) (RAF Museum), 176 (b), 177, 178 (Imperial War Museum), 179 (t&b), 179 (m) (Imperial War Museum), 180 (t) (Imperial War Museum), 181, 182 (both), 183 (m) (RAF Museum), 184 (b), 188 (m), 190 (b), 192 (t), 196 (both), 197 (Imperial War Museum), 198 (both), 199, 200 (both), 201 (t) (Imperial War Museum), 202 (t), 203 (US National Archive), 204 (b), 205 (both), 206 (both), 207 (US National Archives), 209 (both) (Imperial War Museum), 210 (all), 211 (both), 212 (t), 212 (b) (Imperial War Museum), 213 (both), 214 (t), 216 (both), 217 (t), 218, 219, 222-223 (Imperial War Museum), 224 (b), 225 (Imperial War Museum), 241.

ILLUSTRATIONS
All artworks courtesy of Orbis Publishing, with the exception of the following:
Aerospace Publishing Ltd: 173. Amber Books Ltd: 52 (b), endpapers. Mainline Design: 187. Pilot Press Ltd: 16 (b), 25 (t), 50, 68, 74, 85 (b), 127, 141, 158 (t), 177, 214, 218, 226, 227, 228, 230, 232, 234, 236, 237, 238, 240, 242, 243.

Contents

A Close-Run Thing

THE RAF'S NEW FIGHTER, THE SUPERMARINE SPITFIRE,
BEGINS ACTIVE SERVICE WITH NO.19 SQUADRON, THE
FIRST UNIT TO RECEIVE THE TYPE, IN 1938. THESE EARLY
EXAMPLES OF ONE OF THE KEY FIGHTERS IN THE BATTLE
ARE NOTABLE FOR THEIR TWIN-BLADED WATTS PROPELLORS,
WHICH WERE LATER REPLACED BY TRIPLE-BLADED VERSIONS.

RIGHT: A FAMOUS
CONTEMPORARY CARTOON,
SHOWING BRITISH
DEFIANCE IN THE WAKE OF
FRANCE'S DEFEAT AND THE
EVACUATION AT DUNKIRK.
A BRITISH TOMMY WAVES
HIS FIST IN DEFIANCE OF
THE GERMAN BOMBERS ON
THE HORIZON.

"VERY WELL , ALONE "

One of the most pervasive views of the Battle of Britain was that heavily out-numbered but superior British pilots won their victory against overwhelming German forces through grit, courage and skill alone. This common perception, still widely held, also lays great stress on the wartime propagandist belief that the German fighter pilots were no match for their opponents. Yet it is worth reinvestigating the truth of what actually happened, as the Battle was in many ways a victory for the RAF's cautious tactics, tactics that ensured the survival of a Fighter Command which, though more than equal in courage and determination, was no match for the Germans when it came to combat experience and tactical expertise. The Battle was a 'close run thing', and if we ignore the German bomber losses, the *Jagdwaffe* caused greater damage than it sustained from Fighter Command.

There are nearly as many interpretations of the Battle, and its significance, as there are books about the subject. Many of the issues remain matters of great controversy amongst historians and academics, and even among the survivors of those who fought. Most books have tended to 'take sides' and few offer a balanced view of the battle and the arguments surrounding it. This book is therefore intended both as a straightforward narrative history of the Battle, but also as a guide to some of the controversies and arguments.

Unlike a land battle, even dating the Battle of Britain poses problems. The German Luftwaffe began flying sporadic sorties over Britain even as the Battle of France raged, and the campaign against Britain slowly built in intensity, before declining into an ongoing campaign of night attacks against British cities and a sporadic series of single-aircraft 'hit-and-run' raids. This makes precise dating almost impossible, and many different start and finish dates have been suggested. The MoD has used the period from 10 July through to 31 October, or 8 August to 15 September, while other 'start dates' have included 6, 8,

11, 12, or 13 August, and other closing dates
have included 30 September, and 5 October,
most of which are arbitrary. In this book, the
Battle of Britain covers the months of July,
August, September and October 1940.

Even the importance of the Battle
has been questioned. Conventional wisdom
is that by defeating the Luftwaffe, the RAF
saved Britain from invasion, leaving Britain
an unsinkable 'aircraft carrier' and eventual
springboard for D-Day. Hitler was forced to

fight on two fronts, leading to his eventual defeat. But some experts question whether the
Luftwaffe was defeated in 1940, and many question whether an invasion could ever have
succeeded. Others even question whether Hitler ever seriously intended to invade at all.

What is less open to question is that the Battle of Britain was seen by the British as
a 'historic victory' (at a time when Britain badly needed one), and this in itself encouraged
the country to keep up the war effort. Few acknowledged the slenderness of the margin of
victory. Many viewed the battle as marking a humiliating defeat for Germany, undermining
the myth of Nazi invincibility, and encouraging resistance throughout occupied Europe.
It may even have influenced those in power in isolationist America, who perhaps doubted
Britain's ability to carry on the fight, to provide aid for the latter's struggle against Hitler.

I hope that this book helps the reader to make up his or her own mind about the Battle's
importance, but above all, I hope that it can act as a suitable tribute to and reminder of
Churchill's famous 'Few' sixty years on from the Battle.

ABOVE: SCRAMBLE! IN A
SCENE THAT WOULD SOON
BECOME FAMILIAR TO
ALL RAF FIGHTER PILOTS
DURING THE BATTLE, THESE
HURRICANE PILOTS RACE
FOR THEIR MACHINES.

LEFT: BARRAGE BALLOONS,
SEEN HERE OVER
BUCKINGHAM PALACE
EARLY IN THE WAR, WERE
INTENDED TO FRIGHTEN OFF
ENEMY BOMBERS, OR AT
LEAST DISTURB THEIR AIM.
THE HIGH-TENSION WIRES
ATTACHING THEM TO THE
GROUND COULD CUT AN
AIRCRAFT'S WING IN TWO.

CHAPTER 1

The Build-up to War

ADOLF HITLER, LEADER OF THE NEWLY-FORMED NAZI
PARTY, AND HIS HENCHMEN PICTURED AT A RALLY OF THE
SA DURING THE PERIOD OF HIS RISE TO POWER.
WITHIN A DECADE, HE WOULD PLUNGE THE WORLD INTO
A TERRIBLE WAR.

The roots of the Battle of Britain go back long before the outbreak of the Second World War. Some authors on the Battle even go back to the German raids on mainland Britain in the latter part of the First World War. The mighty Zeppelin airships and Belgian-based Gotha heavy bombers had struck terror into the civilian populace, generating a demand for effective air defences, while causing little physical damage. These raids were certainly one of the factors which led to the establishment and survival of an independent Royal Air Force, but their further relevance is at best questionable.

There is little doubt, however, that the punitive and humiliating peace (and the impossibly swingeing reparations bill) imposed on Germany at Versailles in June 1919 left a festering sense of resentment and a simmering desire for revenge, and for the recovery of areas like the Saar and Alsace Lorraine. But many in Britain and France had wanted to 'Squeeze Germany until the Pips Squeak!' and were unable to see that they were creating perfect conditions for totalitarianism and dictatorship. Against this background the rise of Adolf Hitler and the Nazi party should not be surprising.

Once Hitler's Nazi party became the largest force in the German Reichstag in 1932 (a democratic achievement, it should be noted), German rearmament gathered pace. It became increasingly likely that war would result from Germany's efforts to overturn what was seen by many as an unjust and humiliating peace treaty. Germany withdrew from the League of Nations Disarmament Conference on 14 October 1933, and a new air force, the Luftwaffe, began to be formed under Herman Göring (one of Hitler's most trusted Nazi lieutenants) and Erhard Milch, then the head of the German airline Lufthansa. Trainee pilots were given rudimentary military training (initially in secret) at gliding schools or in Russia.

Hitler, already the leader of the largest party in the Reichstag, became Chancellor in 1933 at President von Hindenburg's invitation, on the resignation of von Schleicher. The Chancellor was the effective head of government in Germany, though the ageing and ailing von Hindenburg remained the nominal head of state. Hitler combined the offices of President and Chancellor when he became Führer in August 1934 on the death of Hindenburg. German

rearmament and militarisation gathered speed, and soon
became sufficiently frightening to draw a response in
the rest of Europe. Pacifism seemed to have had its day,
and comfortable assumptions like the ten year rule (the
assumption, renewed annually, that there would be no war
for a decade) were abandoned.

When Hitler announced the existence of his Luftwaffe
on 27 March 1935, he claimed parity with Britain's
Royal Air Force (though this was an idle boast, since
most of the Luftwaffe's aeroplanes were trainers) and
stated his intention to achieve parity with France. The
British and French failed to differentiate propaganda
from fact, and Hitler's boasting merely served to spur
further, and rather more serious, expansion.

Hitler's aims to re-establish a 'Greater Germany'
with borders broadly equivalent to those existing
before 1918 were achieved without much bloodshed.
He gained control of the Saarland following a
plebiscite, and marched into the Rhineland unopposed. But this
represented the re-incorporation of areas which most observers viewed as being 'rightly
German' and few made a fuss. Unfortunately, the lack of opposition encouraged Hitler to
annex Austria in the so-called 'Anschluss' of March 1938. The Austrians were, of course,
a Germanic people, speaking German, and the Nazis (and their Anschluss) did enjoy
considerable support there. There was thus little international reaction.

The next step was taken in September 1938, when the German army marched into the
Sudetenland, border areas of Czechoslovakia occupied by so-called Sudeten Germans.
This was arguably Hitler's biggest gamble, since many believed that he would have had
to back down had Britain and France stood up to him. But instead, a cynical promise
not to invade the remainder of Czechoslovakia ensured British and French complicity in
this latest piece of German aggression. Britain's Prime Minister, Neville Chamberlain,
returned to Croydon from the negotiations at Munich waving his worthless piece of paper

ABOVE: BOMB DAMAGE
IN LONDON FOLLOWING A
RAID BY GOTHAS. TYPICAL
BOMB LOAD ON A CROSS-
CHANNEL RAID WAS SIX
50KG (110LB) BOMBS,
ABOUT HALF THE MAXIMUM
LOAD. THE GOTHAS WERE
WELL DEFENDED AND AGILE.

RIGHT: BY 1918 THE
BRITISH AIR DEFENCES WERE
WELL ORGANISED. AIRCRAFT
LIKE THE BRISTOL FIGHTER
PLAYED A PROMINENT
PART, CONTROLLED BY
AN EXTREMELY ADVANCED
GROUND ORGANISATION.

BELOW: THE CREW
COMPARTMENT OF AN
UNIDENTIFIED ZEPPELIN
BROUGHT DOWN NEAR
LONDON. IN ALL, 380
ZEPPELIN CREWMEN
LOST THEIR LIVES ON
ACTIVE SERVICE.

and prophesying 'peace in our time'. Whether or not he believed Herr Hitler's assurances is perhaps a moot point, since Britain was similarly unprepared for war.

Five months later, in March 1939, Hitler did invade the rest of Czechoslovakia, whose border defences had already been lost along with the Sudetenland. But although Czechoslovakia was a sovereign country, on which Germany had no legitimate claim, it was a relatively new invention, and the international community again stood by and watched as Hitler invaded.

Hitler was then in no position to fight had Britain or France intervened, and the invasion of Czechoslovakia is sometimes seen as having been his greatest gamble. The lack of response from Britain and France was noted, and virtually condemned Poland to the same fate. In 1939, when briefing his commanders for the assault on Poland, Hitler reassured them by saying: 'I have witnessed the miserable worms Churchill and Daladier in Munich; they will be too cowardly to attack and will go no further than blockade.'

EUROPE AT WAR

By mid-1939, Hitler's biggest remaining grievance was the continued separation of East Prussia from the rest of Germany, the two countries separated by Poland's occupation of the German-speaking port of Danzig and the corridor of territory to it. Had Hitler's growing threats against Poland been acceded to, there is some doubt as to whether war was inevitable. Some would suggest that his subsequent campaigns against Britain, France and the Low

Countries were a direct response to the Anglo-French declaration of war, and that he was essentially content with his western borders. Others would maintain that Hitler's ambitions were more grandiose, and that he always harboured designs on the whole of Poland and on a swathe of territory further east to provide *Lebensraum* (living space) for the Germanic, Aryan people. It is also argued that his hatred of Bolshevism was sufficient to make war with Russia inevitable. But any analysis of Hitler's war aims is fraught with difficulties. His stated intentions were often confused and contradictory, and there was little to differentiate planning options from concrete intentions. Compounding the problems of interpretation, the Third Reich operated with an astonishing degree of freedom from written orders, with Hitler's subordinates often left free to interpret their master's wishes.

But, at the end of the day, such speculation is no more than an interesting diversion. Much to Hitler's astonishment, especially after their failure to react to his seizure of Czechoslovakia, Britain and France fulfilled their treaty obligations when he invaded Poland on 1 September 1939. Britain issued an ultimatum for Germany to withdraw, and then declared war on 3 September. This was something of a forlorn gesture, since Britain felt that it could not actually do anything to intervene directly on Poland's behalf. Britain thus found itself forced to stand by and watch impotently as Hitler's *Blitzkrieg* began. It is arguable that with Hitler's attention turned to the East, Britain and France could, and should, have attacked Germany in the West, forcing him to dilute his attack on Poland. Whether that would have changed the outcome, and whether the British or the French were in any position to intervene in September 1939 will forever be a matter for speculation and debate. But the Franco-British declaration of war changed the whole situation. Even this

In 1939, when briefing his commanders for the assault on Poland, Hitler reassured them by saying: 'I have witnessed the miserable worms Churchill and Daladier in Munich; they will be too cowardly to attack and will go no further than blockade.'

ABOVE: THE SPANISH CIVIL WAR (1936-39) GAVE THE LUFTWAFFE IN-VALUABLE COMBAT EXPERIENCE. ADOLF GALLAND, A GERMAN FIGHTER ACE OF WWII, IS SEATED ON THE RIGHT.

LEFT: AN EARLY MESSERSCHMITT BF 109 FLYING LOW OVER SPANISH NATIONALIST TRENCHES. IT OUTCLASSED EVERY OTHER FIGHTER IN THE CIVIL WAR.

ABOVE: UNIT PRIDE WAS AN IMPORTANT FACTOR IN THE DEVELOPMENT OF THE LUFTWAFFE. HERE, GERMAN AIRMEN PARADE THEIR SQUADRON INSIGNIA IN FRONT OF A HEINKEL HE 111 BOMBER.

RIGHT: THE WELLINGTON BOMBER WAS ONE OF BRITAIN'S MOST ADVANCED DESIGNS AT THE OUTBREAK OF WWII, AND WAS HEAVILY INVOLVED IN THE BOMBING OF GERMANY IN THE EARLY YEARS.

half-hearted response forced Hitler to plan a knock-out blow in the West before he could turn his attentions towards what had always been his primary target – Russia.

Hitler's previous territorial gains had been made without a shot being fired, and the Luftwaffe had played only the most minor part (transporting 2000 troops to Vienna during Germany's annexation of Austria in 1938, for example). But in Poland the Germans expected, and met, fierce resistance.

Without assistance, Poland succumbed quickly, although the efforts of its armed forces (cavalry against tanks, obsolete PZL P-11 open-cockpit fighters against Messerschmitt Bf 109s) soon became the stuff of legend. But it would be wrong to accept the simplified view of the campaign, since the battle for Poland was far from being a walkover. The out-numbered and out-gunned Polish air force imposed heavy cost on the invaders, particularly when the fighters were cut free from their rigid links to specific regionally deployed ground formations. Even though the PZL P.11 was slower than any of the frontline German combat types (with the exception of the Junkers Ju 87 and Henschel Hs 123 and Hs 126), it performed surprisingly well. Only 12 P.11 pilots were killed, seven posted missing, and 11 wounded, while 116 of the aircraft were downed (including eight to friendly ground fire). In turn, they accounted for 116 enemy aircraft, and on one occasion a P.11 pilot (Lt Col Pamula of No.114 Squadron) shot down a Ju 87, and a Heinkel He 111 before running out of ammunition. He then rammed an escorting Bf 109 and baled out to fight again! Poland lost 264 aircraft to enemy action, with 116 more fleeing to Romania, and it lost 234 aircrew killed or missing in action. Some pilots escaped to France and Britain, where many continued the fight. The Luftwaffe lost 285 aircraft (with 279 more suffering severe damage), and 189 aircrew killed, 224 missing, and 126 wounded. But while the campaign was not quite the walkover that has sometimes been portrayed, the end was inevitable, even before Russia invaded from the east on 17 September. Warsaw finally fell on 27 September.

Hitler next turned his attentions to Scandinavia, launching an invasion of Norway aimed at safeguarding supplies of Swedish iron ore to the Ruhr, and at securing his left flank for his

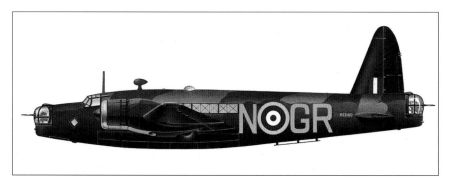

planned assault on Russia. Hitler launched his invasion of Denmark and southern Norway on 9 April 1940, and six days later British land forces went ashore at Narvik. Britain had already planned a limited occupation of northern Norway to deny Germany the use of Narvik, a strategically vital port giving open access to the North Sea and a potential base for German naval raiders. Most of the British Gladiator aircraft supporting the troops were destroyed on the ground during the next few days, and most of the force was evacuated between 30 May and 2 April. The Gladiators did fly 49 sorties, however, recording 37 attacks on enemy aircraft and achieving six confirmed victories and eight 'probables'. The last three aircraft had been destroyed by 27 April.

LEFT: GERMAN TROOPS MARCH TRIUMPHANTLY INTO CZECHOSLOVAKIA, MARCH 1939. ALLIED INERTIA OVER GERMANY'S EXPANSION PERSUADED HITLER TO PROCEED WITH PLANS TO INVADE POLAND THAT SUMMER.

Hitler's previous territorial gains had been made without a shot being fired, and the Luftwaffe had played only the most minor part (transporting 2000 troops to Vienna during Germany's annexation of Austria in 1938, for example). But in Poland the Germans expected, and met, fierce resistance.

> Many Germans harboured a strong desire to take revenge on France, and to humiliate the French as they felt they had been humiliated in 1918.

TOP: AUSTRIAN CUSTOMS OFFICIALS CAST ASIDE A BARRIER ON THE FRONTIER WITH GERMANY. THE 'ANSCHLUSS' WITH AUSTRIA WAS THE FIRST STEP ON THE ROAD TO HITLER'S 'GREATER REICH'.

ABOVE: PZL P.11 FIGHTERS OF THE POLISH AIR FORCE. OF THE 175 AIRCRAFT DELIVERED, 114 WERE LOST, BUT NOT BEFORE THEY HAD DESTROYED 120 GERMAN AIRCRAFT.

The assault on Narvik was renewed with newly arrived Gloster Gladiators and Hawker Hurricanes, and a mixed force of Norwegian, British, Polish and French units finally took the port. The new batch of No.263 Squadron Gladiators flew 389 sorties and gained 26 kills in 69 combats, while the Hurricanes clocked up 26 combats, achieving 11 confirmed kills and eight probables. Hitler was furious, and on 5 May, with the deadlines for his offensive against France and the Low Countries getting closer, he ordered General Stumpff to intensify his attacks on the British enclave at Narvik. Even without the Battle of France diverting away resources and attention, sustaining the isolated garrison at Narvik was never going to be a long-term option, and it was evacuated on 8 June. The eight surviving Gladiators and 10 remaining Hurricanes were flown onto the aircraft carrier HMS *Glorious* on 7 June, but unfortunately the ship was sunk the next day, and only two of the pilots survived.

Even while the Norwegian campaign reached its closing stages, and on the very day that Chamberlain resigned (10 May), the Wehrmacht launched another lightning offensive (*Blitzkrieg*), this time against France and the Low Countries.

WAR IN THE WEST

Apart from the German invasion of Denmark and Norway (seen by many as a prelude to wider European conquests), things remained ominously quiet on the Western Front following the fall of Poland. At one time, Hitler had hoped to launch his assault in the West on 12 November 1939, but was persuaded to delay. During this delay each side studiously avoided overtly hostile actions, shying away from bombing enemy territory (though enemy warships and military ports were considered fair game) and conducting cursory reconnaissance missions. German bombers attacked Royal Navy warships at sea and in open harbours, but great care was taken to avoid bombs falling where they might harm civilians. Thus when Ju 88s set out for Scotland to bomb HMS *Hood* in the Firth of Forth on 16 October 1939, but found it in harbour at Rosyth amidst more densely populated areas, they attacked other targets still in the Firth to avoid civilian casualties. RAF bombers operated under much the same constraints in their attacks on German naval targets. Referred to in Britain as the 'Phoney War' or 'Sitzkrieg', and in France as 'la Drôle de Guerre' (Joke War), the period saw Britain and France strengthening their defences. The UK provided a massive Expeditionary Force in France, including an Air Component of fighter and bomber squadrons, and a separate Advanced Air Striking Force.

As time passed it became increasingly clear that Hitler was planning a massive attack on France, driven partly by the need to avoid fighting on two fronts when he launched his attack on Russia, and partly motivated by his desire to avenge the humiliations of the Versailles Treaty which had ended the First World War. Many Germans harboured a strong desire to take revenge on France, and to humiliate the French as they felt they had been humiliated in 1918. Starting with the Franco-Prussian War of 1871, France and Germany (or more accurately Prussia) had already fought twice within less than a century, and 'round three' was eagerly awaited by the more bellicose members of German society and the military.

But while these attitudes were well known in France, and while even French intelligence was able to detect the massive build-up of forces along its borders, there was an underlying

CHURCHILL BECOMES PRIME MINISTER

The reputation of Neville Chamberlain, the British Prime Minister, was by now tarnished by the fiasco of the Munich negotiations (though many at the time had supported his attempts to avoid the onset of war). He came under increasing criticism in the House of Commons as the war in Norway raged. Even the Liberal leader and former Premier David Lloyd George (who had himself visited Germany and returned warmly endorsing 'Mr Hitler's great achievements') commented that 'The Prime Minister has appealed for sacrifice – he should now sacrifice the seals of office.' Others were more direct. 'In the name of God, Go!', he was told. Bowing to the inevitable Chamberlain resigned, and his Conservative government was replaced by a 'National Coalition' led by the Conservative First Lord of the Admiralty, Winston Churchill.

LEFT: GERMAN GROUND CREW SNATCHING A REST BESIDE A HEINKEL HE 111 BOMBER BETWEEN SORTIES OVER POLAND. THE GROUND MECHANICS WERE KNOWN AS 'SCHWARZE' (BLACKIES) BY THE AIRCREW.

RIGHT: THIS FAKED
PROPAGANDA PHOTOGRAPH
PURPORTS TO SHOW A
HEINKEL HE 111 BOMBER
RELEASING ITS LOAD OVER
THE DOOMED CITY OF
WARSAW. THE MASSED
ATTACKS ON WARSAW,
KNOWN AS OPERATION
SEASIDE, BEGAN ON 13
SEPTEMBER 1939.

The period of genteel jousting over the French borders came to an end on 10 May 1940, when Hitler revealed his strategy for avoiding a frontal assault on France's heavily fortified frontier. He attacked through the Netherlands and Belgium, ignoring the neutral status of the two countries. The Netherlands fell after only four days, its air force being virtually annihilated on the ground, while Belgium lasted little longer.

assumption that the vast fortresses of the Siegfried and Maginot Lines would produce a stalemate, and that any German assault would be enormously costly and doomed to eventual failure.

Thus throughout the autumn and winter of 1939 and the spring of 1940, activity on the Western Front was largely limited to the interception of enemy reconnaissance aircraft. Flying Officer W.O. 'Boy' Mould of No.1 Squadron drew first blood for the RAF, downing a Dornier Do 17 over his own airfield on 30 October. Flying Officer E.J. 'Cobber' Kain shot down another on 8 November, opening what was to be an impressive score. This first engagement took place at 27,000ft and marked the highest air combat recorded to that date. On 23 November, Kain downed another Do 17 and on that same day No.73

Squadron accounted for three Do 17s, while No.1 Squadron bagged a pair of Heinkel He 111s. The tempo of air fighting increased in March 1940, giving Kain the chance to become the RAF's first 'ace' of World War II, downing a single Bf 109 on 3 March, followed by two more on 26 March.

While Nos 1 and 73 Squadrons served with the Advanced Air Striking Force in France, and Nos 85 and 87 with the BEF's Air Component, Fighter Command units in the UK were also getting to grips with the enemy. Nos 43, 111 and 605 Squadrons in particular saw action against German bombers and reconnaissance aircraft attempting to attack Scapa Flow, several Hurricane pilots opening their scores with Dornier Do 17s and Heinkel He 111s.

The period of genteel jousting over the French borders came to an end on 10 May 1940, when Hitler revealed his strategy for avoiding a frontal assault on France's heavily fortified frontier. He attacked through the Netherlands and Belgium, ignoring the neutral status of the two countries. The Netherlands fell after only four days, its air force being virtually annihilated on the ground, while Belgium lasted little longer. The supposedly impregnable Fort Eben Emael fell to a 55-man glider-borne assault force, cracking open the entire Belgian defences.

The Germans captured the key crossings of the Albert Canal and this allowed the Wehrmacht to continue its advance. The German forces involved in the offensive (136 Divisions) were actually smaller than those of the combined British, French, Belgian and Dutch armies which faced them. Yet they were better equipped, considerably more mobile, with more and better armour and artillery, and the advantage of surprise and well-rehearsed plans. Crucially, the German forces on the ground were supported by a bigger, experienced and well-equipped air force, and operated under a unified command structure. Germany fielded 3824 warplanes for the attack on France, including 860 Messerschmitt Bf 109s, 350 Bf 110s, 380 dive bombers, 1300 bombers, 300 long-range reconnaissance and 340 short-range reconnaissance aircraft. This represented massive superiority, with the Bf 110s alone outnumbering the combined strengths of the Belgian and Dutch air forces, and with Germany fielding more Bf 109s than the entire frontline strength of the French Armée de l'Air.

Quite apart from the situation at the front, France was in deep trouble. A pervading pessimism (verging on defeatism) permeated government, the populace and the armed forces. As if this were not bad enough, the armed forces were equipped with obsolete and inadequate weapons, a direct result of the rampant corruption of the recent years. During the immediate pre-war period a favoured furniture manufacturer had been given the contract to build an all-metal aircraft, for example, while a paint-maker had gained the contract for parachutes. The newly-nationalised aircraft industry was in chaos, and modern aircraft ready to enter service failed to reach the front in time to make any real

EARLY BRITISH SUCCESS

A number of pilots gained victories during this period, some of whom subsequently passed on their experience during the early stages of the Battle of Britain. Those who gained large numbers of successes included Flying Officer Leslie Clisby, Flight Lieutenant Peter Prosser Hanks, Flight Lieutenant Peter 'Johnny' Walker of No.1 Squadron, Flying Officer Newell ('Fanny') Orton, Sergeant Harold Paul of No.73 Squadron. By the time the 'Phoney War' ended, No.1 Squadron had accounted for 26 enemy aircraft, while No.73 had downed 30.

difference. Crippling shortages of spare parts and modern servicing equipment further eroded preparedness, while ill-trained aircrew received little direction from a General Staff which had no real grasp of strategy or modern tactics, and lacked a modern reporting system. Small wonder then that the French air force 'Shattered into a thousand pieces at the first blow'. Thus the small (but highly professional) British force in France was of disproportionate value.

Britain's BEF under Lord Gort had moved forward into Belgium as the German offensive began, forming part of a defensive chain stretching between the Meuse, Namur and Antwerp. But any chain is only as good as its weakest link, and when the retreating Belgian Army failed to fill the gap between the BEF and the French Seventh Army, von Rundstedt broke through on 13 May. This cut off the BEF and the Seventh Army from the rest of France, and marked the beginning of the end.

Before the breakthrough, the RAF had eight Hurricane squadrons in France, with Nos 3, 79, 501 and 504 Squadrons reinforcing the BEF's Air Component from 10 and 11 May. These were reinforced by No.11 Group squadrons flying patrols from their English bases. On 13 May, pilots from home-based squadrons were sent to reinforce the French-based units. No.3 Squadron received pilots from Nos 32, 56 and 253 Squadrons, No.85 from Nos 145 and 213, No.607 from Nos 151, 242, and 245, and No.615 Squadron from Nos 151, 229 and 601 Squadrons.

In one week from 10 May, no less than 27 Hurricane pilots became aces, while during the entire Battle of France up until 21 May, Hurricane pilots claimed 499 kills. Some 299 of these were subsequently confirmed as falling to RAF fighters by a post-war study of German records. The battle as a whole produced 41 RAF fighter aces. This was a remarkable achievement, and one accomplished despite the RAF's continuing reliance on discredited tactics, and despite the fact that many of the aircraft involved were early Mark I Hurricanes, with two-bladed wooden propellers. It would be a mistake, however, to regard the Battle of France as having been fought by the Hurricane alone. British fighters based in France formed only a small proportion of the overall Fighter Command effort, and the Spitfire also played a major role, albeit while operating from airfields in southern England. Even the Defiant had a part to play – No.264 Squadron actually amassed a tally of 65 victories by 31 May, and accounted for 17 Bf 109s and 11 Ju 87s and Ju 88s in a single day. But the undoubted

achievements of the RAF fighters in France were quite naturally over-shadowed by the terrible losses suffered by the Battle and Blenheim light bombers, and, of course, by the fact that the campaign ended in humiliating defeat.

Many called for greater efforts, and pushed for the despatch of further squadrons to France to try and stem the German advance. 'Where', asked some, 'were the Spitfires?' Air Marshall Sir John Slessor, for example, pointed out that '500 or 600 good short-range fighters sitting in England' would be unable to influence the course of a war which would effect Britain's future. 'Our quite natural and proper obsession' with the danger of a knock-out blow in France, he thought, was leading to an over-insular outlook. Defeat in France would, after all, inevitably increase pressure on Britain, and the battle to save England was effectively already being fought over Belgium and France.

ABOVE: DRESSED IN THEIR GAMES KIT, BOYS FROM A LONDON PUBLIC SCHOOL DIG THE FOUNDATIONS OF AN AIR RAID SHELTER IN THE SCHOOL GROUNDS.

LEFT: HEINKEL HE 111 SHOT DOWN OVER LAKE LESJASKOG, NORWAY, BY SQN LDR DONALDSON AND FLT LT MILLS OF NO 263 SQUADRON RAF, FLYING GLOSTER GLADIATOR BIPLANE FIGHTERS.

RIGHT: BRITISH ANTI-AIRCRAFT ARTILLERY ON THE WESTERN FRONT IN THE WINTER OF 1939-40. THE BRITISH TROOPS HAD SOME SPLENDID EQUIPMENT, BUT THERE WAS TOO LITTLE OF IT TO COUNT.

BELOW: FRENCH SOLDIERS EXAMINING A SOUND LOCATOR SOMEWHERE IN FRANCE. EARLY WARNING OF AIR ATTACKS WAS PRACTICALLY NON-EXISTENT AT THIS TIME, RELYING ON FRONT-LINE OBSERVERS AND TELEPHONE NETWORKS.

Churchill and his war cabinet were quite ready to respond to French Premier Reynaud's appeals for more fighters, but Air Chief Marshal Sir Hugh Dowding objected in the most forceful manner. On 16 May he reminded the Air Council that it had been agreed that a force of 52 Squadrons was felt necessary to defend Britain against even unescorted raids from the East (let alone raids launched simultaneously from France and the Low Countries, and escorted by single-engined fighters based on the French coast). He pointed out that he was now down to only 36 Squadrons, having lost the equivalent of ten units to the French campaign within the last few days.

In a remarkably candid letter he advised Churchill that 'if the home defence force is drained away in desperate attempts to remedy the situation in France, defeat in France will involve the final, complete and irremediable defeat of this country... I believe that, if an adequate fighter force is kept in this country, if the Fleet remains in being, and if home forces are suitably organised to resist invasion we should be able to carry on the war single handed for some time, if not indefinitely.' Privately, Dowding worried that the 'Hurricane tap is now full on', and that his Command was in real danger of being 'bled white'.

As a result of Dowding's timely intervention, plans to send yet more whole squadrons to France were put on hold, though aircraft and pilots continued to be sent out piecemeal

LEFT: THE DORNIER DO 17 WAS ONE OF THE MAINSTAYS OF THE GERMAN MEDIUM BOMBER FLEET. THIS DO 17Z OF THE STAB III/KG3 WAS BASED AT HEILIGENBEIL IN EAST PRUSSIA DURING THE POLISH CAMPAIGN.

as replacements. Fighter Command also formed three composite squadrons (later six) from single flights of six (later twelve) Hurricane squadrons, and these were despatched across the Channel to operate from French bases on a daily basis. The first of these units (56/213, 111/253, and 145/601) began operations from French bases on 16 May.

Their fight was to be short, however, since the BEF's Air Component began withdrawing to UK airfields on 19 May, and had completed its withdrawal by 21 May. As early as 18 June, Churchill had stated baldly that 'What General Weygand has called the Battle for France is now over. I expect that the Battle of Britain is about to begin. Upon this battle depends the survival of Christian civilisation.' The withdrawal of the Air Component left only the AASF Squadrons (retreating to the south and west) actually in France, though RAF fighters continued flying from their British bases. The BEF soldiers, meanwhile, were themselves becoming encircled, and the possible ports which could be used for an evacuation fell one-by-one, until only Dunkirk remained.

On 23 May, Göring announced that the Luftwaffe would now destroy the British single-handed, and told Milch that he had 'managed to talk the Führer round to halting the Army. The Luftwaffe is to wipe out the British on the beaches.' On 24 May, Hitler did order the Panzers to halt, but probably because von Rundstedt and von Kleist worried that the armoured divisions might be worn out if they pushed on through the lowlands of Flanders, which had, by now, been flooded. The Panzer divisions had also raced ahead of their logistical tail, rendering them vulnerable to counter attack, and they had left the extended southern flank dangerously exposed. Suggestions that the tanks were halted specifically to give the Luftwaffe a chance of glory, or to allow Hitler to negotiate with the British (capturing the BEF being felt to be somewhat provocative, and perhaps likely to undermine peace talks), would seem to be somewhat far-fetched.

BELOW: RAF FIGHTER PILOTS IN FRANCE WAIT, WHILST WEARING THEIR FLYING GEAR, FOR ORDERS TO SCRAMBLE. BOTH SIDES CARRIED OUT ONLY LIMITED OFFENSIVE AIR OPERATIONS IN THE WEST BEFORE THE EARLY SUMMER OF 1940.

History records that an extraordinary fleet (including some small and barely seaworthy rivercraft commandeered for the operation) lifted 338,226 men to safety between 26 May and 4 June, snatching a

ABOVE: RAF PILOTS OF NO 1 SQUADRON DASH FOR THEIR HURRICANES DURING A PRACTICE 'SCRAMBLE' AT VASSIN-COURT IN THE WINTER OF 1939-40. THERE WERE FREQUENT CLASHES WITH GERMAN FIGHTERS DURING THIS PERIOD.

RIGHT: THE DEWOITINE D520 WAS A FINE FIGHTER, BUT DELIVERIES WERE ONLY BEGINNING TO REACH FRENCH SQUADRONS IN MAY 1940 WHEN THE GERMANS ATTACKED.

moral (or morale) victory from the jaws of what remained a military defeat. Churchill had expected that only about 30,000 men would be evacuated, but the total number was more than ten times this, and included about 50,000 French and Belgian troops. This meant that only some 60,000 members of the BEF were left behind in France killed, missing or as Prisoners of War. This was a great achievement, not least for the unpopular Lord Gort, of whom little had been expected beyond personal bravery. But it was the 'brusque and pedantic' Gort who realised that his allotted task (to advance on and relieve Calais and re-join the main body of French troops advancing from the Somme) could no longer succeed, and it had been he who rapidly drew up a new plan to withdraw west to Dunkirk, and to save his soldiers with their hand-guns and personal weapons.

The Battle of France continued after Dunkirk, with the Germans launching Fall Rote (Plan Red) the next day, storming south across the River Somme. Field Marshal Erwin

DUNKIRK

Dunkirk did little for the reputation of the RAF, however, since few realised how hard it fought to protect those on the evacuation beaches. These came under heavy enemy air attack, and many of the army personnel who were evacuated asked 'Where are our fighters?', and some still feel bitter that the RAF did not play a fuller part. In fact, while they saw the low level bombers pounding them below the cloud and smoke, the British soldiers did not see the very real battle raging higher in the air. Fighter Command flew 2739 sorties over Dunkirk (with bombers flying another 651 and recce aircraft another 171) and fought what was the costliest battle of the French campaign, losing 106 fighters and 87 Spitfire and Hurricane pilots killed or captured. In return they destroyed 166 German aircraft (having claimed 217) and undeniably made the crucial difference between the success and failure of the evacuation.

But the loss of these 87 pilots and 106 single-engined fighters was near-disastrous, since it included many of those who had gained combat experience over France. It also saw the deaths of many men who had been the cream of pre-war Fighter Command, who could have been expected to 'lead the fight' during the Battle of Britain.

Rommel broke through at Amiens on 6 June, and the Germans took Paris on 14 June. Mussolini, eager not to lose out, had joined the war on 10 June (the very day that Norway surrendered), but even at this very late stage, it seemed that Hitler was not bent on the total defeat of Britain and France. The original communiqué announcing the formation of the German/Italian axis read: 'Germany and Italy will now march shoulder to shoulder and will not rest until Britain and France have been beaten'. Hitler personally crossed out the last few words and wrote instead '... will fight on until those in power in Britain and France

ABOVE: RAF PERSONNEL EXAMINE TROPHIES FROM A DOWNED GERMAN AIRCRAFT. THE GERMANS LOST NEARLY 1500 COMBAT AIRCRAFT IN THE BATTLE OF FRANCE – A LOSS THAT COULD NOT BE MADE GOOD BEFORE THE AIR OFFENSIVE AGAINST BRITAIN STARTED.

LEFT: GERMAN PERSONNEL BURYING A ROYAL AIR FORCE PILOT. BOTH SIDES TREATED ENEMY DEAD WITH CHIVALRY AND BURIED THEM WITH FULL MILITARY HONOURS. CIVILIANS OFTEN SHOWED LESS RESPECT.

RIGHT: RAF PERSONNEL
EXAMINING AN MG15
MACHINE GUN FROM
THE DORSAL TURRET OF
A SHOT-DOWN HEINKEL
HE 111 BOMBER. A
THOROUGH EXAMINATION
AND ASSESSMENT OF ENEMY
EQUIPMENT HELPED INSPIRE
TACTICS TO COMBAT THEM.

BELOW: GERMAN TROOPS
LAYING OUT A RECOGNITION
SIGNAL. WITH GROUND
FORCES ADVANCING
RAPIDLY, IT WAS VITAL
FOR THE LUFTWAFFE TO
KNOW EXACTLY WHERE THE
GERMAN SPEARHEADS WERE
FROM HOUR TO HOUR TO
AVOID FRIENDLY CASUALTIES.

are prepared to respect the rights of our two peoples to exist.' This made little difference in France, where it was as easy to complete the campaign and take Paris, as it would have been to halt the advance. France finally surrendered on 22 June, with Hitler taking great delight in ensuring that the surrender was signed in the very same railway car that had been used for the German surrender in 1918. This was a powerful symbolic gesture, and at a stroke wiped out the humiliation and shame of Germany's Great War defeat. Hitler himself was so excited that he danced a jig as he waited to enter the railway carriage. But even in France, Hitler stopped short of invading the whole country, and left a massive swathe of territory nominally independent under the Vichy regime headed by the Great War hero, Marshal Pétain. That portion of France actually under direct German control was fairly small, and arguably sufficient only to safeguard Germany's own borders and prevent the Allies having an easy 'back door' for invasion.

But France was, decisively, out of the fight. Former President Reynaud had wanted to send the army to Switzerland to be interned

and to move his government, air force and navy to North Africa to continue the fight (just as British contingency plans saw a move to Canada). Unfortunately, his deputy Pétain, and General Weygand, the head of the armed forces, had been more in tune with the defeated mood of the country, with many famously preferring 'slavery to war'. When Reynaud's group was finally outnumbered in the cabinet by the defeatists, he resigned and was replaced by Pétain, and full surrender became inevitable. His order to hand over 400 Luftwaffe pilots (held as POWs by the French) to the British for safe-keeping were overturned, and Pétain refused to let the fleet escape to Canada, fearful of German reprisals should he agree.

Meanwhile, large numbers of British troops remaining in France retreated in good order to western ports for evacuation, covered by the three remaining AASF Squadrons and by UK-based fighters . Nos 17 and 242 Squadrons briefly joined the AASF in France on 7 June, but all fighters had been withdrawn from France by 18 June, the last No.73 Squadron Hurricanes flying from Nantes to Tangmere on that date.

By 22 June, RAF losses in the West had reached 959 aircraft of all types, including 66 in Norway. Of these, 509 were fighters, with 435 pilots killed, missing or captured. Only 66 of the hundreds of Hurricanes dispatched to France made the return journey, and many of these were severely damaged – some so badly that they were scrapped on the spot. Even as early as 5 June, Fighter Command had an operational strength of only 331 single-engined fighters. But fortunately German losses had been heavy too, including 247 of the much-feared Bf 109s and 108 Bf 110s.

On 18 June, Churchill had warned that the Battle for Britain was about to begin, and urged the British people to prepare in what was to become one of his most famous speeches. 'Let us therefore brace ourselves to our duty, and so bear ourselves that if the British Commonwealth and Empire last for a thousand years, men will still say: "This, was their finest hour." '

On 30 June, German troops occupied the Channel Islands which had been partially evacuated and 'demilitarised' on 18 June in the vain hope that this would save them from occupation. German troops were now standing on British soil for the first time. People wondered whether the English mainland would be next.

CHAPTER 2

The Rise of the Luftwaffe

LEFT: THE HEINKEL HE 51 WAS THE MAINSTAY OF THE
NEW LUFTWAFFE'S FIGHTER FORCE DURING MOST OF THE
1930S, AND EQUIPPED THE CONDOR LEGION'S FIGHTER
SQUADRONS IN THE SPANISH CIVIL WAR.

Adolf Hitler is often described as having had a profound suspicion and dislike of aircraft and air power. While this may be an over-statement, there is no doubt that Hitler was essentially a land-based military thinker, obsessed with the concept of taking and holding territory. The development and growth of the Luftwaffe can only be seen in this light. Because Hitler shaped overall strategic thinking to an unparalleled degree, it was inevitable that air power could only ever be an adjunct to the land forces of the Wehrmacht, a force whose sole purpose was to 'clear the way' and make things easier for the advance of ground troops and tanks. When the Battle of Britain became an independent air campaign, with Germany aiming to achieve victory through air power alone, Hitler lost interest in it, turning his attention eastwards. The failure of the Luftwaffe in the Battle of Britain only confirmed Hitler's prejudices, and led to a steady erosion in Göring's power and influence, and in the importance of the Luftwaffe itself.

After the First World War, the terms of the Versailles Treaty limited Germany to tiny armed forces (little more than a militia), barely sufficient to guarantee internal security, and inadequate even for defending the nation's territorial integrity. The air force and navy were disbanded entirely, and Germany was banned from operating warships and military aircraft.

But from the very beginning, even during the brief period of the Weimar Republic, Germany was determined to evade the restrictions imposed by the victorious Allied nations. General Hans von Seeckt, head of the Reichswehr between 1919 and 1926, took some 180 talented officers of the Imperial Air Service and retained them specifically to form the nucleus and air staff of a new air force, which would be built up in secret.

German aircraft manufacturing companies kept going, sometimes by basing themselves abroad, and civil aviation was quietly allowed to expand. The German airline Lufthansa

RIGHT: HERMANN GÖRING, DESTINED TO COMMAND HITLER'S LUFTWAFFE, WAS THE LAST COMMANDER OF THE RICHTHOFEN GESCHWADER IN WWI, AND HAD 22 VICTORIES TO HIS CREDIT. HE IS SEEN HERE ON THE RIGHT.

BASIC FLYING TRAINING

From 1920, basic flying training was given to large numbers of potential air force members through the Luftsportverband – ostensibly a civilian sports flying organisation – using mainly gliders. Later, many of the best Luftsportverband members subsequently went to the Verkehrsfliegerschule (the airline pilot's school) via the NSFK (National Socialist Flying Corps). From 1924, proper military flying training began (in secret) at Lipetsk in Russia, following a December 1923 agreement with the Soviets. Hundreds of pilots and engineers quietly retired from the army, went to Lipetsk, and re-enlisted. After the end of the Lipetsk school, the Verkehrsfliegerschule took over much the same role, taking both civilians and military officers. The civilians (and those military personnel who had not served in the Great War) went on short military courses at the school's 'out-station' at Schleissheim, courses that included air-to-ground firing and combat manoeuvring and aerobatics. Later, no-one seemed to notice that the output of pilots from the Verkehrsfliegerschule far exceeded the number that the civil airline Lufthansa could possibly require.

was formed in 1926 by amalgamating a number of smaller concerns. Deutsche Lufthansa was headed by Erhard Milch, a former air force officer, and became a cover for military activity after the first Nazi election victories of 1928. The airline subsequently acted as the operator of a number of ostensibly civil aircraft which had in fact been designed for dual use as bombers. This allowed a large number of pilots to gain experience of long-range navigation and modern aircraft, and Lufthansa also developed long-range radio navigation aids, predecessors to the equipment used by pathfinders like the KG 100 during the Second World War. As time passed, the German cover-stories became steadily more outrageous, and eventually included Do 11C bombers flying night bomber-navigation exercises under the auspices of the State Railways Inspectorate!

After the appointment of Hitler as Chancellor in 1933, Milch was appointed Secretary of State in the Air Ministry, under Göring as Minister. But because Göring had many other positions, and was busily engaged in stamping out opposition to the Nazis, Milch did most of the work in creating the new Air Ministry, and in laying the foundations for the new air force with General Wever as Chief of the Air Staff. Hitler announced the existence of his Luftwaffe on 27 March 1935, officially inaugurating the new force and confirming the appointments of Göring as Commander in Chief, Milch as Secretary of State for Air and General Wever as Chief of Staff. The Luftwaffe immediately took over various flying schools, paramilitary and police units, including an SA squadron which became the Richthofen Geschwader at Berlin's Döberitz aerodrome.

BELOW: ALL FUTURE LUFTWAFFE PILOTS HAD TO UNDERGO AB INITIO GLIDER TRAINING, IN WHICH THEY RECEIVED A THOROUGH GROUNDING IN THE PRACTICAL ASPECTS OF FLIGHT BEFORE MOVING ON TO POWERED AIRCRAFT.

On its official creation, the Luftwaffe had 20,000 men, and with 1888 aircraft Hitler claimed parity with Britain's Royal Air Force. This was little more than empty blustering, since most of the new air arm's aeroplanes were trainers or interim types, and real operational combat aircraft were notable chiefly by their absence. At the same time, Hitler announced his intention to keep building to achieve parity with France. Inevitably this provoked the British and French to expand their own forces, but in anticipation of this, the foundations were laid for a huge expansion of the Luftwaffe. Milch's first production programme (with orders for 4021 aircraft) was intended to equip six bomber, six reconnaissance and six fighter Geschwaderen (squadrons), each with nine Staffelen (squadron units) in three Grüppen (Groups). These were to act as 'operational instruction units', allowing for a rapid and massive expansion which would leave the Luftwaffe as the largest air arm in Europe. Milch's production programme, launched in 1934, drew surprisingly little reaction abroad, even though only 115 of the aircraft involved were destined to serve with Lufthansa.

Bombers were given priority initially, but Milch's intention to switch the emphasis to fighter production after 1937 (when the bomber force would be all but complete) was abandoned when he lost influence and power. This would have serious consequences, not least in 1940. Milch's most important confederate was the new Chief of the Air Staff, Wever, who had a tremendous grasp of air power theory, and who was also a great organiser. Together they planned the next stage of Luftwaffe expansion, including a vital long-range bomber (Ural-bomber) programme. This was drawn up to produce a bomber with sufficient range to reach targets in the north of Scotland or across the Ural mountains, and resulted in orders for the Junkers Ju 89 and the Dornier Do 19 (four-engined bombers broadly equivalent to the RAF's Stirling).

The death of General Wever left the all-important long-range bomber programme vulnerable to cancellation. The programme was already at risk, thanks to the prevailing culture of short-termism, which discriminated against any project which would not

BELOW: A CADET IN DFS GLIDER PREPARES TO BE WINCH-LAUNCHED. DFS PRODUCED MANY DIFFERENT TYPES OF GLIDER BEFORE AND DURING THE WAR, INCLUDING TROOP-CARRIERS USED FOR AIRBORNE ASSAULTS.

produce near-immediate results. Both Göring and the head of his technical department were dyed-in-the-wool fighter pilots, with little understanding of the finer points of bombing, and Wever was replaced as Chief of the Air Staff by Albert Kesselring, who had begun his career as an army officer, transferring to the Luftwaffe relatively late. This made him naturally predisposed to the needs of the army, and he became a fierce advocate of tactical air operations. He did not share Wever's enthusiasm for long-range heavy bombers. The remaining heavy bomber adherents were handicapped by their lack of influence, and by the lack of strategic understanding displayed by their commander, Göring, and by Wever's successor.

Cleverly, Kesselring pointed out to Göring that three twin-engined bombers would cost the same (and take up the same industrial capacity) as two four-engined bombers. Göring reportedly replied that Hitler would ask how many bombers the Luftwaffe had, and not how many engines they had, and the fate of the Dornier Do 19 and Junkers Ju 89 was sealed, to the good fortune of the British. The types were simply abandoned, and their prototypes were scrapped. In the excitement surrounding the victories of the Condor Legion and its lighter tactical bombers in Spain, no-one seemed to care. Those who had no qualms about the lack of long-range bombers were typified by World War One fighter ace Ernst Udet, who justified the omission by postulating that 'Hitler will never let us in for a conflict that might take us outside the confines of the continent.'

ABOVE: ADOLF HITLER ON TOUR IN A GERMAN TOWN. GERMANS SAW THEIR CHARISMATIC FÜHRER AS A SAVIOUR WHO COULD RESCUE THEIR COUNTRY. INSTEAD, HE DRAGGED IT DOWN TO EVEN GREATER DISASTER.

However, the cancellation of these aircraft was, to many, astonishing. In the 1930s, belief in the long-range strategic bomber as a potentially war-winning weapon was widely accepted, and every air force had its followers of the theories of Trenchard, Billy Mitchell and the Italian Douhet. Civilian politicians gloomily predicted that the 'bomber would always get through' and many expected any future war to bring 'terror from the skies' to cities and civil populations. Indeed it is generally believed that had the Luftwaffe gone ahead and procured a long-range bomber, the whole course of the Battle of Britain could have been changed. In fact, though the Ju 89 and Do 19 were cancelled, the Heinkel He 177 had already been launched (as the Bomber A), promising to make the scrapping of the Junkers and Dornier heavies rather less significant. Although technical problems prevented the big Heinkel from being in service by 1940, it had a longer range and a heavier bombload than either of the cancelled aircraft. But for whatever the reason, the Luftwaffe was left with no heavy long-range bomber with which to fight the Battle of Britain.

Jealous of Milch's power and influence (he had become the Führer's main adviser on aviation, with Göring's concentration on police and other matters), Herman Göring manoeuvred to take away responsibilities from Milch, re-assigning them to other officers, while allowing him to remain Secretary of State. Hoping to consolidate his own position, Göring appointed many World War One cronies to positions of power and influence, sowing the seeds of what would become crippling Luftwaffe weaknesses. Thus Ernst Udet became Director of the Technical Department, a post for which he could scarcely have been less well suited. The wartime fighter pilots did include some highly capable professionals who were an incalculable asset to the fledgling Luftwaffe, including Wolfram von Richthofen (cousin of the famous Red Baron), who would become a leading commander and one of the major forces behind the Luftwaffe's successful Blitzkrieg doctrine. But gifted technocrats typified by Milch and Wever were in a minority, and Milch began to worry that he would be the scapegoat if Göring (or his appointees) blundered.

Accordingly he requested to be allowed to go back to running Lufthansa full-time. Göring refused, forbade him to retire, but allowed that he might 'commit suicide if he wished.'

By 1935, the Luftwaffe was well on the way to becoming a large and technically well-trained air force, but lacked only recent operational experience. Even this was soon to be remedied. 85 volunteers (with 20 Ju 52s and six He 51s) were sent to Spain in 1936, and these were first employed to transport Franco's Foreign Legion troops from Tetuan to Seville. In November 1936, the Condor Legion was formed under Generalmajor Sperrle (with General Wolfram von Richthofen as Chief of Staff). Manned by volunteers (including an initial 370 pilots who travelled to Spain on a 'Strength through Joy' cruise ship), the Condor Legion marked a major expansion in German aid to the nationalists in the Spanish Civil War, functioning as a semi-autonomous air force supporting General Franco's forces.

Spain provided an excellent training ground for the hundreds of Luftwaffe pilots who were rotated through the Condor Legion, and also allowed the Luftwaffe to develop and refine tactics suited to the new generation of combat aircraft. Wolfram von Richthofen, for example, developed dive bomber and close air support tactics, while Werner Mölders conceived of new and innovative fighter tactics. Like Mölders, many fighter pilots who subsequently rose to fame in the Second World War (including some of the most successful Battle of Britain aces) had their baptism of fire in Spain. Condor Legion veterans then returned to their units and passed on their hard-won experience to others.

The Spanish Civil War also provided the Luftwaffe with the opportunity to develop the doctrine and strategy it would later employ in the European war. Tasked with backing ground offensives by Franco's army, the Condor Legion developed a new concept of using aircraft for close support, with fighter-bombers attacking targets immune to high-level bombing, and with dive-bombers operating as precise 'airborne artillery', while escort fighters brushed off enemy air opposition. But the development of this form of air warfare over-shadowed development in other vital areas and led to an over-reliance on the use of dive bombers, and a doctrine which only worked best under conditions of total air supremacy. When this was absent, Luftwaffe tactics would prove to be less effective. Thus

LEFT: IN THIS PHOTOGRAPH, A TRAINEE GLIDER PILOT MEMBER OF THE HITLER YOUTH HAS HIS EYES FIRMLY FIXED ON THE SKY. THE NAZI PROPAGANDA MACHINE MADE MUCH CAPITAL OUT OF YOUNG PEOPLE'S ENTHUSIASM.

THE LUFTWAFFE'S NEW AIRCRAFT

The aircraft which would form the backbone of the Luftwaffe during the Battle of Britain were all evaluated at the Luftwaffe's test centre at Rechlin during 1936 – these being the Messerschmitt Bf 109, the Junkers Ju 88, the Dornier Do 17 and the Heinkel He 111. The Ju 87 had been evaluated and ordered into production the previous year. This new generation of German combat aircraft out-classed contemporary British service machines, but because they appeared prior to the war, during the Battle itself they were generally out-classed by the British aeroplanes which had been designed in response. Only in the field of light bombers were the British unable to catch-up. This was because the RAF's rigid requirement to operate from grass runways made its bombers too small, too old-fashioned and too light. Aircraft like the Bristol Blenheim could never hope to match the Ju 88 or Heinkel He 111.

RIGHT: THE JUNKERS
JU 87V-4 WAS THE
PRODUCTION PROTOTYPE OF
THE A-SERIES DIVE-BOMBER,
THE FIRST OF THE 'STUKAS'
THAT WERE TO PROVIDE
SUCH EFFECTIVE SUPPORT TO
THE GERMAN ARMIES IN THE
EARLY MONTHS OF WWII.

OPPOSITE: DORNIER DO
17 BOMBERS FLYING OVER
A NAZI PARTY RALLY IN THE
1930S. THE DO 17 WAS
DEVELOPED FROM A DESIGN
FOR A FAST MAILPLANE
CAPABLE OF CARRYING SIX
PASSENGERS.

when war came in 1939, the Luftwaffe was well-trained for a tactical air support role in relation to highly mobile ground forces, but was less well prepared for the campaign it was forced to begin against Britain in 1940.

Despite massive production, the Luftwaffe remained a small frontline force at the time of the Munich agreement, with only 453 serviceable fighters, 582 serviceable bombers and 159 serviceable dive-bombers. But expansion continued, particularly with the absorption of Austrian aircraft factories and aircrew, and by 1939, the Luftwaffe was ready to support a full-scale war.

REICHSMARSCHALL HERMAN GÖRING

The leader of Hitler's Luftwaffe has been caricatured and parodied so often that a true picture of this complex character is sometimes difficult to discern. It is too easy to dismiss Göring as a fat and slightly effeminate buffoon, ignorant of modern tactics and technology, and too intent on elaborate uniforms, hunting and plunder to lead his air force. Like all really persistent myths, such a picture has some basis in fact, but it is also a grotesque distortion of the truth, too partial to be useful.

It is too easy to dismiss
Göring as a fat and
slightly effeminate
buffoon, ignorant of
modern tactics and
technology, and too
intent on elaborate
uniforms, hunting and
plunder to lead his air
force. Like all really
persistent myths, such a
picture has some basis
in fact, but it is also a
grotesque distortion of
the truth, too partial to
be useful.

Herman Göring had been badly wounded in the trenches before transferring to the Imperial German Air Service as an observer, subsequently qualifying as a pilot. During the First World War, he rose to command the Richthofen 'Circus' after the death of the 'Red Baron', winning the highly prized Pour le Mérite medal.

Joining the Nazis in 1922, Göring led the SA (Sturm Abteilung, or Storm Troopers) during their early years. As the Nazis made the transition to mass movement, winning elections, Göring provided the NSDAP (Nationalsozialistische Deutsche Arbeiter Partei – National Socialist Workers Party) with a symbol of respectability and responsibility. Entering the Reichstag in 1928, he was soon put into a number of high profile positions, becoming President of the Reichstag, Air Minister and Prime Minister of Prussia. He

also established the Gestapo and the concentration camps, becoming the second most powerful figure in Germany. His war wounds (and injuries suffered in the Munich Putsch in 1923) famously led him to become addicted to morphine, though he was able to cure himself, briefly, before he began a descent into further addiction and illness.

Corrupt, vain and indolent, Göring nevertheless oversaw the rebuilding of the Luftwaffe in the 1930s, initially using his political influence and connections to help and protect Erhard Milch (a former Great War Jasta commander) as he went about the hard work of creating an air force. But at the same time, Göring was prone to cronyism, and this resulted in some famously unwise appointments, the best-known of which was Ernst Udet (a Richthofen Geschwader ace who achieved 62 victories during the Great War) as the head of the Luftwaffe's Technical Department. Further down the chain of command, the infant Luftwaffe filled with ex-Great War fighter pilots, many of whom were aces, and many of whom remained in active service during the Battle of Britain.

While fanatically proud of his Luftwaffe, Göring had not made any real effort to prepare himself to lead it. He did not understand modern air power, and lacked any intellectual grasp of the potential or the limitations of air warfare. As an ex-fighter pilot he was naturally interested in fighters, and he was an enthusiastic promoter of tactical air support which was self-evidently glamorous and exciting. But transport aircraft, logistics and the technicalities of air power bored him. Had Göring been merely a figurehead, his enthusiasm and pride would have been useful, but he wanted to be a hands-on commander. His decisions tended to be based on instinct rather than insight or intellect, and he was only too pleased to delegate (often to poorly chosen subordinates) to save himself work. Yet unfortunately for the Luftwaffe, he was also prone to taking personal command if there was any promise of personal glory, or if he thought he could ingratiate himself further with his beloved Führer.

The Luftwaffe had been ideally constituted for the campaigns in Poland and the Low Countries, where it had gained air superiority at an early stage, and if the Battle of France

ABOVE: AIRCREW OF THE GERMAN CONDOR LEGION ENJOYING A MEAL BETWEEN SORTIES. THE AIRCRAFT IN THE BACKGROUND IS A HEINKEL HE 45, A SMALL NUMBER OF WHICH WERE USED FOR RECONNAISSANCE IN SPAIN.

RIGHT: THE PROTOTYPE MESSERSCHMITT BF 109 MONOPLANE FIGHTER, WHICH FIRST FLEW FROM AUGSBURG IN SEPTEMBER 1935.

proved more costly, the extent of the
eventual victory was decisive enough to
cover over any deficiencies. Experience
against the RAF over France led some
Luftwaffe fighter pilots to anticipate that
the Battle of Britain would be their most
difficult task yet. At the same time, an
overjoyed Hitler conferred on Göring
the unique rank of Reichsmarschall,
blinded by the success of the Luftwaffe
over France and the Low Countries,
and reassured by Göring's boasting.

The Luftwaffe was, as we have seen,
inadequately equipped for an air campaign against Britain,
but Göring's poor leadership was an equally powerful factor in the eventual German
defeat. He seized primacy for the Luftwaffe in the Battle by promising Hitler that his air
force would bring the British to their knees by bombing alone, but Göring failed to take
advantage of Britain's weakness immediately after Dunkirk. Göring was shamefully slow
in launching his bombers even against British convoys and coastal targets, giving the RAF
an invaluable breathing space. And even after battle was joined, Göring had no clear idea
of how to achieve the results he had promised. Even as late as 16 July he was asking his
subordinates how to attain air superiority. And as if this were not enough, Göring attempted
to mastermind the operation at arm's length, forcing his subordinates to shuttle back and
forth between their French headquarters and his Prussian estate. Apart from brief visits in
his armoured train, Göring did not actually base himself at the front in France until after 7
September, after the Battle had been lost.

Göring initially used his bombers as little more than bait, attempting to draw the RAF
into a battle of attrition. Yet Air Chief Marshal Dowding and Air Vice Marshal Park's

TOP: THE FOCKE-WULF
FW 56 STÖSSER WAS AN
ADVANCED TRAINER FOR
THE LUFTWAFFE. ERSNT
UDET FLEW IT WHEN
DEVELOPING DIVE-BOMBING
TECHNIQUES LATER USED BY
THE STUKA.

LEFT: THE HEAD OF THE
LUFTWAFFE AND ONE
OF HITLER'S RIGHT-HAND
MEN, HERMANN GÖRING
HAD BEEN AN ACE DURING
WORLD WAR I, FLYING
IN THE FAMOUS 'FLYING
CIRCUS' OF THE RED
BARON.

measured and cautious response baffled the Luftwaffe, but conserved RAF strength while still minimising the effectiveness of German raids. Max Hastings described the Luftwaffe's bombing campaign as following 'an erratic pattern that defied logic', and certainly it was characterised by rapidly shifting objectives and by a failure to correctly analyse the effectiveness of different strategies before changing them. Göring's Luftwaffe also failed to concentrate attacks on vital targets, or to follow up successful raids to maximise damage on particular targets.

The switch from attacks on Fighter Command aerodromes to London and the cities is a well-known example of this tendency, but it was a pattern which was to be repeated again and again. When the Luftwaffe mounted its devastating attack on Coventry, for instance, industrial production returned to its normal levels within five days. Had the Luftwaffe returned once or twice, Coventry could have remained unproductive for a long period, but months elapsed before the next attack. Even more significantly, the Luftwaffe failed to match its target list to the size of its bomber force. The Luftwaffe might have been able to knock out Fighter Command had it concentrated on that one objective, or it might have been able to destroy the control and reporting system. Alternatively, an all-out offensive against London might have forced the British to sue for peace, had it been launched earlier and more decisively. But the Luftwaffe chose to attack all of these targets, and proved to be simply too small to support the campaign that Göring anticipated.

Göring's optimism that the Luftwaffe could win a victory within two or three weeks was never realistic, and becomes inexplicable when pre-war German planning studies are taken

LEFT: SENIOR OFFICERS OF THE NEW LUFTWAFFE SHARE A JOKE ON A GERMAN AIRFIELD. WERNER MÖLDERS, AN ACE IN THE SPANISH CIVIL WAR AND THE BATTLE OF BRITAIN, STANDS ON THE RIGHT.

BELOW: A YOUNG RADIO OPERATOR/GUNNER IN THE NOSE POSITION OF A HEINKEL HE 111 BOMBER. GERMAN BOMBERS AT THIS STAGE OF THE WAR WERE NOT PARTICULARLY WELL ARMED, AND SUFFERED ACCORDINGLY.

into account. In 1938, General Felmy pointed out the need for a massive increase in Luftwaffe strength (to 58 bomber wings) if war against Britain were to be contemplated – including no less than 13 dedicated anti-ship Geschwaderen. He concluded that the Luftwaffe could actually achieve no more than a 'disruptive effect' against Britain, and that war would be 'fruitless'. Less than a year later, in early 1939, General Geiseler confirmed that the Luftwaffe was inadequate to attack and succeed against Britain without a major expansion.

But Göring should not take all the blame for the Luftwaffe's failure in the Battle of Britain. Even had they received better leadership and direction, some believe that Göring's subordinates were not up to the job in hand. Milch, for example, was over-burdened and unpopular, while Udet was temperamentally unsuited to the desk work that was his lot. But worse still were the arguments between rival commanders. Just as Fighter Command's chief, Dowding, had

to contend with bickering among his two main Group Commanders, so Herman Göring had to watch as his primary Luftflotte chiefs argued about the best strategy for attacking Britain. Hugo Sperrle wanted an all-out effort, especially against ports and supply depots, while Albert Kesselring wanted to attack Britain through its peripheries – including Gibraltar and the Mediterranean, concentrating on a relatively limited target set within Britain itself but especially London. Göring was able to impose some discipline, and his Luftflotte commanders did work together to a common plan, though (as we have seen) this common plan changed too often to be effective, and the Luftwaffe never had the resources to carry it out.

MOTIVES AND WAR AIMS

Any attempt at analysing Hitler's real war aims is enormously difficult. The Third Reich famously operated with few written orders, and Hitler's subordinates manoeuvred for favour with a great deal of autonomy, but without much direction, according to what they thought would please Hitler. Hitler himself gave little real indication of his motivation, except, perhaps, in the earliest days and in the impenetrable 'Mein Kampf'. In truth, he was probably driven by a series of constantly changing attitudes, reacting to the ideas of some of his subordinates and to perceptions of what national pride and honour might dictate. More

and more, the situation in the West became an unwelcome distraction as he prepared for what he saw as a 'historically ordained' crusade against the Bolshevik, the Slav and the Jew – an expansionist war which would provide living space (Lebensraum) for the Aryan Germans. In the end, everything became subservient to Hitler's own 'holy war', even if it meant that Germany would have to fight a country which Hitler himself had once hoped would be an ally.

As the Second World War broke out, Hitler was probably profoundly disturbed to find himself at war with Britain, although Führer Direktiv 6 (of 9 October 1939) had envisaged taking the Low Countries to provide a base for 'the successful prosecution of an air and sea war against England'. But this was almost certainly unrepresentative of his views in the first year of the war. Hitler's intuition was

ABOVE: THE HEINKEL HE 118 WAS A PROMISING PROTOTYPE DIVE-BOMBER, BUT THE PROGRAMME WAS EFFECTIVELY CANCELLED WHEN UDET WAS FORCED TO BALE OUT DURING A TEST FLIGHT.

RIGHT: CLOSE-UP OF THE NOSE OF AN EARLY-MODEL MESSERSCHMITT BF 109B. THE 109B HAD AN ARMAMENT OF THREE MG17 MACHINE GUNS, ONE OF WHICH FIRED THROUGH THE PROPELLER BOSS. IT WAS LATER REPLACED BY A 20MM CANNON.

that war against Britain could only end in disaster for Germany, even if she emerged victorious. Hitler admired the English, and valued the British Empire as a force for stability in the world, and only wanted British recognition of his position (and territorial gains) on the European continent. There were, of course, Nazis who did want to fight the British – men like foreign minister von Ribbentrop who believed that 'two great trees could not prosper too close together'.

One prominent historian of the period commented that 'the German view of Britain was formed by unusually stupid men like von Ribbentrop'. This may or may not have been true, but it is certain that Hitler himself had little real knowledge or understanding of Britain. His view was distorted by his experiences of Neville Chamberlain, and by over-exaggerated reports of the power, extent and influence of the British Union of Fascists, and other pro-German organisations. He was also unaware of the way in which Britain's attitude to Germany had changed since his invasion of Czechoslovakia. Before 1938, even moderate politicians had fallen for Hitler's charm, and had been impressed with what he had created in Germany. Thus David Lloyd George and even the Duke of Windsor had made openly admiring remarks following early visits to Germany. But after 1938, even British fascists tempered their praise of Nazi Germany.

Hitler believed that Britain remained semi-feudal, with only the most tenuous grip on democracy. In Britain itself, the fascists made little impact (as evidenced by their performance in General Elections), but in Germany they were thought to be of great importance and significance. The Nazis believed that Churchill was personally unpopular, that there was a real potential for massive social unrest in Britain, and that peace with Germany would meet with general approval. The British Secret Service encouraged British fascists to transmit false and misleading reports back to Germany, and watched with amusement as Germany broadcast radio messages to non-existent or impotent cells of revolutionaries and anti-Churchill 'resistants'.

Hitler was a politician who was driven by instinct, perverse racial ideology and a degree of mysticism, but had no initial anglophobia. Even after the Battle of France, Hitler saw his

BELOW: A PRODUCTION
JUNKERS JU 87A-1 IN
SERVICE WITH STUKA-
GESCHWADER 162 IIN
1937. LIKE OTHER
GERMAN TYPES, THE JU 87
WAS EVALUATED IN SPAIN,
WHERE IT WAS FLOWN BY
A UNIT KNOWN AS THE
IOLANTHE-KETTE.

BOTTOM: THREE STUKAS
ON GROUND-SUPPORT
DUTY OVERFLY A GERMAN
ARMOURED CAR AT VERY
LOW LEVEL.

HITLER'S RESPECT FOR BRITAIN

There can be no doubt that Hitler had not wanted to fight against Britain, a country whose people and institutions he respected enormously. He once described the British parliamentary system as 'a sublime self-government by a nation' and respected Britain's army, navy and public schools. In Mein Kampf, he described the British as a 'Germanic Brother Nation' and a 'Herrenvolk' (master race), equal in value even to the Germans. Hitler's dream was for the German Reich (concentrated and confined to the European continent) to co-exist beside Britain's maritime power and widely-spread overseas empire. Even much later in the war, during the advance on Moscow, Hitler remarked that the British were 'of an impertinence without equal, but still I admire them. We have a lot to learn there.'

quarrel as being with Winston Churchill, and a certain portion of the English 'ruling class' – probably an element which he would have characterised as being dominated by Jews. He felt that the British and German peoples were not 'natural enemies' and admired and valued Britain's empire as a force for stability in the world. Fricke, a senior naval planner, cleverly summed up the Nazi attitude to Britain: 'Throughout the world, England epitomises the reputation of the white man, therefore the destruction of England would have a negative effect on the whole white race.'

While Britain was still seen as being a potential ally (if only the anti-German Churchill regime were removed or made to see reason), actual friendship with Britain was no longer viewed as being essential. As it became increasingly clear that Britain would not make peace on German terms, continuation of the war was accepted as a necessity. The real problem was seen as the fact that Britain's pre-condition for peace would inevitably be a German withdrawal from Poland. Since Poland was to be the springboard for the German assault on Russia, this was impossible, and deadlock was inevitable. As Hitler became more and more preoccupied with the forthcoming attack on Russia, the need to finish business in the West became increasingly urgent. Although Britain was not viewed as representing a serious obstacle to German ambitions, there was felt to be a need to win a quick victory before launching the attack on Russia. Some within the Nazi hierarchy cautioned against under-estimating the British, but their warnings went unheeded.

Even as late as 19 July 1940, Hitler still hoped that agreement could be reached with Britain, and he made an appeal for peace. 'In this hour I feel it to be my duty before my own conscience

ABOVE: THE LUFTWAFFE
WAS AN IDEAL VEHICLE FOR
GERMAN PROPAGANDA,
WHICH FOSTERED THE
'NORDIC GOD' IMAGE
WITH ITS PHOTOGRAPHS OF
STEELY-EYED AIRCREW.

to appeal once more to reason in England. I consider myself to be in a position to do so, since I am not begging for something as the vanquished, but as the victor, speaking in the name of reason. I can see no reason why this war need go on.'

Although some government papers relating to the period remain closed to public access, there are good reasons for believing that Britain did, at the very least, enter into secret negotiations for peace, and continued these for some time after the formal declaration of war. But by mid-1940, no British government could have hoped to negotiate with Hitler, since the people themselves would not have countenanced it. Churchill's uncompromising rhetoric struck a chord, and the public mood was bellicose.

No response was made to Hitler's 'appeal' beyond a terse comment from Lord Halifax that 'We shall not stop fighting until freedom is secure.' The British reaction was made more clear to the King of Sweden, who offered to act as an intermediary. 'These horrible events', wrote Churchill 'have darkened the pages of European history with an indelible stain. His Majesty's Government see in them not the slightest cause to recede in any way from their principles and resolves set out in October 1939. On the contrary, their intention to prosecute the war against Germany by every means in their power until Hitlerism is finally broken and the world relieved from the curse which a wicked man has brought upon it has been strengthened to such a point, that they would rather all perish in the common ruin than fail or falter in their duty.' But even in the face of rejections and hostility like this, Hitler still hoped that Britain might be encouraged to make peace without the necessity for inflicting complete and catastrophic defeat, and in one respect at least, the Battle of Britain (an air campaign alone, initially aimed at military and industrial targets, and not the British people themselves) can be seen as a last attempt to achieve some kind of peace.

OPERATION SEA LION – THE PLAN

Although there is great controversy as to whether the Germans ever really intended to invade Britain, and as to whether any invasion could have succeeded, sketchy plans for an invasion, code-named Seelöwe (Sea Lion), were hurriedly drawn up in early July, building on a speculative study (Löwe, or 'Study Red') drawn up by Admiral Raeder in 1939. Raeder had made the study because he didn't want to appear unprepared if Hitler or the army suddenly demanded transport and protection for an invasion scheme. Though nominally an invasion plan, Raeder's study was effectively a well-organised set of arguments as to why invasion was impossible.

Göring's deputy, Erhard Milch, had already proposed an immediate paratroop-led invasion of Britain as France fell, intending to take advantage of the Wehrmacht's momentum and sky-high morale, and to exploit the confusion and chaos which followed Dunkirk. He had flown his own aircraft to Dunkirk on 4 June, and had seen the huge amount of heavy equipment left behind by the retreating BEF. The BEF had survived in terms of numbers of men, but lost its armour, transport, heavy weapons and supplies. Even ammunition and rifles were in short supply immediately after Dunkirk. And while British Pathé newsreels presented Dunkirk as having been almost a victory, there was no doubt that the shocked, dispirited and exhausted men pictured trooping off the small ships were members of a beaten army. With time they would recover their pride and morale, and were soon rearmed and re-equipped, but not in the days immediately after the evacuation. 'If we wait four weeks it will be too late' stated Milch, prophetically.

Milch appreciated the temporary nature of the weakness and vulnerability of the British Army. He calculated that an immediate bold strike, using all available paratroopers to take and hold a cluster of 'bridgehead' aerodromes (such as Manston and Hawkinge) might succeed, with Ju 52s providing resupply and the Ju 87 Stukas operating as airborne artillery. But Hitler (perhaps convinced that Britain would sue for peace) preferred to wait, eager

'These horrible events', wrote Churchill 'have darkened the pages of European history with an indelible stain. His Majesty's Government see in them not the slightest cause to recede in any way from their principles and resolves set out in October 1939.'

LEFT: GERMAN ARMOURERS LOADING PRACTICE TORPEDOES ON TO A HEINKEL HE 111H6. THE HEINKEL PROVED AN EXTREMELY EFFECTIVE TORPEDO-BOMBER, BUT WAS TOO SLOW TO BE EFFECTIVE AGAINST WELL-PROTECTED LAND TARGETS.

RIGHT: HEINKELS UNDER PRODUCTION. IN THE FOREGROUND IS A HE 115 FLOATPLANE, WHILST IN THE BACKGROUND ARE SEVERAL HE 111 BOMBERS. GERMAN PRODUCTION RATES WERE VERY SLOW, MEANING THAT LOSSES COULD NOT BE QUICKLY REPLACED.

BOTTOM: THE JUNKERS JU 52, WHICH WOULD GO ON TO HAVE SUCH A PROMINENT ROLE IN WWII AS A TRANSPORT, SEEN HERE AS A BOMBER IN THE SPANISH CIVIL WAR.

to tour the battlefields of France, and to prepare elaborate victory celebrations, while the army wanted time to finish off the French and then regroup.

Even the Luftwaffe was somewhat tardy in turning its attention to the RAF. The German air force was slow to reintegrate newly released prisoners of war, and home leave was granted to many air and groundcrew. Göring did finally issue orders for a preliminary air offensive against the UK on 30 June. It was stated that a full-scale assault would begin on Adlertag (Eagle Day) and confident boasts were made that the RAF would be wiped out within two or three weeks, providing Germany with the measure of air superiority that would be necessary for any invasion. This seemed no idle boast, since Göring had at his disposal three Air Fleets (Luftflotten) in France, Belgium and Norway, controlling nearly 1400 bombers, 320 Bf 110 long-range fighters, and 813 single-engined fighters, together with the usual reconnaissance and support aircraft.

But while these were impressive figures, the delay between the fall of France and the start of the Battle of Britain proved inadequate for the Germans to replace the losses suffered in Poland and France. These losses had included 30 per cent of the Luftwaffe's fighters and 40 per cent of the Stuka dive-bombers. And as if this were not bad enough, Britain's more efficient industry was granted sufficient breathing space to come close to replacing RAF losses, and the British armed forces were able to re-group and prepare

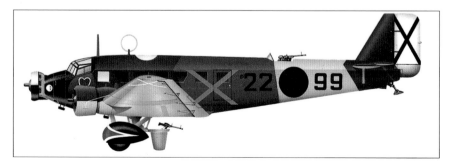

for the assault. But Germany was lulled into a false sense of security by the extent of its previous victories, and it was widely assumed that victory was inevitable, even with depleted forces. Complacency and arrogance allowed senior officers to conclude that complete re-equipment and regrouping would not be necessary just to finish the job of beating the English, who, it was assumed, were half-beaten already. German confidence rode very high, at least at higher levels of command. At the frontline, attitudes varied. Despite being buoyed up by the speed and decisive nature of their victories, many members of the armed forces believed that Britain might prove a tougher opponent than others presumed. Most German fighter pilots who had encountered the RAF during the fierce fighting over France (and especially over Dunkirk) viewed their opponents with respect, and many expected the forthcoming Battle of Britain to present them with their toughest challenge to date.

It was not until 2 July 1940 that Hitler even ordered the updating of the provisional invasion plans prepared before the war. The very next day, the Royal Navy destroyed the French fleet at Oran, preventing any chance of it falling into German hands, and reinforcing Britain's maritime superiority. This daring raid represented a humiliating reminder that the British were still capable of causing trouble. It also prevented the Kreigsmarine (navy) from obtaining some potentially useful capital ships. The operation was necessary, since huge elements of the French navy had transferred their allegiance to the Vichy regime, reassured by the fact that Pétain (a national hero in the First World War, and a patriot) was its leader. Churchill later admonished the French authorities to the effect that: 'A puppet government has been installed in Vichy, which can at any time be coerced into becoming our enemy. The Czechs, the Poles, the Norwegians, the Dutch and the Belgians are still fighting. Only France has humbled herself, and that is not the fault of this great but noble nation but of those whom are called men of Vichy.' Churchill's jibe was unpalatable, but accurate, and at this stage of the war, the blandishments of de Gaulle to join the 'Free French' (then more widely known as the 'Fighting French') often fell on deaf ears. Many French regarded the Vichy regime as their legitimate government, reassured by the presence of the great Pétain. Oran caused a massive decline in Anglo-French relations, and a furious Hitler angrily demanded that work on the invasion be stepped up. But he had been deprived of three potentially invaluable battleships, and the English public gained a much-needed victory to celebrate.

The leaders of the German Kreigsmarine was only too aware of Britain's naval might, and after the mauling meted out in Norway it was also fearful that an invasion could not be mounted without at least local air superiority. The Kreigsmarine was probably the

BELOW: LUFTWAFFE AIRCREW AT A BRIEFING. GERMAN CREWS, FLUSHED WITH THEIR SUCCESSES DURING THE POLISH AND FRENCH CAMPAIGNS, WERE TO FIND THE AIR BATTLES OVER ENGLAND MUCH TOUGHER THAN EXPECTED.

only part of the German armed forces not infected by the complacency brought about by the apparently easy and quick victories in Poland, the Low Countries and France, and were the only element who did not fundamentally under-estimate Britain's capacity to defend itself. Raeder's original Study Red had outlined an invasion (by only about 7500 men!) on the English south coast on a 100km (62.1 mile) section between Portland and the Isle of Wight. The first army counter-study ('Study Northwest') moved the invasion to the east coast, with an airborne assault capturing the ports of Lowestoft and Great Yarmouth, followed by an infantry division and a brigade of cyclists landing at the ports, and by an infantry division going ashore at Dunwich and Hollesley Bay. Second and third waves were to include ten panzer and infantry divisions and there was to be a diversionary attack north of the river Humber. The total force committed rose to over 100,000 men, a force far beyond that which the German navy could move, even over a short distance.

The army plan was completely unworkable, not least because unloading in the ports would be no easier than on the open coast, there were insufficient resources for the proposed diversion, and the risk of very rapid intervention by the Royal Navy was considerable. As France fell, Raeder became terrified that someone would suddenly drop responsibility for an invasion of Britain into his lap, and he determined to forestall this by telling the Führer how and why such an operation was impossible, but to do so by presenting an invasion plan in which the objections and difficulties were clearly laid out. The Naval Staff thus modified its 'Study Red' into a new 'Study England', and drew up a plan for a landing (by about 160,000 men) on a narrow front (between Eastbourne and Dover) with participating vessels using a corridor swept of mines and protected by strings of U-boats and minefields. The German Wehrmacht favoured a more ambitious undertaking, with 250,000 men landing along a

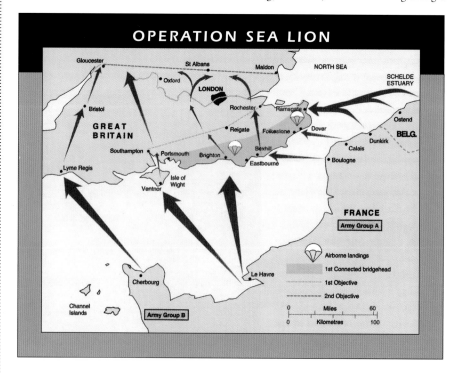

much broader 160km (100 mile) front, stretching from the Isle of Wight to Margate in Kent, launched from ports between Rotterdam and Le Havre. With the Battle of France over, and with plans already underway, General Halder, the Chief of the General Staff, realised that available troops, German-occupied Channel Ports and existing planning at last made an invasion more of a possibility, and he worked hard to come up with a definitive, single plan.

Under Halder's plans, von Rundstedt's Army Group A were to attack in Kent and Sussex, with the 16th Army (under Busch) on the right (between Ramsgate and Dungeness) and the 9th Army (under Strauss) further west (between Brighton and Worthing). The 16th Army was to drive north to London, with the 9th pushing up towards Aldershot. Even further west, Army Group B was to make a second landing, with the 6th Army (under von Reichenau) driving northwards from Lyme Bay towards Bristol, advancing to cut off London from the West, and aiming to take the high ground on a line curving up from Plymouth to the Thames Estuary. The plan envisaged multiple bridgeheads, but ironically included non along the stretch of coast between Portland and the Isle of Wight which the Kreigsmarine had assessed as being the most suitable stretch of coast for a landing.

Army Group B's spearhead alone was to have consisted of three divisions, and the entire Sea Lion first wave was of ten divisions, totalling 90,100 men and 650 tanks, supported by an astonishing 4443 horses. The second wave included 170,300 men, with 34,200 vehicles, 57,550 horses and 26,000 bicycles. The Luftwaffe, meanwhile, announced that it had 25,000 airborne troops available, including some 7000 paratroopers, and began scouring the newly captured countries for parachute silk in order to produce more parachutes and thereby create more paratroopers. But while the numbers of troops to be committed were impressive, and while the strategic plan looked convincing, the invasion was planned in two weeks, and draft plans were presented to Hitler on 13 July, 11 days after he'd asked for them. But little thought was given to the detailed logistical requirements, nor of how the Royal Navy might be neutralised, or at least prevented from intervening in the Channel. Halder was also unprepared for the furious reaction of the Kreigsmarine, who felt that the resources available would allow only a much narrower front, between Folkestone and Beachy Head, without the Ramsgate and Brighton Bay landings planned by Halder. And rather than attempting to be conciliatory, Halder began drawing up plans for diversionary landings (or simulated landings) in East Anglia, the Thames Estuary and even Ireland. The Kreigsmarine, meanwhile, planned its own diversion for Scotland. On 16 August, Hitler intervened, ruling out the Lyme Bay landing and reducing the Brighton Bay landing to an option, and then only for a one-wave light landing.

To carry this huge force across the Channel, Germany amassed a prodigious invasion fleet, and while there were only 155 transport ships, these were augmented by a fleet of more than 3000 converted barges and other sundry small boats. Dutch and Belgian barges were not available, having been taken across the Channel or destroyed in the fighting, while the French inland fleet was bottled up in the impassable network of canals, many of whose bridges and locks had been destroyed. But Germany itself relied on Rhine traffic for moving raw materials and food, and its own barges were hastily requisitioned. The barges were rapidly converted to incorporate bow loading ramps which would allow them to be driven right up onto the beaches, and some were strengthened to allow them to carry heavy armoured vehicles. Some were even fitted with auxiliary powerplants, in the shape of redundant aero engines bolted to gantries on the rear deck.

An invasion attempt began to seem imminent. On 16 July, Hitler issued Führer-Direktiv 16 which included the ominous words: 'Since England, despite her hopeless military situation, shows no signs of coming to terms, I have decided to prepare a landing operation'. The same communiqué underlined that the 'English air force must be so disabled in spirit' as

RIGHT: THE MESSERSCHMITT BF 110 PROVED A FAILURE IN ITS ROLE OF LONG-RANGE ESCORT FIGHTER, AND SUFFERED HEAVY LOSSES AT THE HANDS OF RAF FIGHTER COMMAND. IT WAS LATER USED WITH SUCCESS AS A NIGHT FIGHTER.

to be incapable of disrupting the crossing, and Göring reassured his leader that this would be achieved. The Channel ports and ports in the Low Countries began to fill with this rag-tag armada, and RAF reconnaissance aircraft regularly brought back high-quality photos of the build-up. Sea Lion appeared to be imminent.

Yet despite British worries, the German High Command had produced what was, at best, a makeshift invasion plan (one that has since been described as a 'Dunkirk in reverse') taking two weeks to try and achieve what the Allies, for the D-Day invasion, later spent two years preparing for. Many now believe that with this level of planning Sea Lion could never have been more than a bluff.

ABOVE: RAF
RECONNAISSANCE
PHOTOGRAPH OF A FRENCH
AIRFIELD NOW IN GERMAN
HANDS. THE TWO AIRCRAFT
AT RIGHT CENTRE ARE
HEINKEL HE 111S, WITH
A JUNKERS JU 52/3M
TRANSPORT AT TOP RIGHT.

SEA LION – FACT OR FANTASY?

There is documentary evidence that provisional invasion plans were drawn up, and that orders for certain preparations were issued. At the same time there remains considerable controversy as to whether Operation Sea Lion ever amounted to more than a generously resourced bluff – a deception operation on a grand scale. A successful bluff, after all, requires great effort if it is to look like the real thing, and requires the pretence of full preparations.

If an enemy is to be deceived, so too must many of the supposed 'participants', in this case including many senior officers in the Wehrmacht and Kreigsmarine. This is not as difficult to achieve as it might sound. Except at the very highest level, confidentiality ensures that even quite senior officers are only aware of the aspects of an operation which directly involve them, and this helps explain how some of the Generals failed to see through the charade, and failed to realise that an invasion could not work. Most simply assumed that other parts of the operation would deal with any difficulties they anticipated.

Preparations for Sea Lion were certainly extensive, and detailed. At least 250 Panzers were modified as amphibious assault vehicles, with water seals and long 'Schnorkels', while the number of horses to be embarked was reduced when Halder decided that his Cavalry would use bicycles instead of horses. Newsreels were even prepared for use in the immediate aftermath of a landing (shot during rehearsals, and convincingly cut with real footage from the Battle of France), while food for the various troops, horses and dogs was gathered. But in the end, this was as much wishful thinking as the plans to deport all British males between 17 and 45 to the Reich, or as the appointments of Nazi bureaucrats to run Britain after a successful invasion. Nor was the planned removal of Nelson's column from London (to be re-erected in Berlin as a symbol of victory) any more real!

There is a great deal of evidence to support the hypothesis that Hitler never intended to invade Britain at all. Some suggest that the flotilla of barges supposedly assembled for the invasion actually served two purposes. They were primarily assembled as a bluff, but one which could have been turned into reality had circumstances persuaded Hitler (the supreme opportunist) that an invasion could have succeeded. Interestingly, the number of barges assembled in the Channel ports declined steadily after mid-September, dropping from 1004 on 18 September to 691 by the end of the month. Similarly, on 10 September,

ABOVE: THE FLANKS OF THE PROPOSED GERMAN INVASION OF BRITAIN WERE TO BE PROTECTED BY GERMAN SCHNELLBOOTE (S-BOATS, ERRONEOUSLY CALLED E-BOATS BY THE BRITISH) SEEN HERE MANOEUVRING AT SPEED.

RIGHT: INVASION BARGES
MASSED IN THE HARBOUR
OF DUNKIRK. THE RAF
AND THE FLEET AIR ARM
ATTACKED THE CHANNEL
PORTS CONSTANTLY,
DESTROYING HUNDREDS
OF THE CONVERTED RHINE
BARGES.

Hitler himself never
showed much interest
in the planning for
Sea Lion, in marked
contrast to the planning
which had led to the
conquests of Austria,
Czechoslovakia, Poland,
Denmark, Norway, the
Low Countries and
France.

the first two divisions that had been on standby for Sea Lion quietly moved east. More would soon follow. This was hardly consistent with the build-up prior to an invasion, and conclusively demonstrated that by mid-September, at least, Sea Lion had ceased to be a reality, if it ever had been real at all.

Yet S-Day was eventually scheduled for 21 September, with a final go-ahead date on 11 September. The operation was officially ordered, but was postponed on 17 September. This was, officially at least, a postponement and not a cancellation and preparations and rehearsals continued unabated into October. But on 12 October, General Wilhelm Keitel, the Chief of Staff of the *Oberkommando der Wehrmacht* (OKW – Hitler's replacement for the War Ministry), acknowledged that it was now continuing 'only as a means of exerting political and military pressure on England' and that its execution would 'possibly' take place the following year. In the meantime, this 'bluff' had been an expensive one, dramatically slowing down industrial production, producing food shortages at home, and putting at risk the 1941 harvest. Iron ore and coal built up at the Baltic ports, with insufficient barges to transport it to the Ruhr, and even priority programmes (U-boat construction for example) began to slip. Barges were actually converted and crewed for their new role, consuming 75,000 cubic metres of concrete, 30,000 tonnes of iron girders and 40,000 cubic metres of wooden planks, plus 4000 towlines and huge quantities of canvas, chain and armour plate. Huge numbers of former seamen were transferred from the army and Luftwaffe, and the Kriegsmarine mobilised its reserves.

Hitler himself never showed much interest in the planning for Sea Lion, in marked contrast to the planning which had led to the conquests of Austria, Czechoslovakia, Poland, Denmark, Norway, the Low Countries and France. When the Kriegsmarine and Wehrmacht initially produced various invasion studies, Hitler expressly forbade any real preparations, concentrating first on the drive to capture Paris, and then on celebrating his victory. This lack of involvement may have had little significance, since Hitler was very much a land-based military thinker, unable to understand the problems of air and sea power. Those who believe in the reality of Sea Lion use Hitler's land-based thinking to explain that he was thus bound to leave detailed planning in the hands of his subordinates. But others see in this lack of involvement a confirmation that Sea Lion was never more than a 'planning option'. Hitler was, after all, psychologically driven to be directly involved in the planning of all of his great victories.

While Hitler often relied on luck, daring and surprise to 'carry the day', and was often inadequately prepared to meet well-ordered opposition, the Wehrmacht's lack of preparation for an invasion of Britain was in an entirely different league. The Allied D-Day landings took two years to prepare, with huge logistical problems to overcome. Some now ask how, if Hitler ever intended mounting a real invasion, he ever dreamed that he might succeed with so little preparation and planning? Incredible as it may now seem, the complete lack of detail in the Sea Lion plan, and the failure to take account of logistics, opposition and other factors may simply have represented a complete lack of understanding of the scope of the proposed undertaking, and the nature of the English Channel itself. As if to confirm this, a High Command memo compared the proposed operation to a 'river crossing on a broad front'.

But lack of preparation may not have been the main factor in preventing an invasion. After one meeting to discuss invasion plans, General Halder noted in his diary that Hitler 'believes that England must be forced into making peace. The reason: if we destroy

"HAVE I COMMAND OF DER SEA?"
"NEIN, MEIN FÜHRER"

"HAVE I COMMAND OF DER AIR?"
"NEIN, MEIN FÜHRER"

"THEN LET DER INVASION BEGIN!"

Göring   Raeder   Hitler

FLAT BOTTOM FLOOGIE FLEET

PREPARATIONS FOR CONQUEST

RIGHT: THE WAR GAVE BRITAIN'S CARTOONISTS ENDLESS SCOPE TO EXERCISE THEIR TALENT, AND PROVIDED A MUCH-NEEDED BOOST TO BRITISH MORALE, WHICH WAS OFTEN NOT AT ITS BEST IN THE SUMMER OF 1940.

BELOW: GERMAN TROOPS PRACTISING UNLOADING A HALF-TRACK ARMED WITH AN ANTI-AIRCRAFT CANNON, WHICH APPEARS FAR LESS POLISHED THAN THE ALLIED LANDINGS IN NORMANDY ONLY FOUR YEARS LATER.

England militarily, the British Empire will fall. Germany will gain nothing from this. German blood would have been spilt for Japan, America, and others.' There is no doubt that Hitler had some difficulty in seeing the British people (as opposed to their leaders) as being a natural enemy, and because of this, he had little stomach for a war against (or an invasion of) Britain, particularly while communist Russia was still in existence on his doorstep, so to speak. While Nazi peace overtures were rudely rebuffed by Churchill's government, Hitler still held back from the kind of all-out war against another Aryan nation which an invasion would have represented. He was never quite sure what an invasion of Britain would achieve, and when asked about the invasion plan is quoted as having said 'Let us by all means conquer Britain. But what then, and what for?' Hitler knew that even if an invasion were successful, the effort of holding on to the island nation would prevent him from launching the attack on Russia.

Even if it is accepted that Hitler himself ever seriously contemplated an invasion, there is plenty of evidence that any such plans had been shelved indefinitely long before the Battle of Britain reached its climax. The lack of transport ships, the unsuitability of the Rhine barges

BRITISH FEAR OF INVASION

While few in a position to really know the truth expected Sea Lion to come to fruition, the fear of invasion in England was very real. Hitler's astonishing series of military successes led some to assume that he was some kind of military miracle worker, to whom the usual rules of what was possible did not apply, and whose actions were inherently unpredictable. Britain's Chief of the Naval Staff wrote that 'We cannot assume that past military rules as to what is practicable will be allowed to govern the action undertaken.' Meanwhile, fear of invasion grew among the British public, and panic measures were adopted, with the removal or over-painting of roadsigns and railway station names, and a rapid development programme which turned Britain into a 'Fortress Island'. Hysteria about the danger posed by 'Fifth Columnists' spiralled out of control, while clever German disinformation and a foolish British government reaction raised suspicions such as German paratroopers being disguised as nuns. As a result of such stories there were supposedly occasions on which the thighs of elderly nuns were closely examined for the 'tell-tale bruising caused by a parachute harness'. Whether or not this fear of invasion was worth the resources dedicated to Sea Lion is impossible to judge.

commandeered for the operation and the Kreigsmarine's lack of naval superiority cast doubt on the viability of any landing operation. There was little chance that any invasion fleet could have survived the Channel crossing in the face of Royal Navy intervention, and even with air superiority, the Luftwaffe as equipped in 1940 could not have prevented such an intervention.

But whatever Hitler's motivation, and whatever he thought about Sea Lion's prospects, there is little doubt that many in the German High Command never took it seriously. Even after the issue of Führer-Direktiv 16, Generals Jödl and Jeschonnek remained convinced that there would be no invasion, and profoundly doubted that Germany could actually mount such an operation. Even Göring, fanatically loyal to Hitler, lacked much faith in the planned invasion. He would probably have enjoyed the opportunity to show off his Luftwaffe, but was always worried that the proposed invasion would not, or could not work, and was astonished and angry to find that his air campaign was subordinated to the needs of the army and navy in the invasion.

Göring remained hungry for glory and prominence, and hoped that his Luftwaffe would make Sea Lion an unnecessary irrelevance by forcing Britain to surrender or sue for peace through bombing alone. His overall concept for an independent air campaign was sensible enough, aiming as it did to probe Britain's defences, then destroy the RAF on the ground and in the air, simultaneously destroying Britain's aircraft industry and attacking harbours and shipping to cut off vital imports. Göring felt that this campaign in itself could bring Britain to its knees. Göring's total faith in the efficacy of air attacks may now appear to be profoundly unrealistic, but for anyone schooled in the air power theories of the 1920s, the belief that a war could be won by bombing alone was by no means unusual, and was almost an orthodoxy. In any case, had the Luftwaffe been properly equipped for a true strategic bombing campaign, then perhaps Göring's high expectations would not have been so wide of the mark. But in 1940, the Luftwaffe was a tactical air force, tailored to the needs of army support, and ill-equipped and ill-prepared for autonomous strategic operation.

ABOVE: AFTER DUNKIRK BRITISH FACTORIES WORKED FEVERISHLY TO REPLACE THE ARMAMENTS LOST IN THE EVACUATION. TANKS IN PARTICULAR WERE IN SHORT SUPPLY.

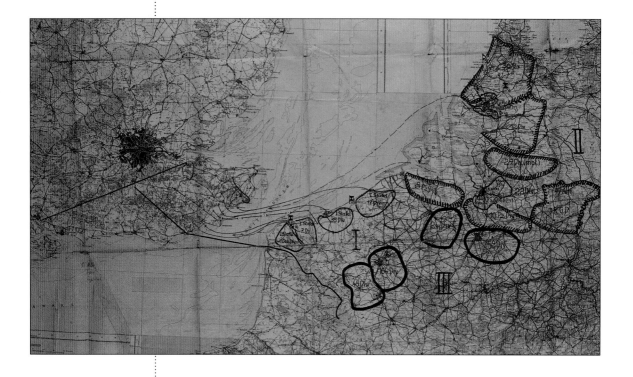

GERMAN INTELLIGENCE

German perceptions of the English political scene, and of the government's popularity and intentions, were wide of the mark even before the war, when political and social observation should have been easy. Pre-war military intelligence was even less impressive, though Erhard Milch and Ernst Udet were able to make a personal tour of important RAF stations and aircraft companies, and Milch ordered an extremely useful and highly detailed book on Britain's industrial capacity from a London bookseller, in his own name, using Reichsluftfahrtministerium headed note-paper. It was paid for by the Luftwaffe Intelligence Department, though whether they used a cheque bearing their real departmental name is unknown!

Hitler's Third Reich had two primary intelligence organisations: the military Abwehr under the enigmatic Admiral Canaris, and Himmler's Sicherheitsdienst. Quite apart from an unhealthy degree of rivalry and a complete lack of co-operation, the two organisations had overlapping areas of interest and responsibility, this leading to a great duplication of effort. Neither organisation was well organised for the collection of information on military targets – Himmler's SD being used principally to hunt internal opposition and to conduct political warfare, and the Abwehr being too much the personal fiefdom of Canaris. Some still suspect that Canaris was working for the Allies, but this seems unlikely (although he was eventually executed for complicity in the plot to kill Hitler). He was, however, an officer of the old-school, a Great War U-boat commander and a patriot, but with a fastidious distaste for Nazism and its bourgeois leaders. In 1940, Canaris may not have been working for a German defeat, but he certainly had his own agenda. The effect of this on the Battle of Britain may never be known.

Once war broke out, the Germans sent over a succession of pitifully inadequate spies, landing them from U-boats, ships, or by parachute. Ridiculously under-trained and ill-prepared, these unfortunates inevitably gave themselves away, sometimes by their heavy German accents, and sometimes by their total unfamiliarity with English customs or currency. Most were captured within hours of landing, and those who were not converted to work as double agents were inevitably hanged. The biggest problem was that no network of agents, safe houses and the like had been put in place before the war, so the new arrivals had to operate independently. German author Egbert Kieser wrote that 'It can be said with some confidence that no German agent remained undiscovered.'

Despite the ineffectiveness of the main intelligence organisations, the Luftwaffe was slow to establish its own intelligence department. It eventually did so in the form of the 5th Abteilung, an organisation with a lowly Major, Joseph 'Beppo' Schmidt, in command. Schmidt was a middle-ranking officer of limited ability and imagination, and his office was little more than a cuttings bureau.

The 5th Abteilung was remarkably inefficient, and made poor use of the reports it received from German Air Attachés (such as General Wenniger in London), although these were, in truth, of little use anyway. Nor was proper use made of radio intercepts provided by the 3rd Abteilung, or of the photographic coverage provided by the ostensibly civil 'route-planning' Heinkel 111s operating from Staaken. These assets could have provided much more useful raw data, but were never properly tasked, and as such their operations were always rather random, and lacked a clear direction.

From all these sources, Schmidt worked up a report riddled with errors, small and large. The radar systems went unnoticed, while almost every aspect of the Royal Air

LEFT: GERMAN PERSONNEL AT WORK CONVERTING A RHINE BARGE FOR A MORE SINISTER PURPOSE – THAT OF TRANSPORTING TANKS AND HEAVY VEHICLES ACROSS THE CHANNEL.

RIGHT AND BELOW: TWO
IN A SERIES OF POSTERS BY
FOUGASSE, ALL ON THE
SAME THEME. THE BRITISH
AUTHORITIES WERE QUITE
PARANOID ABOUT SPIES;
IN FACT, THE GERMAN
INTELLIGENCE NETWORK IN
BRITAIN WAS LAUGHABLY
INEPT.

Force was underestimated. Although every RAF Station Commander was an ex-frontline pilot, and though all were required to remain in current flying practise on the aircraft based at their airfields, Luftwaffe intelligence concluded that they were elderly men who did not fly at all. This was a criticism far more applicable to the Luftwaffe, many of whose senior officers were not even qualified as pilots, and many of whom had served in the Great War. Great War experience was rare in Fighter Command at station level, and Schmidt would doubtless have been astonished to learn that Keith Park, Air Officer Commanding (AOC) No.11 Group, flew over Dunkirk in his personal Hurricane, while at least one Station Commander (Victor Beamish) scored kills during the Battle.

Schmidt under-estimated the strength of Fighter Command (his 1939 estimate was 200 fighters when the Command actually had 608) and completely failed to take account of the capacity of British industry to manufacture new fighters, or to repair and return damaged aircraft to service. Once the two air forces were at war, the disparity between Schmidt's estimates and combat reality grew ever wider. Schmidt also under-estimated the quality and ability of Fighter Command aircrew and the comparative effectiveness of their aircraft. The fabric-covered Hurricane was regarded as little more than an easy target, while it was conceded that only a 'well-flown Spitfire' might be superior to a Bf 110 – the inference being that the Bf 110 would usually triumph. Schmidt misunderstood the nature of Fighter Command, and the way it operated. He assumed that squadrons were rigidly tied to their peacetime bases, and were tightly controlled by radio telephony and visual observation in only a very small geographic area.

Strangely, Schmidt over-estimated the capabilities of Britain's night defences, worried by the combination of twin-engined Blenheim night fighters and searchlights. This was the only element of Britain's air defences to which he did give any credence, and yet, in reality the system was immature and of limited usefulness (admittedly his assessment of AA guns as being 'ineffective' was not very far from the truth).

Target information was little better, and although Schmidt rightly stressed the importance of Royal Navy warships, ports, docks, warehouses, oil storage and distribution facilities, many of these were misidentified. Even the real purpose of some RAF airfields was not detected, and during the Battle of Britain much effort was wasted attacking Training Command and Fleet Air Arm stations like Detling, or minor airfields like Lympne. This was due in part to very poor photographic interpretation. Tangmere's Blenheim night fighters were misidentified as bombers, while

"........ but for Heaven's sake don't say I told you!"

CARELESS TALK COSTS LIVES

Keep mum she's not so dumb!
CARELESS TALK COSTS LIVES

Supermarine's Woolston Spitfire factory was identified as a bomber plant belonging to the manufacturer Avro.

The Schmidt report has been described as 'the worst piece of intelligence since the Trojans believed that the Greek wooden horse was just a present', but this is not completely fair. While spectacularly unreliable and inaccurate in detail, Schmidt did at least recognise the threat posed by Britain as being the only enemy of Germany actually capable of carrying on the war on its own. He was wise enough to urge immediate action before Britain could improve and perfect its defences, and before Britain's empire and dominions could throw their weight into the conflict.

ABOVE: SENIOR BRITISH OFFICERS EXAMINE A SUSPICIOUS PARACHUTE THAT HAS BEEN FOUND IN SCOTLAND. AGENTS WERE ALSO DELIVERED BY SEA, EITHER FROM A U-BOAT OR S-BOAT.

German intelligence should have improved once war broke out, but it proved unable to extract much useful intelligence from PoWs, and most crucially failed to notice the rapid development and deployment of a radar-based fighter control system. Most importantly, the assumptions of Schmidt's original Studie Blau were taken as read, and evidence which supported its conclusions was noted, while that which undermined it was ignored. Not that there was much good new evidence. Throughout July 1940, most of the Luftwaffe reconnaissance aircraft operating over Britain concentrated on tactical, short-term tasks (principally tracking convoys) and suffered very heavy losses.

Consequently, the Luftwaffe lost faith in its own intelligence at the height of the Battle. A radical underestimation of the RAF's strength, coupled with dramatic over-claiming of kills (by between 300 and 500 per cent) led to early expectations that the RAF was on its last legs. As the RAF Spitfires and Hurricanes kept appearing, day after day, jokes turned to despair. In August, Luftwaffe pilots began laughingly saying 'Here they come again, those last 50 RAF fighters!' over their radio transmitters. But the joke wore thin as increasing numbers of Bf 109Es and their pilots were lost, and as the Luftwaffe failed to make good its losses. On 7 September, Osterkamp complained that 'We keep shooting them down, but they don't get any fewer in number.'

Good intelligence was perfectly possible, as was demonstrated by the Royal Air Force, who placed a higher priority on it. In the RAF, Major Schmidt's nearest equivalent was an Air Commodore, and a network of intelligence officers stretching down to station and squadron level was soon in place. By the time war broke out, the RAF had amassed an accurate and complete Luftwaffe order of battle (and had identified every Grüppe and Staffel by Eagle Day), and they made good use of PoWs, with a well-crafted system of interrogation and debriefing. The RAF's estimate of Luftwaffe strength was correct (within five per cent, estimating 4500 aircraft, when the correct figure was 4295), and it was also aware that its pilots over-claimed their successes, and was broadly aware of how much by. This meant that its estimates of real German losses were fairly accurate (as opposed to the figures released to the media). There were problems, of course. A Rolls Royce technical representative in Yugoslavia obtained a Messerschmitt Bf 110's DB.601 aero engine

A radical under-estimation of the RAF's strength, coupled with dramatic over-claiming of kills (by between 300 and 500 per cent) led to early expectations that the RAF was on its last legs. As the RAF Spitfires and Hurricanes kept appearing, day after day, jokes turned to despair. In August, Luftwaffe pilots began laughingly saying 'Here they come again, those last 50 RAF fighters!' over their radio transmitters.

which was lost en route home, while the complete Bf 109 handbook was 'borrowed' and photographed, only to then be mis-filed and effectively lost! Nor did Fighter Command's AOC get access to the Enigma decoding machine until after the Battle (16 October, 1940), though this omission was probably not critical.

A GATHERING OF EAGLES

By July 1940, the Luftwaffe had amassed a great deal of combat experience, and had refined and developed the tactics and techniques it had learned in Spain flying against the Republican forces. Although it had suffered losses (and even though, typically, these had not been fully replaced), Milch's early concentration on training had paid dividends. There was no shortage of aircrew to fly for the Luftwaffe, and the 100 or so flying schools had an annual output of between 10,000 and 15,000 pilots. Shortages of bombs and oil had been made up since the attack on Poland, and the Battle of France had not seriously depleted stocks, though reserves of aircraft were low. But after the success of the Blitzkrieg, no-one seriously expected attrition to be heavy. New aircraft (like the Ju 88) and new sub-variants of existing types (like the Do 17Z and Bf 109E) were replacing or had replaced the types with which the Luftwaffe had started the war. And while many acknowledged that the British represented tough opponents, the Luftwaffe felt itself ready to begin the assault on Britain, confident that it would win. The Luftwaffe's personnel were thus in high spirits.

But behind the scenes, the Luftwaffe was not quite the invincible machine that many thought it was. The air arm remained poorly commanded, with Göring still in overall control, and with an unhealthy degree of rancour and bickering among his subordinates. The highly capable Erhard Milch had clawed back some of his power and influence, having been appointed Luftwaffe Inspector General (while remaining Secretary of State), but remained isolated and lacked real power. Kesselring had been replaced as Chief of Staff, first by Stumpff and then, in February 1939, by Hans Jeschonnek. While Jeschonnek was one of the Great War aces appointed by Göring, and a tactical airman to his marrow, he was also a hard-working technocrat in the mould of Milch, though the two men were not destined to get on well together, and the inexperienced Jeschonnek proved unable to avoid being sucked into some of Göring's incompetent schemes, including the unsuccessful attempt to destroy the BEF on the beaches at Dunkirk.

Further down the chain of command things were little better. The rigid division between flying and support personnel was not as efficient or as flexible as the RAF system, and led to rivalries and petty jealousies. In the RAF, airfields were commanded by senior pilots who actually flew, usually on operations, to keep their skills fresh, while senior administrative officers, adjutants and fighter controllers were similarly drawn from the ranks of older pilots. They thus had an understanding of the needs of the pilots, and fought hard for 'their boys'. In the Luftwaffe, an aerodrome commander was a dedicated administrator, who had never been in a fighter cockpit, and who reported through a different chain of command to his flying unit commanders.

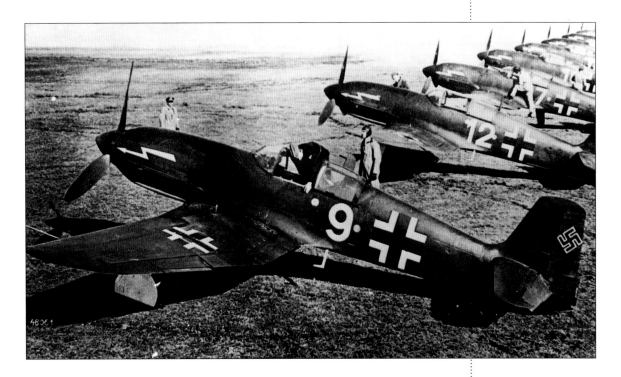

**ABOVE: ALTHOUGH
APPEARING TO BE IN
LUFTWAFFE SERVICE,
THE HE 100 (OR 112U)
WAS ONLY USED BY
THE GERMANS FOR
PROPA-GANDA PURPOSES
AFTER THE DECISION WAS
MADE NOT TO ADOPT IT AS
A FIGHTER.**

While the Luftwaffe had some very capable and highly experienced section leaders and Staffel commanders, there was little in-depth experience since few pilots had been flying in the Luftwaffe for more than about five years. There were many excellent pilots, with good combat skills, but very few had sufficient command experience to even lead a Staffel effectively. This left command of many of the Grüppen in the hands of men who had also flown in the First World War – men who, in truth, were too old to be flying fighters in 1940. Losses in combat were extremely hard to replace. By contrast, many RAF Squadron Commanders had been flying for ten years, with eight years on frontline fighters, and some had even more experience. The Luftwaffe had no equivalent to the RAF's Group Captains and Air Commodores who had flown operationally between the mid-to-late 1920s and the early 1930s, before going on to staff work while still fairly young and flexible.

Although the Luftwaffe had shown a clear technical superiority over its previous opponents, whose air forces had been tiny and equipped with obsolete types, its own aircraft were no longer at the cutting edge of technology, and against the RAF they would begin to show some deficiencies. This was particularly true of the Luftwaffe's bombers, which were slow (though both the Do 17 and Ju 88 were capable of running away quickly in a steep dive) and woefully under-armed and lightly armoured. Had the RAF's fighters been properly armed, with 20mm cannon instead of their ineffective batteries of rifle-calibre machine guns, they would have been destroyed in droves. In skies ruled by the Spitfire, the Ju 87 was even more vulnerable, while the twin-engined Bf 110 Zerstorer (on which such high hopes were pinned) was similarly unable to cope with modern single-engined fighters.

Even the much-vaunted Bf 109 was no match for the Spitfire and Hurricane, and during the Battle BF 109 pilots were directed not to attempt to match the turn ability of the RAF

fighters, but to use their superior speed to make high-speed slash attacks. But more serious than the Bf 109's poor turn performance was its lack of endurance and range, which left it unable to engage in prolonged air battles, and unable to escort friendly bombers all the way to their targets.

Replacements for the Luftwaffe's obsolescent types were slow to reach the frontline. The inadequacies of some aircraft types were not always obvious until they were put into combat, and development and production was slow. German aircraft production, in particular, was unable to match that of Britain's revived aircraft industry, not least because there was no effective structure to direct it. Thus as soon as the Battle of France was over, potentially invaluable aircraft production capacity was used instead to make pre-fabricated aluminium huts, and even folding ladders for Rhineland vineyards. There was certainly no equivalent to the mass mobilisation of every conceivable industry to help the war effort, as there had been in Britain. For example, a powerful justification for the production of the Mosquito night fighter/bomber was that it would use the skills and production plants of the furniture industry.

Germany also lagged behind Britain in the application of technology. In the development of radar, for example, German scientists produced sets that were more sophisticated, and had greater potential than the crude equipment pressed into service by the British. But the advanced German technology was trouble-prone and unsuitable for frontline use, and little urgency was injected into the programme. The German radars which worked best were used for sea surveillance, and Germany assumed that Britain's coastal chain stations served the same purpose, albeit using a less suitable frequency band.

Yet in some ways, the Luftwaffe was better prepared in organisational terms for its assault on Britain, with Air Fleets already fully formed, ready to take position on newly-captured French, Belgian, Dutch and Norwegian airfields. The old Grüppen-Kommandos

had been replaced in 1939 by five numbered Air Fleets or Luftflotten. These were integrated autonomous tactical air forces in their own right, unlike the RAF's separate functional Commands. There were advantages and disadvantages to both approaches, and it is certainly true that the Luftflotten enjoyed great success in Poland and France. However, the development of German fighter and bomber tactics and doctrine was stultified, as there was no central organisation which encouraged innovation and advances. For the Battle of Britain, Luftflotte II under Kesselring was headquartered in Brussels, supporting Army Group B, with Luftflotte III under Sperrle headquartered in Paris, supporting Army Groups A and C. Luftflotte V was based in Norway (though some of its units had transferred to Luftflotten on the continent).

At a lower level on the organisational ladder, the Luftwaffe's structure encouraged use of the Grüppe as the standard tactical unit, rather than the Staffel. During the Battle of Britain, this meant that Fighter Command was often out-numbered (since it operated in squadrons, or pairs of squadrons), but it also meant that the Luftwaffe used unwieldy formations that were easy to intercept, and that the German forces were seldom able to overwhelm the defences by attacking at several points simultaneously. Weaknesses such as this, and the many other deficiencies in the Luftwaffe's equipment and infrastructure, would dramatically affect the direction and outcome of the Battle of Britain.

BELOW: THE COCKPIT OF A GERMAN BOMBER. WHILST THE PILOT FLIES THE PLANE, THE CO-PILOT KEEPS A CAREFUL EYE OUT FOR ANY ENEMY FIGHTERS. DESPITE SUCH CAUTION, GERMAN BOMBER LOSSES DURING THE BATTLE WERE TO BE HIGH.

CHAPTER 3

The Royal Air Force 1918–1940

LEFT: THE PILOT OF A 1930S HAWKER AUDAX ARMY CO-OPERATION AIRCRAFT MAKING LAST-MINUTE MAP CHECKS BEFORE BOARDING HIS AIRCRAFT. NOTE THE AIR MECHANICS STANDING AT EACH WINGTIP, READY TO RELEASE THE WHEEL CHOCKS.

At the end of the Great War, Britain had what was then the largest air force ever seen, with 293,532 officers and men and 22,000 aircraft, although this shrunk to 31,500 officers and men and 371 aircraft within just one year! Only the determination of Lord Trenchard and his officers prevented complete disbandment, with the Army and Royal Navy absorbing aircraft and aircrew to re-form their own air arms. Trenchard cleverly structured the tiny infant RAF as a collection of cadres, around which later expansion could be based. Great emphasis was therefore placed on founding training establishments, including the RAF College at Cranwell, for training those officers granted permanent commissions. These men would go on to command the service, while the School of Technical Training at Halton trained boy entrants or apprentices, and the

Central Flying School trained flying instructors and had responsibility for maintaining standards. From the beginning, there was a deliberate policy of training an elite permanent cadre, with short-duration personnel receiving a less rigorous training, although even this compared very well with that given to personnel in any other air arms.

Rather than staffing his squadrons only with long-serving career pilots, Trenchard recruited large numbers of officers on what were called 'Short Service Commissions', under which they spent only five years in the regular RAF, but then provided a reserve of trained aircrew who could, in time of crisis, be refreshed and re-trained quickly and simply. Trenchard also pressed for the creation of an Auxiliary Air Force, with frontline flying squadrons equipped with machines recently discarded by the regular squadrons. The Auxiliary squadrons were to be built up around a full-time regular core, but would be manned principally by enthusiastic part-timers, some of whom would be former Short-Service Commission aircrew. Trenchard foresaw the Auxiliaries as providing a well-motivated reinforcement in times of crisis, a faith borne out by the record of the Auxiliaries in the early years of the Second World War. Trenchard also urged the creation of University Air Squadrons, with flying schools for undergraduates at Oxford, Cambridge and London colleges aimed at making supporters of air power among graduates who might then join the Civil Service, professions or Government, and to encourage high-calibre graduates to consider the RAF as a career. The Auxiliary and University Squadrons were initially seen as an expensive luxury, and were not established until the mid-1930s.

It took several years for the RAF to define a role for itself, and as it did so it grew to meet new responsibilities, which initially consisted largely of monitoring and enforcing the armistice in Europe, and colonial policing. Home defence was particularly neglected in the early years, following so soon after the 'war to end all wars'. But the French had retained a large force of bombers and fighters (about 300 of each) after World War I, and these made the RAF's

OPPOSITE TOP: A WESTLAND WAPITI OF NO 60 SQUADRON, KOHAT, BOMBING DISSIDENT TRIBESMEN ON THE NORTH-WEST FRONTIER OF INDIA.

OPPOSITE BOTTOM: THE LUMBERING HANDLEY PAGE HEYFORD, SEEN HERE UNDER MOCK ATTACK, WAS THE LAST OF THE RAF'S BIPLANE HEAVY BOMBERS. BY THE BEGINNING OF WWII IT HAD BEEN REPLACED BY THE VICKERS WELLINGTON AND OTHER TYPES.

LEFT: HAWKER FURY I BIPLANE FIGHTERS OF NO 43 SQUADRON MUSTERED AT RAF MILDENHALL, SUFFOLK, FOR A ROYAL REVIEW IN 1938. THE FURY WAS THE DIRECT ANCESTOR OF THE HURRICANE, WHICH WAS ORIGINALLY KNOWN AS THE FURY MONOPLANE.

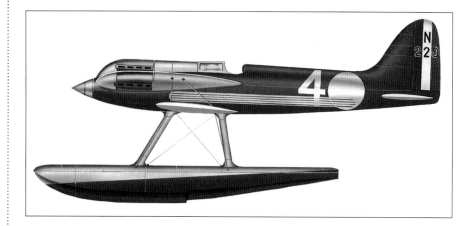

equivalent home defence force of about 40 aircraft, in three squadrons, look rather inadequate.

In 1922, the decision was taken to form a Metropolitan Air Force with some 14 bomber and nine fighter squadrons (about 266 aircraft), the high proportion of bombers reflecting the Trenchard orthodoxy that offence was the best form of defence. In 1923, the Government accepted that the 'Home Defence Air Force' should be expanded to 52 squadrons, but almost immediately the Conservative Premier, Bonar-Law, appointed Sir Eric Geddes to cut defence expenditure, a task made palatable to the public by the prevailing climate of pacifism and disarmament. The Government postulated a 'Ten Year Rule', assuming that Germany would rigidly adhere to the terms of the Treaty of Versailles and that there would thus be no danger of war for at least ten years.

It was 1928 before Trenchard was able to restore the expansion programme, winning permission for a force of 394 bombers and 204 fighters. Even then, it was laid down that the scheme would not reach fruition before 1935 or 1936, and it was subsequently delayed by Ramsay MacDonald's second Labour administration (who added two years to the timetable)

and then indefinitely postponed in 1932 under the 'armament truce' which accompanied the League of Nations' Disarmament Conference.

But meanwhile, existing forces had been carefully reorganised from 1925 with the formation of the Air Defence of Great Britain. Within the ADGB, three so-called 'Bombing Areas' were augmented by a 'Fighting Area', the latter controlling all the fighter aircraft and fighter airfields. With the main threat still perceived as coming from France, Trenchard built up a defensive belt of fighter aerodromes running from Devizes in Wiltshire to Cambridge, curving

around London and roughly parallel to the coast. This belt consisted of eight 24.1km (15-mile) wide 'sectors' with one fighter squadron per sector, except in the two sectors south and south-east of London, which each had two squadrons. Three further fighter units were based at coastal aerodromes from where, it was hoped, they would harass enemy formations before they reached the fighter belt, and as they retreated. (Bomber aerodromes were similarly arrayed to meet the needs of a war between England and France, lying behind the fighter belt in Wiltshire, Hampshire, Berkshire and Oxfordshire.) The permanent 'Sector Airfields' of the fighters were augmented by new aerodromes, and by satellite and emergency landing grounds which were cleared of obstacles, rolled flat and properly drained before being leased back to farmers, ready for requisition for use by the RAF in any emergency.

The foundations for a control and reporting system were also laid, initially relying upon the Observer Corps, telephone lines and mobile sound locators. Apart from the introduction of radar and radio, and the extension and strengthening of the fighter belt, the system was recognisably similar to that of Fighter Command as it fought the Battle of Britain. The perception of France as the major threat in the 1920s and early 1930s was extremely fortuitous, since the Luftwaffe mounted its Battle of Britain offensive from French aerodromes.

Expansion was re-started in 1934, following the break-up of the League of Nations' Disarmament Conference. The first stage of British military expansion, authorised as 'Scheme A' in July 1934, was little more than a high-profile attempt to impress the Germans

K
7986

K7986

with what amounted to little more than superficial changes and low-budget rearmament. Although the existence of Germany's own new air force was then still supposedly secret, there was deep suspicion that Germany was gearing up for war of some sort.

Britain's new Secretary of State for Air, Sir Philip Cunliffe-Lister, newly ennobled as Lord Swinton, soon pushed through a more dramatic expansion programme, which aimed to increase RAF strength by 588 aircraft and 49 squadrons. This was to take the RAF to 122 squadrons (including 20 heavy bomber, 18 medium bomber, 30 light bomber, 35 fighter and 18 reconnaissance) and 1512 aircraft. Lord Swinton also began urging industry to gear-up for what amounted to wartime levels of production in peacetime.

Exhortation is seldom enough to achieve radical change, and various practical measures were put in place to achieve the necessary expansion of industrial output. The 'Shadow Factory' scheme, announced in March 1936, built state-owned plants equipped and managed by non-aerospace industrial concerns. These produced products designed by aircraft or engine makers, usually components or sub-assemblies for final assembly elsewhere. The first Shadow Factories were run by motor car manufacturers, and produced components for Bristol Aero Engines. Lord Nuffield's company, Wolseley, declined to participate unless it could build whole engines, which was not an option, and instead was later given control of the Castle Bromwich factory, whose task would be to build whole Spitfires under the

ABOVE: HURRICANES ON THE PRODUCTION LINE. THE HURRICANE'S STRUCTURE WAS ROBUST, LIGHT, RELATIVELY EASY TO MANUFACTURE AND REPAIR, AND WAS CAPABLE OF ABSORBING AN ENORMOUS AMOUNT OF BATTLE DAMAGE.

guidance of Vickers Supermarine. In the end, the Nuffield organisation proved unable to run the Castle Bromwich works effectively, and it was only after the transfer of the factory to the control of Vickers Supermarine – nearly too late for the Battle of Britain – that the factory began churning out huge numbers of Spitfires. Had Vickers been in control of the plant from the beginning, many more fighter squadrons could have been Spitfire-equipped during the Battle of Britain. But Nuffield was not alone in having problems. The first batch of Spitfire wings produced by Pobjoy did not fit the fuselages built by Supermarine, for example.

Studies in the early 1930s shaped the design of the RAF's first wartime fighters. The need for monoplanes of stressed skin, monocoque construction had already been demonstrated by the success of the Schneider Trophy-winning Supermarine seaplanes, although many older Air Staff officers felt that enclosed cockpits were not a good idea, and pressed hard for the retention of open cockpits. Ballistics experts had shown that at least eight machine guns would be required to destroy a bomber in the two seconds available in a typical firing pass, and this led to the adoption of the eight-gun battery of 0.303in Colt-Brownings as the standard for the Hurricane and Spitfire. Research using a contemporary bomber as the target would have shown even this to be inadequate, and would have demonstrated that a two-second burst was longer than would often be possible. But without the necessary theoretical work to demonstrate a need, no-one realised that a fighter actually would require fewer, much heavier weapons (four 20mm cannon was

probably ideal). Even eight rifle-calibre machine guns was a tremendous improvement over the two guns carried by most of the RAF's frontline fighters during the early 1930s, however. Fighter specifications drawn up in 1934–35 also demanded provision of a reflector gunsight, oxygen for the pilot, a retractable undercarriage, and performance figures exceeding 442.6km/h (275mph) at 4572m (15,000ft), a climb to 6096m (20,000ft) within seven and a half minutes, a ceiling of 10,058m (33,000ft) and a landing run of 229m (750ft).

All of this ensured that the expansion programme eventually produced an air force equipped with large numbers of truly modern aircraft (unlike in France, where the bulk of the aircraft in service on the outbreak of war were obsolete). Certainly in 1938, the RAF's fighter units were still equipped with biplanes which stood little chance of catching Germany's new monoplane bombers, but by the outbreak of war, fighters like the Spitfire and Hurricane were firmly in the ascendancy.

'Scheme F' of the expansion, authorised in February 1936, strengthened the RAF frontline further, and placed increased emphasis on the provision of fighters. Meanwhile, the new Chief of the Air Staff, Air Chief Marshal Sir Edward Ellington, fought hard to

ANTI-AIRCRAFT COMMAND

The aircraft of Fighter Command were augmented by an array of searchlights and anti-aircraft guns, which were coordinated and collected together in April 1939 with the formation of Anti-Aircraft Command. Anti-Aircraft Command was actually a branch of the army, commanded by an army officer (General Sir Frederick Pile) though it was headquartered at Bentley Priory, within Fighter Command's own Headquarters. By the time the Battle began, the Command had seven divisions controlling 1200 heavy and 587 light guns, supported by 3932 searchlights. Some 300 of the heavy guns were in permanent concrete emplacements, but the rest could theoretically be deployed where needed. Usually deployed in batteries of four, linked to a local Gun Operations Room, the guns had a limited effect. Most were sited to protect the Royal Navy's shore bases, thus the Rosyth Dockyard (probably outside the range of most bombers) had 96 guns, while Headquarters Fighter Command had only four. Anti-Aircraft Command had its problems, of course, not least that its personnel often worked in the most primitive conditions. Sighting the guns was extremely difficult, even against targets flying straight and level, and there was a shortage of Kerrison predictors. Gun-laying radar was in extremely short supply, and most guns relied on useless sound locators to find their targets. Nor was the Command given proximity fuses – so the shells were ineffective unless the target happened to be at exactly the same altitude as the pre-set fuse. Against low-flying targets there were not enough of the fast-firing Bofors guns, although the command did have some Parachute And Cable (PAC) devices which proved surprisingly effective.

Anti-aircraft guns were undeniably useful as morale boosters, especially when the Luftwaffe started mounting night attacks. Some victories were credited to the guns, but questions remain as to whether these enemy aircraft were actually downed by the guns, or by fighters whose claims were disallowed. Some even believe that the guns accounted for more friendly aircraft than hostile, and it is virtually certain that AA shells killed more British civilians than they did German airmen as they rained back to earth. Even if Anti-Aircraft Command's kill claims are accepted, it has been calculated that at least 30,000 rounds were expended for every enemy aircraft destroyed. Yet the anti-aircraft guns did succeed in breaking up formations of enemy bombers, reducing the accuracy of their bombing, and sometimes forcing them to fly higher than they would have wanted. Shellbursts also drew attention to the position of enemy aircraft.

The balloon barrage was not part of Anti-Aircraft Command, being controlled by the RAF's own Balloon Command. Some 1466 balloons were operational by the end of July 1940, and these proved to be an excellent deterrent to low-level aircraft (especially at night) and also provided a useful diversionary target for Bf 109s during their daylight sweeps. A balloon was, of course, easy and cheap to replace, yet was a difficult target which could help deplete a Bf 109's limited fuel reserve, and could even provoke an enemy pilot to fly into the ground.

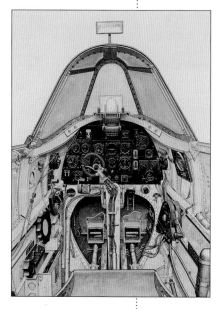

ABOVE: THE COCKPIT
OF A SPITFIRE, WITH A
CENTRALLY-MOUNTED
CONTROL YOKE, COMPLETE
WITH TRIGGER BUTTON.

RIGHT: BRISTOL BLENHEIM
MEDIUM BOMBERS ON
THE PRODUCTION LINE
AT FILTON, BRISTOL, IN
1938. BY THE SPRING
OF 1940 THE MK I HAD
BEEN REPLACED BY THE
MK IV, THE MK IS BEING
CONVERTED TO THE NIGHT
FIGHTER ROLE.

ensure that his service was based on quality and not just sheer quantity. Without an equivalent to Göring (who distributed top positions on the basis of patronage), Royal Air Force appointments during the late 1930s were on the whole eminently sensible, and included the posting of Sir Hugh Dowding to command the newly formed Fighter Command in 1936. The formation of Fighter Command recognised the growing importance attached to Britain's air defences, though the highest priority and prestige was still attached to bombers. The new Fighter Command controlled two subordinate geographic groups, No.11 in the south and No.12 in the north. From November 1939, there was also a Balloon Command overseeing the many barrage balloons, while Anti-Aircraft Command was formed in April 1939 to control and coordinate the searchlights and guns.

By the time of the Munich crisis, Fighter Command was larger than it had ever been, but only three of its 19 operational fighter squadrons were equipped with Hurricanes, and the rest used a variety of ageing and obsolete biplanes. Three more units were non-operational while converting to Hurricanes, while No.19 Squadron at Duxford had just taken delivery of its first Spitfire. With no heating for their gun bays, the Hurricanes were less useful than they appeared, being limited to a ceiling of only 4572m (15,000ft) to avoid their weapons freezing. The Munich agreement bought time for an intensification of the RAF expansion, and a changeover for the RAF, which went onto what amounted to a war footing. Silver fighters with gaudy squadron markings were hastily camouflaged and received inconspicuous two-letter identifying codes, and aircraft routinely began flying with loaded weapons.

The RAF had to find men to fly and service its new aircraft, and this was achieved by offering more Short Service Commissions and enlistments, and by offering to extend the

service of those coming to the end of their short-service engagements. Those who signed on for extended service were naturally denied to the Reserve, and to compensate for this, a new Volunteer Reserve was formed, giving elementary flying training to some of its members at a number of civilian-operated Reserve Flying Schools. By the time war broke out, the RAFVR was 63,000 strong, with 5000 aircrew trained or undergoing training. In June 1939, the Women's Auxiliary Air Force was formed with the aim of freeing men for aircrew and frontline ground duties by replacing second-line staff with WAAFs. In December 1939 (too late to influence the Battle of Britain), Flying Training School capacity was dramatically expanded through the Empire Air Training Scheme, under which RAF and Dominion aircrew received their basic and advanced flying training at RAF schools set up in Canada, Australia, New Zealand, South Africa and Southern Rhodesia.

Where British airmen really lagged behind their German counterparts between the wars was operational experience. Some RAF pilots did take part in combat operations, but these tended to be low-intensity actions against rebellious tribesmen in the Arabian interior or on the North West Frontier. Such operations tended to involve the RAF's oldest and most obsolete aircraft types, and provided no opportunity to develop tactics or weapons suitable for a real modern war.

When war broke out, the RAF's expansion programme had really started to bear fruit. Five Spitfire squadrons were operational or soon to become operational, with a further 11

ABOVE: SPITFIRE MK I OF NO 19 SQUADRON IN FLIGHT. BASED AT DUXFORD, NO 19 WAS THE FIRST SQUADRON TO REARM WITH THE SPITFIRE IN THE SUMMER OF 1938. THE SQUADRON NUMBER ON THE TAIL WAS SOON REPLACED BY FUSELAGE CODE LETTERS.

RIGHT: HAWKER
HURRICANES OF NO 242
SQUADRON ON PATROL
OVER SOUTHERN ENGLAND.
MANNED MAINLY BY
CANADIANS, NO 242
WAS COMMANDED IN THE
BATTLE OF BRITAIN BY
THE LEGENDARY DOUGLAS
BADER.

OPPOSITE PAGE: QUEEN
ELIZABETH INSPECTING
MEMBERS OF THE ATS
(AUXILIARY TRANSPORT
SERVICE), OF WHICH SHE
WAS COMMANDANT-IN-
CHIEF.

In many quarters the fall of France was quietly welcomed, with a widespread feeling that the French had let Britain down again and again. Such attitudes went to the top of British society. The King remarked that 'Personally I feel happier now that we have no Allies to be polite to and pamper', while Churchill welcomed the fact that Britain's destiny was now in its own hands.

operational with the Hurricane. Fighter Command was becoming a modern force, though it remained below the 52-squadron total Dowding had calculated as being the minimum necessary to protect the country from unescorted German bomber attacks from German bases. Nor had Dowding anything like his required number of heavy AA guns (1264), searchlights (4700) twin-barrelled light AA guns for low-level air defence (300) or barrage balloons (400 for London alone). But things were getting better, and there was, at last, the political will to do the job of defending Britain properly.

THE FEW

Air Commodore John Slessor, the Air Ministry's Director of Plans, was an intelligent and realistic military thinker. He was not prone to the despair and pessimism (or the groundless optimism) which infected many senior military men and political leaders during 1940. His assessment was that the Royal Navy and the RAF could together prevent any German landing, but that without the RAF, the Royal Navy would not be able to prevent invasion indefinitely. He also realised that, in its weakened post-Dunkirk state, the British Army might be unable to stop a 'serious invasion'. This made it vital that the Germans should be defeated before they could launch an invasion, or that the necessary pre-conditions for invasion be denied. This in turn placed the RAF in a key position, since to prevent invasion the Luftwaffe had to be deprived of air supremacy. Even in this measured analysis, the vital importance of RAF Fighter Command is thus apparent.

The Royal Air Force lost 509 fighter aircraft over Western Europe (of a total of 959 aircraft lost) in the 3 weeks following the German invasion of the Low Countries on 10 May. This shocking figure included 67 Spitfires and 386 Hurricanes. By 5 June, Fighter Command fielded only 331 single-engined fighters, having lost 106 fighters over Dunkirk, an evacuation which also saw the deaths of over 80 RAF pilots. By late June, some 435 pilots were listed as killed, missing or captured. And of the 261 Hurricanes despatched to fly from French aerodromes, only 66 returned, and some of those were so badly damaged that they were unceremoniously scrapped.

But although it had been badly depleted in the fierce fighting in France, and indeed in Norway, Fighter Command had performed surprisingly well against the Luftwaffe's seasoned veterans, and during the French campaign had accounted for 247 Messerschmitt Bf 109s and 108 Bf 110s. As the campaign drew on, and as its pilots gained experience, it became steadily more effective. Over Dunkirk, for example, the RAF's fighter pilots destroyed 166 enemy aircraft (claiming 217) for the loss of 131 aircraft and 87 pilots. Although some of the RAF's most experienced peacetime officers had been lost, relatively large numbers of middle-ranking and junior pilots (who would become the Section, Flight and Squadron Leaders of the Battle of Britain) had opened their scores, gaining invaluable combat experience, tactical know-how and confidence. Even more importantly, the hard-won combat knowledge gained in France began to show up the inadequacies of pre-war tactics, moving the Command towards accepting change during the early days of the Battle of Britain. And while France had fallen, and while the RAF had suffered its own setbacks, the myth of German invincibility was undermined.

In many quarters the fall of France was quietly welcomed, with a widespread feeling that the French had let Britain down again and again. Such attitudes went to the top of British society. The King remarked that 'Personally I feel happier now that we have no Allies to be polite to and pamper', while Churchill welcomed the fact that Britain's destiny was now in its own hands. Dowding, the Commander-in-Chief of Fighter Command, had been even more contemptuous of the French, and was even more relieved to see them out of the war. 'I went down on my knees and thanked God!', he said later.

On his elevation to the post of Prime Minister on 14 May, Churchill had established a Ministry of Aircraft Production, and appointed the energetic Lord Beaverbrook to run it. The Shadow Factories established before the war were galvanised into action. The Castle Bromwich works, run by Nuffield, had still not produced a single Spitfire, so the organisation was put under the control of Vickers Supermarine, with astonishing results. By 30 September it had produced 125 Spitfire Mk IIs. Between June and

BELOW: THE POLISH FIGHTER SQUADRONS PLAYED A VITAL PART IN THE BATTLE OF BRITAIN. NO 303 SQUADRON, WHOSE PILOTS ARE PICTURED HERE, WAS BASED AT NORTHOLT DURING THE BATTLE.

BOTTOM: WOMEN OF THE AIR TRANSPORT AUXILIARY, SEEN HERE, DELIVERED AIRCRAFT TO THE FRONT-LINE RAF SQUADRONS IN ENGLAND. THEY FLEW EVERYTHING FROM LIGHT TRAINERS TO HEAVY BOMBERS.

October, Britain's monthly fighter production totals were 446, 496, 476, 467 and 469 – a total of 2354 aircraft. At the start of the Battle, the Maintenance Units held 222 Hurricanes and 119 Spitfires in storage for issue as attrition replacements, or to equip new units, and at their very lowest, reserves never dropped below 78 Hurricanes and 38 Spitfires (equivalent to nine squadrons). By comparison, German industry managed to produce 14, 220, 173, 218 and 144 between June and October – a total of only 919 aircraft.

Britain's speedy production of new fighters was augmented by a great effort in the rapid repair and return to service of damaged aircraft, such that 35 per cent of replacement aircraft delivered to frontline squadrons during the Battle were repaired rather than newly built. Some 60 per cent of the aircraft regarded as being unrepairable at Station level were rebuilt to fly again by the revitalised Civilian Repair Organisation, which was rebuilding 160 aircraft per week by mid July, and which delivered 4196 aircraft between July and December. In some cases, aircraft were repaired on a 'while you wait' basis, with Hurricanes flying into Henlow with battle damage, only to be repaired in time for their pilots to fly them again that day. The record time for changing both wings and to fit and load all eight

BELOW: BEFORE AMERICA'S ENTRY INTO THE WAR, THREE RAF FIGHTER SQUADRONS – THE SO-CALLED 'EAGLE SQUADRONS', NOS 71, 121 AND 133 – WERE MANNED BY AMERICAN PERSONNEL, BUT THEY WERE FORMED TOO LATE TO SEE ACTION IN 1940.

machine guns on a Hurricane was one hour and 55 minutes!

Fighter Command was never threatened by the aircraft shortages which sometimes loomed large on the other side of the Channel, and also avoided being affected by shortages of fuel, oil or ammunition. Britain even managed to secure regular supplies of 100 Octane aviation fuel from the USA (such high-octane fuel then being beyond the capabilities of most British refineries), allowing all Fighter Command Merlin-engined fighters to be converted to run on the more efficient, higher performance fuel by March 1940. Fuel reserves rose steadily throughout the Battle of Britain, despite heavy use.

Aircraft availability was thus not much of a problem, though finding pilots for them sometimes was. Some 3000 aircrew fought in the Battle of Britain, but relatively few of them were regular, peacetime Fighter Command men, even after the massive expansion in pilot numbers during the late 1930s. 1700 extra Short Service Commissions had been awarded, and 800 new NCO (Non Commissioned Officer) pilots had been trained. The number of Flying Training Schools had grown from six to eleven. The best fighter pilots from Army Cooperation Command and Coastal Command were posted in to eke out the Fighter Command squadrons, along with hand-picked pilots from Bomber Command. The peacetime Auxiliaries also played an important part, especially at the beginning of the Battle. The shortage of pilots also prompted the transfer of 45 part-trained and semi-trained Royal Navy pilots on 6 June 1940 for conversion to eight-gun fighters. 30 more followed by the end of June, though 10 were subsequently recalled for service in the Mediterranean. But those who remained were scattered through Fighter Command, and several achieved Ace status.

And then there were the foreign volunteers, drawn from Britain's empire, dominions and commonwealth, from the occupied countries of Europe, and even from the USA.

ABOVE: CZECH PILOTS, LIKE THIS YOUNG OFFICER, MADE A VITAL CONTRIBUTION TO THE RAF'S VICTORY. ONE OF THEM, SGT JOSEF FRANTISEK, DESTROYED 17 ENEMY AIRCRAFT DURING THE BATTLE OF BRITAIN, MORE THAN ANY OTHER PILOT.

LEFT: THE HAWKER HURRICANE, NOT THE SPITFIRE, WAS TO BE THE MAINSTAY OF THE RAF DURING THE BATTLE OF BRITAIN.

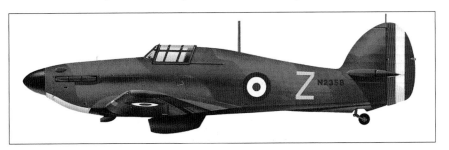

ABOVE: A BRITISH 'BOBBY'
SHAKES HANDS WITH
SOME INDIAN AIR FORCE
OFFICERS, NEWLY ARRIVED
IN BRITAIN. THE PILOTS
WHO DEFENDED THE
COUNTRY IN THE SUMMER
OF 1940 CAME FROM
MANY CORNERS OF THE
GLOBE.

Numerically the most important were the Poles, 147 of whom enlisted in the RAF, some of them newly qualified and inexperienced, some having fought against the Germans in 1939 before moving on to fly and fight with Polish formations within the French Armée de l'Air. The Poles had little command of the English language, few had any experience of modern aircraft, and the majority were not committed until quite late in the Battle, when the two Polish Squadrons were formed. But they were aggressive and determined, and rapidly gained a reputation as formidable fighter pilots and as crack shots. By November, the Polish No.303 Squadron had outscored every RAF unit in the Battle of Britain, while in 1941 Polish squadrons took the top three places in Fighter Command's gunnery competition, with scores of 808, 432 and 193. The top-scoring 'English' Squadron came fourth, with a score of 150.

In addition to the Poles there were 101 New Zealanders, 94 Canadians, 87 Czechs, 29 Belgians, 22 Australians, 22 South Africans, 14 French, 10 Irishmen, seven Americans and one pilot each from Palestine, Jamaica and Newfoundland. The Canadians included many fully-trained RCAF officers, and even before the Battle began they were able to man a combat-ready Hurricane squadron (No.242).

The public perception of 'the Few' was once that they were predominantly English public schoolboys, barely out of their teens, with a hefty proportion of adventurers from Australia and the Empire. The list of top-scorers in the Battle (presented in the appendices) is broadly representative of the Few as a whole, and certainly contradicts the simplistic picture of the RAF's fighter pilots. Eight of the top-scoring pilots, fully one quarter, were NCOs, while these eight were augmented by two pilots who had been commissioned from the ranks. Of these ten NCOs or former NCOs, no less than five were ex Halton apprentices (known as 'Brats') and two were from the solidly 'lower middle class' RAFVR, as were three of the commissioned pilots. Six of the remaining top scorers were, admittedly, from the Auxiliary Air Force (often seen as being socially exclusive), although one of these had been a plasterer's apprentice. The remainder had obtained Short Service Commissions after school or university, but only two were from notable public schools.

Nor were there many non-British top-scorers in the early stage of the war. The sole American to score more than eight victories had actually received an English public school education and was an Auxiliary Air Force pilot. The top scorers included, however, two New Zealanders, one Australian (and one Brit whose parents had emigrated to Australia, from where he returned soon after he'd arrived!), a South African, a Czech and one Pole. Antipodean and Canadian pilots certainly made a major contribution later in the war, but they were still a rarity during the Battle of Britain.

Perhaps the biggest difference in the Battle of Britain between Fighter Command pilots and their opposite numbers in the Jagdwaffe was the disparity in operational experience.

Although relatively large numbers of Fighter Command pilots had seen action over France and the Channel during the Battle of France, many of the most experienced pilots from that campaign had been withdrawn from the frontline to rest, or to pass on their experience as instructors. Furthermore, only a handful of Fighter Command pilots had any experience dating back before the Battle of France. There were exceptions, of course, including some of the Poles, and Fighter Command even had at least one pilot (a Belgian) who had fought with the Nationalists alongside the Condor Legion in Spain. By contrast, few Luftwaffe fighter Gruppen did not include a brace of veterans of the Spanish war, and large numbers of pilots had found their combat skills in Poland while even larger numbers had fought over France.

Movies and propaganda photos often depict the RAF pilots as being handsome and fit young men. But the popular perception of fresh-faced youths barely out of school is not very accurate. The top-scoring pilots ranged in age from 20 to 32, the majority being more

ABOVE: 'WE SHALL FIGHT THEM ON THE BEACHES...' PRIME MINISTER WINSTON CHURCHILL INSPECTING A DEFENSIVE POST SOMEWHERE ON THE COAST OF NORTH-EAST ENGLAND DURING THE FATEFUL SUMMER OF 1940.

LEFT: FUTURE RAF AIR GUNNERS LEARN TO SHOOT STRAIGHT BEFORE PROGRESSING TO MORE COMPLEX ASPECTS OF THEIR COURSE.

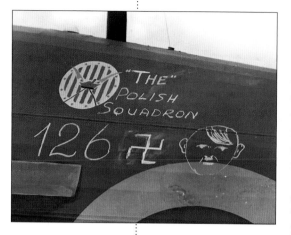

ABOVE: GROUND CREWS OF NO 303 (POLISH) SQUADRON CELEBRATE THE UNIT'S 126TH 'KILL' IN THE BATTLE OF BRITAIN WITH SOME GRAFFITI ON THE SIDE OF A HAWKER HURRICANE. THE SQUADRON SUCCESSIVELY FLEW HURRICANES, SPITFIRES AND MUSTANGS DURING WWII.

RIGHT: GROUNDCREW WORKING ON A HURRICANE HAVE AN IMPROMPTU PICNIC ON THE TAILPLANE BEFORE THE WAR.

than 26 years old. They were generally physically fit, though the RAF's Battle of Britain fighter pilots were not all models of physical perfection. As children, many had grown up in the hard times of the 1920s, and some had poor teeth and were under-sized as the result of childhood malnutrition. And with the pressing need for pilots, aircrew medical inspections were not always used as a means of weeding out those whose fitness might not have met peacetime requirements. Without a war, the legless Douglas Bader would probably not have returned to the cockpit, while the American 'Shorty' Keough, 1.46m (4ft 10in) tall, would not have been able to fly a Spitfire (for which he needed two extra seat cushions). Christopher 'Wombat' Woods-Scawen (an ace with No.43 Squadron) bluffed his way into the RAF despite having appallingly poor eyesight. He memorised the vision chart to pass the initial medical, and then had special goggles made for flying.

Before the invasion of France, the distance from German airfields to Britain meant that the German threat was one of unescorted bombers attacking across the North Sea from Holland and Belgium. Against this threat, Dowding carefully calculated that 52 Squadrons would be required to defend the UK, and he watched helplessly as the French campaign reduced his Command to only 36 squadrons. With the German invasion of France, Britain faced a threat from German, Dutch, Belgian, French and even Norwegian airfields, and relatively large swathes of southeast England fell within the radius of action of the single-

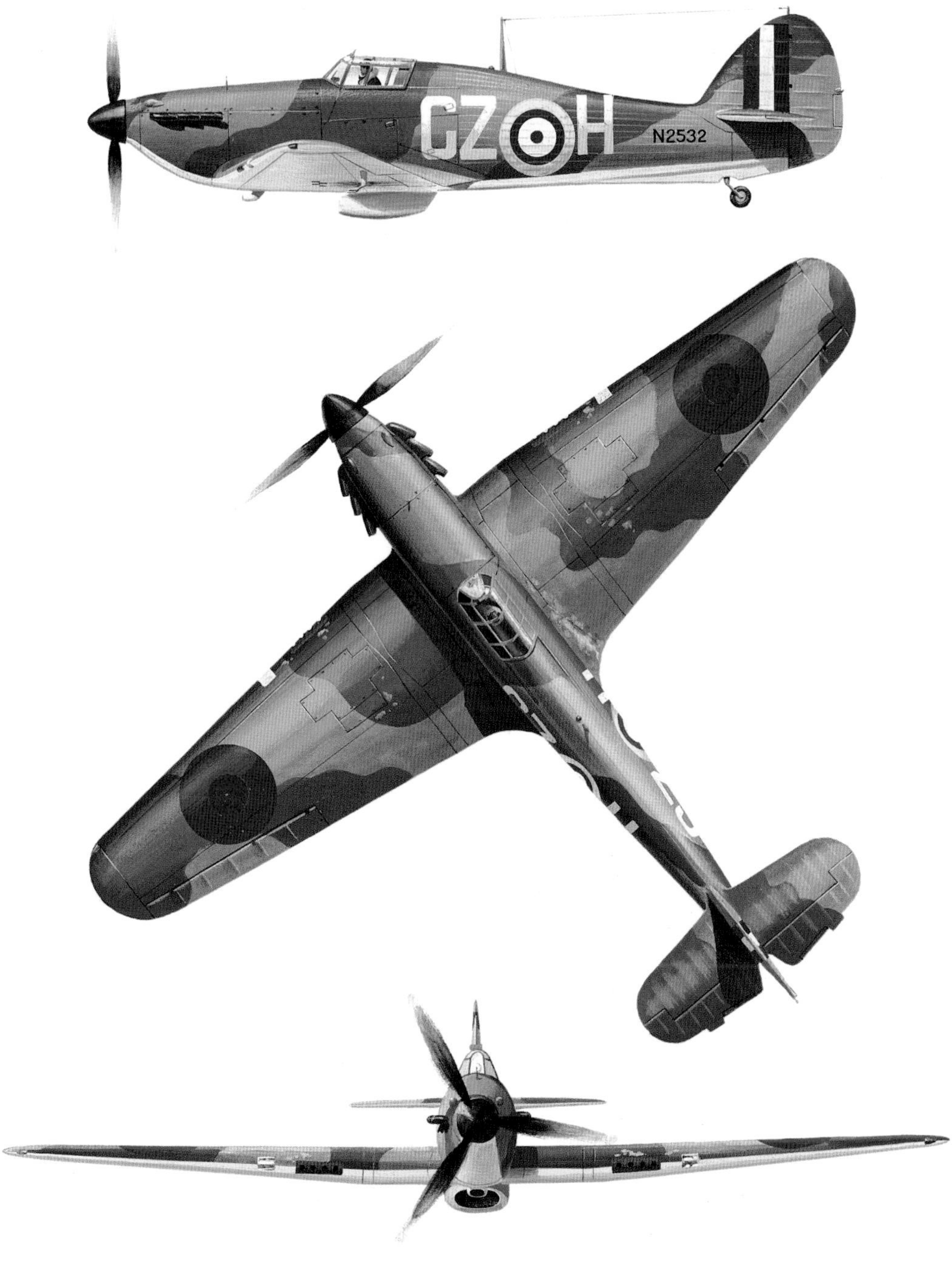
GZ H
N2532

engined Messerschmitt Bf 109. Against this expanded threat, Fighter Command needed to be even stronger. Fortunately, expansion and re-equipment after the fall of France left the Command fielding 58 squadrons by early July, spread between four Groups.

Some felt that Dowding should have concentrated his best fighters in the No.11 Group area (covering the south east), where fighter opposition was most likely, leaving the Blenheims and Defiants in the north, where they could (it was simplistically assumed) deal with unescorted bombers. Instead, Dowding spread his resources, with 12 Hurricane, six Spitfire and four Blenheim squadrons in No.11 Group, five Hurricane, five Spitfire, two Blenheim and one Defiant squadron in East Anglia's No.12 Group, and three Hurricane, six Spitfire, one Blenheim and one Defiant squadron in No.13 Group in the north. The newly formed No.10 Group, covering the West Country, included two Hurricane and two Spitfire squadrons. These were the operational units in the 'front line', while each Group also had some non-operational units working up to readiness.

Dowding appreciated that the forthcoming Battle would be one of attrition, and he aimed to keep a mix of units and aircraft types in the less dangerous areas, forming a ready-made reserve whose elements could be used to reinforce No.11 Group when its squadrons became exhausted. No.11 Group was the largest Group, and had almost half of the RAF's single-seat fighter units. Fortuitously, the Group was also provided with well-equipped permanent airfields, the legacy of the 1920s, when France was felt to be as likely a potential enemy as Germany, and when the bulk of Great Britain's peacetime fighter squadrons were based in the southeast of England. This left the RAF remarkably well prepared to combat raids launched from French airfields.

As the Battle began, Fighter Command was thus in remarkably good shape, and most squadrons were actually over-manned, often with as many as 20 operational pilots on their books. (The normal peacetime establishment of 18 pilots typically included several young pilots still under training).

But once the Battle began, getting replacement pilots was more difficult. Ironically, in late 1939 and early 1940, thousands of trainee pilots (many of them with extensive flying hours in their logbooks) were transferred into other trades because of the chronic shortage of training aircraft. Some of these potential pilots were lost to the system after gaining more flying hours than the young frontline Luftwaffe pilots shot down in the opening stages of the Battle, and many were far more experienced than the RAF's own replacements, some of whom arrived on squadrons with only ten hours basic flying experience and without having completed any Operational Training Unit courses. Churchill's Chief Scientific Adviser, Professor Frederick Lindemann (later Lord Cherwell) had been the driving force behind a reduction in OTU courses from six months to only four weeks, leaving the squadrons to apply the final training. As a result, Fighter Command began receiving replacement pilots

who had not yet mastered their powerful new monoplane fighters, and who had received little training in blind or night flying, navigation, or gunnery.

Battle of Britain mythology has always intimated that most pilots who managed to bail out were rapidly returned to their units, since most fell over friendly territory, or close to the coast. Certainly those who came down over land who were not badly burned or otherwise wounded were able to fight again, but the story was rather different for those who bailed out over the Channel. The Luftwaffe was very good at recovering shot down aircrew (who were generously provided with dinghies and dye markers, and who had excellent life jackets) even from waters close to the English coast, and had an efficient and well-equipped search and rescue organisation. By contrast, British search and rescue efforts were ill coordinated and patchy, and a disgraceful number of those who survived bailing out of their aircraft died of exposure or drowned before they could be recovered.

FATHER OF THE FEW

The young pilots who fought the Battle of Britain seized the public imagination, as did the sleek, beautiful and evocatively named aircraft which they flew. But every bit as important as the men on the frontline (and perhaps even more important) were their leaders. These men were, generally, less colourful than some of their subordinates, but their characters and intelligence were hugely influential when it came to the outcome of the Battle. Just as the Luftwaffe was handicapped by the inadequacies of its supreme commander, so the Commander-in-Chiefs of Fighter Command and No.11 Group made possible much of the eventual RAF victory.

Air Marshal Sir Hugh Dowding, invariably known as 'Stuffy', was a complex and controversial character, whose achievements were never properly recognised at the time, and whose services were contemptuously dispensed with as soon as the Battle was over. Dowding was never an easy man to like, shy and diffident yet also stubborn and difficult, and sometimes very rude.

Like most of the RAF's very senior officers, Downing was coming to the end of his career, having fought during the Great War. In fact, Dowding had been an army officer (a gunner) and had learned to fly at the age of 32 (against his father's express prohibition) and had then been called up into the RFC, commanding a squadron and becoming a Brigadier by 1918. In 1916, he had been dismissed by Trenchard as a 'dismal Jimmy obsessed by the

AIR VICE MARSHAL SIR TRAFFORD LEIGH-MALLORY

Leigh-Mallory had served with distinction in the RFC during the First World War, and pioneered the use of aircraft against tanks. He gained a reputation as an intellectual and a strategic thinker and was extremely ambitious, perhaps because he had been over-shadowed by his brother, the famous mountaineer, George Mallory, who had disappeared on Everest. His pomposity and vanity was explained by some as a cover for his shyness, and he gained a reputation as a caring and loyal commander, devoted to his young pilots, and a lively participant in mess games when he visited his fighter stations.

During the Battle of Britain, Leigh-Mallory commanded Fighter Command's No.12 Group in East Anglia, and was undeniably frustrated at taking a subordinate role to No.11 Group in Sussex and Kent. He had a personal antipathy for No.11 Group's commander, Keith Park, who had been his junior in rank, and he expended more effort in winning a prominent role for his Group and its squadrons than in working to support Park's direct requests for assistance. This directly led to mounting controversy and saw Leigh-Mallory and Sholto-Douglas allied against Dowding and Park.

Following the Battle of Britain, Leigh-Mallory presided over Fighter Command's disastrous series of offensive operations over France in 1941. During the second half of 1941, Fighter Command accounted for 154 enemy aircraft (although claiming 731!), but lost four of its own fighters for every victory. He maintained 75 fighter squadrons in Britain (more than were committed to the Battle of Britain), sustaining a 75 per cent erosion, and yet failed to send the latest Spitfires to the Far East, North Africa and Malta, where they might have done more good.

But nothing seemed able to halt Leigh-Mallory's meteoric rise. He took over Fighter Command in late 1942, and in 1943 became C-in-C of the Allied Expeditionary Air Force, retaining overall control of Fighter Command. By 1944, Leigh-Mallory was an Air Chief Marshal and the Allied Air Commander at SHAEF, reporting directly to General Eisenhower. But in the aftermath of D-Day, he gained a reputation for incompetence, and was resented by some for his pompous, arrogant attitude. Tedder (Eisenhower's deputy and the commander of 2 ATAF, the Allied Tactical Air Forces) and Spaatz (Commander of the USAAF's strategic air forces) regarded his carpet bombing in support of the break-out from Normandy as madness, and were reportedly infuriated by his lack of strategic grasp, and by his lack of bomber experience. General Montgomery dismissed him as a 'gutless bugger'. But others were more impressed, including Eisenhower, who admitted that his 'early doubts' had been entirely erased, and that Leigh-Mallory had given excellent service.

In 1945 Leigh-Mallory was killed in an air crash en route to take up his appointment as Allied Air Commander, South East Asia.

fear of further casualties', a telling criticism which indicated his difficult relations with senior officers, and his concern for his subordinates – both traits which would remain with him throughout his career.

By the late 1930s, Dowding was the most senior of the RAF's Air Marshals, and accordingly he was bitterly disappointed not to be appointed to succeed Sir Edward Ellington as Chief of the Air Staff (CAS) in February 1937, and, in effect, to be passed over by the younger Cyril Newall. During the early 1930s, Dowding had been the Air Member for Supply and Research, and as such had authorised the first radar experiments, watching the development of radar and the radio control of fighters with great interest. He had much in common with Ellington (CAS from 1933), who appointed him C-in-C of the new Fighter Command when it was formed in 1936. In the bomber-obsessed RAF of the 1930s, this was far from being the top job for a man of Dowding's rank and experience. The rest of the Air Staff tended to see fighters as being no more than a comforting placebo for a bomber-fearing public. Fighters had hitherto come under the control of the so-called Air Defence of Great Britain, which had actuallly been principally a bomber arm. Neither Ellington nor Dowding had been adherents of Trenchard's bomber doctrine to any degree, and Dowding set about providing the British Isles with a proper, co-ordinated, fighter defence for the first time with great enthusiasm.

TOP: BEFORE TRAINEE PILOTS GOT THEIR FEET OFF THE GROUND THEY HAD TO MASTER THE LINK TRAINER, AN EARLY FORM OF SIMULATOR IN WHICH THEY LEARNED ABOUT FLYING AND ENGINE CONTROLS.

ABOVE RIGHT: AN AIR GUNNER EXAMINES THE DROGUE AFTER AN AIR-TO-AIR FIRING EXERCISE TO SEE HOW MANY HITS HE HAS REGISTERED.

Under successive expansion programmes, the RAF's budget sky-rocketed (from 17.5 million pounds in 1934, to 27.6 million in 1935, 50.7 million in 1936, 56.5 million in 1937, and finally to 73.5 million pounds in 1938) and Dowding fought to gain a useful share for Fighter Command. In September 1939, he stated that the 'best defence of the Country is the fear of the fighter. If we are strong enough in fighters we will not be attacked in force, whereas limited strength will draw attacks'. Crucially, he divided the country into four geographic areas and set about creating the system of direction and control which would later win the Battle of Britain. He fought for the provision of underground operations rooms, bulletproof windscreens for his new monoplane fighters and concrete runways.

He was a great Commander for Fighter Command, though his tunnel vision and contempt for the needs of other Commands won him few friends. He was also withdrawn and humourless and could be rude and offensive. During the 1939 Air Defence Exercises, for example, he told Sir Trafford Leigh Mallory (one of his Group Commanders) that 'The trouble with you, Leigh-Mallory, is that you sometimes cannot see farther than the end of your little nose.' When Arthur Harris (later the Commander-in-Chief of Bomber Command) was appointed as Dowding's Senior Air Staff Officer, he reported that his 'heart went into my boots!' and that Dowding was 'as stubborn as a mule, but a nice old boy, really.' Dowding was not, in truth, much of a team player, and is usually regarded as a prickly and eccentric loner.

As the Battle of Britain drew near, incredibly, the bureaucrats did their best to distract Dowding's attention from the job in hand. He had originally been given a guarantee of employment until he reached the age of 60 (1942), but in August 1938 this was rescinded and he was told that he would retire in June 1939. His service was extended until 31 March 1940, and on 30 March he was finally told he could stay on until 14 July, though he was not told to whom he would be handing over. On 5 July he was asked to stay on until October. Dowding accepted this, but not without some characteristic moaning about consideration and discourtesy.

This job insecurity came on top of his active argument against wasting precious aircraft in France. His objections were proved to be quite reasonable by history, but at the time his view was not widely accepted, and he was openly contemptuous of other members of the Air Staff who vacillated or who disagreed with him. In opposing the dispatch of fighter aircraft to France, he set himself in opposition to the Prime Minister, who had promised aid to the French. Perhaps surprisingly, this eventually helped Dowding to win Churchill's support, and on 10 July, while bickering about retirement dates continued, Churchill wrote to the Air Staff that Dowding was 'one of the very best men you have got. He should be kept in office indefinitely while the war lasts.' Churchill even began suggesting that Dowding might usefully replace Newall as Chief of the Air Staff. Unfortunately, this support was destined to be short-lived, and may never have been more than expedient.

As the Battle of Britain went on, Dowding's star waned. The Deputy Chief of the Air Staff, Air Vice Marshal Sholto Douglas, and Dowding's own subordinate, Trafford Leigh-Mallory, the AOC No.12 Group, manoeuvred ruthlessly to discredit Dowding, and to engineer his removal. To a certain extent, this was Dowding's own fault, since he signally failed to resolve the row between his two Group Commanders (Leigh-Mallory and Park) during the Battle, and thereby laid himself open to charges of poor leadership. He also suffered because he lacked the kind of flamboyant extrovert confidence that Churchill liked to see in his subordinates,

ABOVE: RAF PERSONNEL PREPARING LEAFLETS TO BE DROPPED FROM A WHITLEY BOMBER OVER SOME ENEMY TARGET. LEAFLET-DROPPING OPERATIONS CONTINUED THROUGHOUT THE WAR.

LEFT: AIR CHIEF MARSHAL SIR SHOLTO DOUGLAS (LEFT) WITH KEITH PARK, THE NEW ZEALAND-BORN COMMANDER OF NO 11 GROUP IN THE BATTLE OF BRITAIN. DOUGLAS REPLACED SIR HUGH DOWDING AS C-IN-C FIGHTER COMMAND IN NOVEMBER 1940.

and was, indeed, just the kind of diffident pessimist that the Prime Minister could not abide. But although he was a 'grey man' Dowding was hard-working and energetic, and (with some exceptions) was an excellent judge of men, appointing extremely competent subordinates to whom he was willing and able to delegate.

Unfortunately, it was relatively trivial and peripheral matters of appearance that combined to fatally undermine Dowding's position, and Dowding's few allies were unable to help him. He had always enjoyed good relations with Beaverbrook, with whom he shared a common dislike for the 'Air Ministry and the bloody Air Marshals' and a strong mutual respect. Dowding was grateful for the production and repair organisations Beaverbrook had created, and in return was even willing to give up precious Spitfires for reconnaissance duties at Beaverbrook's request. But 'the Beaver' was himself under some pressure, resented for his ambition and increasing power, and feared as a potential rival to Churchill. By the end of the Battle of Britain, he was unable to do anything to save Dowding. And while Sir Frederick Pile (the commander of the anti-aircraft defences, and one of Dowding's few friends) summed him up as 'a difficult man, a self-opinionated man, (but also) a most determined man and a man who knew more than anybody about all aspects of aerial warfare', his ability, in the end, was not enough to save him.

By the end of the Battle of Britain, it should have been apparent that Dowding's careful husbandry of his resources had actually won the Battle. He had always feared being drawn into some kind of airborne Battle of Jutland which might have entirely destroyed his force, and he had taken great care to keep sufficient reserves ready to reinforce the frontline No.11 Group

as its individual squadrons became exhausted by bearing the brunt of the German attacks. In retrospect, Dowding's strategy was undeniably the right one, but it drew the ire of Leigh-Mallory, who bitterly resented the vital (but subordinate) role he had been forced to play. Others within No.12 Group felt that Dowding had allowed Park to fight a 'No.11 Group battle' that should have been a Fighter Command battle, profoundly misunderstanding the importance of Dowding's limited engagement in conserving resources and winning what became a battle of attrition. Such people included the charismatic wing leader and CO of No.242 squadron, Douglas Bader, whose adjutant was a Member of Parliament with easy access to the Prime Minister, and who was thus able to put No.12 Group's complaints directly to Churchill.

Dowding's cautious, unspectacular strategy also failed to fire Churchill's imagination, who as a layman (his military knowledge being hugely out of date) appreciated the bold and colourful approach to warfare. Despite his gloriously powerful rhetoric, Churchill

ABOVE: A RADAR STATION ON THE SOUTH COAST. THESE INSTALLATIONS WERE EARLY TARGETS FOR THE GERMAN BOMBERS.

LEFT: A WAAF (WOMEN'S AUXILIARY AIR FORCE) SCANS HER CATHODE RAY TUBE DISPLAY FOR SIGNS OF ENEMY ACTIVITY. THE TERM 'RADAR' DID NOT COME INTO USE UNTIL AFTER THE BATTLE; THE SYSTEM WAS KNOWN AS RDF (RADIO DIRECTION FINDING).

never saw the Battle of Britain as being more than a holding operation while the country gathered its strength for the offensive operations he longed to unleash. Even at the height of the Battle, Churchill was more interested in how the RAF might be able to launch a full bombing campaign. And while Dowding had known what was necessary to defeat the night Blitz (AI radar and more Beaufighters) his unwillingness to undertake less effective measures simply for the sake of show did not endear him to those who wanted something to be 'seen to be done'. Dowding actually opposed wider use of the Hurricane at night, worrying that the use of single-engined night fighters would achieve little, but which would cost precious lives. But his objections were carefully presented by his enemies as evidence that he lacked the dynamism necessary for the next (offensive) stage of the war.

Dowding's enemies were not confined to the higher reaches of the RAF, however. An anonymous paper circulated to Conservative MPs criticised Dowding for his 'inadequate mental ability and very slow brain', and described Fighter Command as a 'one man show'. Some suspect that the paper originated from Downing Street. Max Hastings commented that 'Churchill behaved with great brutality to those whom he decided were serving the war effort badly' and that Dowding 'like Wavell, was a victim of the Prime Minister at

BELOW: WHILE A MODERN, WELL-EQUIPPED CONTROL CENTRE WAS BEING BUILT AT HQ FIGHTER COMMAND, BENTLEY PRIORY, A TEMPORARY OPERATIONS ROOM WAS SET UP LATE IN 1939.

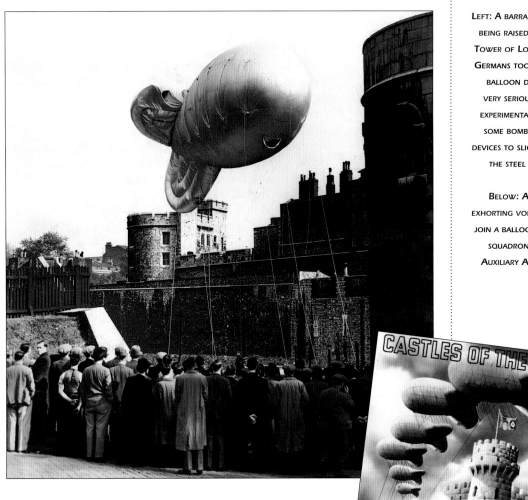

LEFT: A BARRAGE BALLOON
BEING RAISED NEAR THE
TOWER OF LONDON. THE
GERMANS TOOK BRITAIN'S
BALLOON DEFENCES
VERY SERIOUSLY, AND
EXPERIMENTALLY FITTED
SOME BOMBERS WITH
DEVICES TO SLICE THROUGH
THE STEEL CABLES.

BELOW: A POSTER
EXHORTING VOLUNTEERS TO
JOIN A BALLOON BARRAGE
SQUADRON OF THE
AUXILIARY AIR FORCE.

CASTLES OF THE AIR

Man the walls!

Join a BALLOON BARRAGE SQUADRON
AUXILIARY AIR FORCE

his most callous.' It will never be known how hard Churchill pushed for Dowding's removal, but he certainly put up no resistance to the pressure from Sholto Douglas and Leigh-Mallory.

Dowding was dismissed on 17 November 1940, giving way to Sholto Douglas. Dowding was (according to some sources) told to vacate his office within 24 hours, and was told bluntly that 'The Air Council have no further work to offer you.' In fact, Dowding was employed on a vital mission to the USA, and later on staff work in the Air Ministry, finally retiring in 1942. But this was, at best, extremely shabby treatment for the man who had been the architect of victory. It was accompanied by an equally poor reward for his most important and gifted commander, Keith Park. In December, Park was relegated to Training Command (with Leigh-Mallory moving sideways to take over No.11 Group) where he watched Leigh-Mallory's meteoric rise. Much later, Park commented that 'To my dying day I shall feel bitter at the base intrigue which was used to remove Dowding and myself as soon as we had won the Battle of Britain.'

CONTROL, DIRECTION AND DETECTION

Every schoolboy knows that radar was one of the decisive factors which allowed the RAF to win the Battle of Britain. This is quite true, although the name 'radar' was not applied until 1943, and it is often forgotten that Germany had actually deployed radar too, and that German radar was probably more advanced than that used by the British. But while simple and crude, British radar (disingenuously and confusingly known as 'Radio Direction Finding') actually worked, and was reliable and rugged enough to be operationally trustworthy. Moreover, British radar was properly integrated into a well-planned and efficient control and reporting system. German radar, by contrast was limited to use for sea surveillance. German technical experts refused to believe that Britain could have solved the problems of using radar for air surveillance, and assumed that they were using a less than optimum frequency band for their coastal sea surveillance radars.

The roots of Britain's control and reporting system were established in 1933 with the direction of fighters from the ground using radio telephony to convey instructions, and High Frequency radio Direction Finding (HF DF) to work out their position when out of sight of the controller. By 1935, the system had been sufficiently refined to allow a fighter to be vectored onto a bomber target above cloud, at night.

By 1936, Fighter Command was experimenting with simulated radar-controlled intercepts, with target position (of 'unknown origin' as far as the controller was concerned) being passed to the controller who then vectored the fighter aircraft. Complex triangulation and computers did not provide the best and quickest method of providing the fighters with the optimum intercept course, and a system was developed in which controllers were

AIR VICE MARSHAL SIR KEITH PARK

Originally an army officer who fought in France and at Gallipoli, Park transferred to the Royal Flying Corps in 1917. Later, as Dowding's former SASO (Senior Air Staff Officer), Park had helped Dowding prepare Fighter Command for war, and was familiar with the way his superior thought and operated. He was thus an ideal choice as Air Officer Commanding in No.11 Group, the RAF formation against which the main weight of any Luftwaffe offensive would fall, and he was promoted into the post in April 1940.

Park was extremely competent, brisk and efficient, a quick and decisive thinker with a great grasp of detail. But he was not interested in easy popularity and his enemies claimed that he was highly-strung, sensitive and egotistical. Some accused him of enormous vanity, and others of borrowing ideas from others and claiming them as his own. Park won the respect of his pilots, however, through sheer force of personality and through his results. His habit of flying to his stations in his personal Hurricane was also a gesture much appreciated by the frontline pilots – an AOC who flew his own Hurricane was half way to understanding some parts of their job.

Park was said to be 'exhausted' after the Battle, but this was little more than a convenient excuse for his removal and replacement by Leigh-Mallory. Park later had a succession of commands in the Middle East, including responsibility for the tremendously successful air defence of Malta. After Leigh-Mallory was killed in an aircraft crash en route to take up his post as Allied Air Commander, South-East Asia, he was replaced by Park.

trained to work out the solution by their own judgement and gathering experience. They were soon gaining a 93 per cent success rate.

Radar itself was actually used from 1937, with HF DF being applied to keep track of friendly fighters. Each aircraft transmitted its DF signal for 14 seconds in every minute, and these signals were coded to allow the controller to know which signals were coming from which aircraft, using a system of synchronised colour-coded clocks. The system, known as 'Pip Squeak', was simple, and virtually foolproof. It was code-named Cockerel, so that if, for example, a pilot took off without turning Pip Squeak on, the controller might ask: 'Is your cockerel crowing?'

VHF (Very High Frequency) Direction Finding was trialled (by No.66 Squadron) from October 1939, and replaced HF DF at the end of September 1940. But the use of HF or VHF Direction Finding to triangulate the position of friendly fighters was only one element in the overall system.

The other element in the system lay in the detection, location and tracking of the target, which would not obligingly be giving away its location through 'Pip Squeak'. Initially, high hopes were expressed for the use of sound locators, though these proved useable only under certain conditions, and only then at ranges of eight miles or less, and with no height or range indication. The 1934 Air Defence Exercises showed only too clearly that even ancient Vickers Virginias, lumbering along at 2133m (7000ft), were difficult to intercept.

Every schoolboy knows that radar was one of the decisive factors which allowed the RAF to win the Battle of Britain. This is quite true, although the name 'radar' was not applied until 1943, and it is often forgotten that Germany had actually deployed radar too, and that German radar was probably more advanced than that used by the British.

Mr H.E. Wimperis, the Government's Director of Scientific Research, was thus given a wide-ranging brief to see how technology might be used to make fighters more efficient. Wimperis took his brief seriously enough to approach the Scottish physicist Robert Watson-Watt to enquire as to the practicality of producing a radio-based 'death ray'. It was immediately apparent to the scientists that there was no way (at that time, at least) of generating beams of sufficient power to harm either humans or aircraft, but Watson-Watt did point out the potential of using radio beams for target detection, and asked whether the Air Ministry might be interested in how aircraft could be detected by transmitting radio waves which would be reflected by the target aircraft.

Mr H.E. Wimperis, the Government's Director of Scientific Research, was thus given a wide-ranging brief to see how technology might be used to make fighters more efficient. Wimperis took his brief seriously enough to approach the Scottish physicist Robert Watson-Watt to enquire as to the practicality of producing a radio-based 'death ray'.

RIGHT: 'EXPOSING' A SEARCHLIGHT. IN THE DAYS BEFORE AIRBORNE RADAR BECAME A VIABLE WEAPON, NIGHT FIGHTER CREWS RELIED ON SEARCHLIGHTS AND SHELL BURST TO INDICATE THE PRESENCE OF AN ENEMY BOMBER.

The Tizard Committee, charged with a scientific survey of air defence, requested a paper, and this (titled 'The detection and location of aircraft by radio methods') was presented to the Air Ministry on 12 February 1935. Like so many great inventions, radio's potential to detect aircraft had originally been discovered by accident. Watson-Watt was aware of Post Office complaints that passing aircraft could interfere with radio signals and then re-radiate them. He concluded that the time lag between a signal being transmitted and then reflected back by an aircraft to the ground could be displayed on a cathode ray tube, and used to measure the range between the transmitter and the target aircraft.

Hugh Dowding, then the Air Member for Research and Development, was enthusiastic, and a demonstration was organised on 26 February 1935. This used the BBC's short-wave transmitter at Daventry and a passing Handley Page Heyford. Observers on the ground were able to watch a green dot on a CRT grow and then shrink as the aircraft approached and receded. On this somewhat flimsy basis, a grant of £10,000 was given to develop a practical system.

Designated RDF (to convey a relationship with HF Direction Finding), development of the new radar was extremely rapid. By July, radar was able to detect aircraft at ranges of up to 38 miles, and to track them out to 42 miles. In the same month, the scientists correctly identified a formation of three Hawker Harts which flew near their Westland Wallace target aircraft, and by September they were reliably tracking aircraft at ranges of up to 58 miles. This was enough to be militarily useful, though radar was still finding height and precise bearing difficult to achieve. It was recommended that a chain of radar stations be established between Southampton and the Tyne. The first radar antenna mast was erected at Orforness in February 1936, and the scientists moved to Bawdsey, which became the first station in the chain, and the site of a radar training school. The first five stations were at Bawdsey, Canewdon, Great Bromley, Dunkirk and Dover. In March 1936, a Hart was located beyond 62 miles, and in September, Bawdsey participated in the annual Air Defence Exercises. The first stations were officially handed over to the RAF in the summer of 1937, Bawdsey in May, Dover in July and Canewdon in August.

The building of radar stations was accelerated after Munich, with compulsory land purchase and the use of wooden towers. Still officially referred to as 'Air Ministry

Experimental Stations', the radar stations became operational in 1938, and began a 24-hour watch on Good Friday, 1939. A series of small exercises refined the system and allowed the radar operators to practise their skills, improving their ability to judge the strength and composition of mass raids. By this time, basic radar was providing usefully accurate bearing information and some height data, and was used in conjunction with a new 'converter' (essentially a crude electronic calculator) which took range and bearing and displayed them on a standard grid map. The RAF was also busy installing IFF (Identification Friend or Foe) equipment in its aircraft. IFF consisted of a small transmitter which gave the radar 'blip' of the aircraft carrying it a distinctive character, allowing radar operators to differentiate between friendly and hostile aircraft. The 1939 Air Defence Exercises allowed a proper exercise of the radar chain, and provided a forum for the RAF to practise the coordination between radar stations and the Observer Corps. The exercises vindicated all the hard work on radar, and proved the usefulness of IFF.

The original chain of 21 radar stations (known as Chain Home) used fixed antenna arrays, with aerials strung like nets between four masts. These had a range of 40.2km (25 miles) against targets flying at 304.8m (1000ft), 56.3km (35 miles) against targets at 609.6m (2000ft), 80.5km (50 miles) against targets flying at 1524m (5000ft), and 133.6km (83 miles) against targets flying above 3962.4m (13,000ft). They were augmented by the 30 Chain Home Low stations, originally planned as coastal defence radars. Chain Home Low used a rotating antenna atop a tower, transmitting a narrow 'searchlight' beam, giving a capability against low-level targets, albeit over a shorter range and without any height information. The Chain Home and Chain Home Low stations were linked by telephone and were able to pass radar plots between themselves, and to the 'Filter Room' at Fighter Command, which gave the Fighter Command controllers an overall 'air picture'.

When the Battle of Britain began, the Chain Home and Chain Home Low stations gave an average of 20 minutes warning of incoming raids. This was invaluable, since German aerodromes in the Pas de Calais were only 95 miles from inland fighter stations like Kenley (and even closer to the coastal stations, like Manston). A Spitfire required 13

minutes to scramble and climb to 6096m (20,000ft), while a Hurricane needed 16 minutes. Radar therefore gave Fighter Command an invaluable edge in the Battle.

While radar provided early warning of incoming raids, and tracked their progress, the Observer Corps also took responsibility for tracking raids as they crossed the coast. Both organisations provided their plots and tracks to Fighter Command. The Chain Home and Chain Home Low plots were received in the underground Filter Room (which moved out of its ballroom basement in March 1940), where they were checked by cross-reference with IFF plots. The Fighter Command Operations Room (in the ballroom itself) was manned by the C-in-C, the C-in-Cs of the Observer Corps and Anti Aircraft Command, and liaison officers from Bomber and Coastal Commands, the Admiralty and the Ministry of Home Security. The plotting table displayed aircraft tracks over the whole of the UK and its sea approaches, while the underground operations rooms of Nos 11 and 12 Groups showed only those plots in and immediately adjacent to their own areas of operation.

The Group Operations Rooms received their radar plots from Bentley Priory, and received visual plots directly from the Observer Corps Groups. The Group Operations Rooms were then able to direct sectors to deal with incoming raids as appropriate. Each sector had its own operations room, and had emergency standby operations rooms ready

RIGHT: MEMBERS OF THE
VOLUNTEER AMBULANCE
SERVICE GOING THROUGH
ONE OF THEIR DRILLS.
SUCH VOLUNTEERS NIGHTLY
RISKED THEIR LIVES DURING
THE 'BLITZ' AMID THE
RUBBLE OF BRITAIN'S CITIES.

BELOW: WITH BRITAIN
DEPENDENT ON SEABORNE
COMMERCE FOR HER
SURVIVAL, POSTERS SUCH AS
THESE CARRIED A DEFINITE
MESSAGE. THE U-BOAT
CAMPAIGN HAD BROUGHT
BRITAIN TO THE VERGE OF
STARVATION IN WWI; IT
WOULD DO SO AGAIN.

WASTE THE FOOD
AND
HELP THE HUN

to take over if the main centre were to be knocked out in an air raid. The emergency operations rooms were located in a variety of unusual buildings – in one case a butcher's shop, and in another between a fish and chip shop and a public house. The operations rooms were linked to both Group and Command by telephone landline and 'Defence Teleprinter', and the Post Office did an excellent job in maintaining and repairing these, even at the height of the battle, when the sector and Group Operations Rooms became priority targets. The Sector Operations Rooms had their own plotting tables, with radar and Observer Corps plots provided from Bentley Priory's filter room (via landline) and with the position of friendly fighters plotted using Pip Squeak.

A controller in the Sector Operations Room ordered aircraft to scramble, and then vectored individual squadrons into position to make an intercept. He would then sit back and leave fight control to the formation leader when he heard the call 'Tally Ho!' (Enemy in Sight), but would maintain a listening watch until the engagement was complete, interrupting only to warn the formation leader of new enemy formations, etc. The controller then directed the formation to 'pancake' (land back at their home base).

Whereas none of the Luftwaffe's previous opponents had had a control system at all, the RAF had a well-planned and highly efficient system of control and direction. This came as a surprise to the Luftwaffe, who had assumed that aircraft were controlled only when in sight from the ground, close to their own bases. They were quite unable to react and adapt their tactics to meet the new situation, in which the enemy had ample warning of the course, speed, position and altitude of the Luftwaffe's attacking formations.

THE CIVILIAN POPULATION AT WAR

Most people in Britain today either lived through the Battle of Britain, or, more commonly, have family members who lived through the period. This has intensified interest in what was the only major battle of the Second World War to take place on (or more accurately over) British territory, not least because it was a battle which directly involved the civilian population. As a result, the Battle of Britain has become a staple of cinema films, TV documentaries, dramas (and even formed the backdrop for a sitcom, 'Dad's Army'), novels, and newspaper articles. There is therefore now a powerful folk memory of the Battle of Britain, based as much on contemporary propaganda and the contemporary and subsequent interpretation of screenwriters, journalists and fiction-writers as to what really happened. And as time passes, the number of eyewitnesses to the events of 1940 diminishes, and the memories of these survivors is itself modified by what other people say about the Battle. Such memories are also shaped by an altogether natural tendency towards nostalgia as time passes, and the end result is that the heroism and the nobility of the time is fondly remembered, and perhaps even exaggerated, while the harsh realities of the period may sometimes be diminished or ignored.

BELOW: FACTORY WORKERS PRODUCING GAS MASKS FOR INFANTS. GAS WAS NEVER USED AS A WEAPON IN WWII, ALTHOUGH BOTH SIDES EXPERIMENTED WITH EVER-DEADLIER TOXIC AGENTS.

RIGHT: A MEMBER OF THE HOME GUARD, ARMED WITH A THOMSON SUB-MACHINE GUN, ABOUT TO GO ON DUTY. THE MEN OF THE HOME GUARD WERE PREVIOUSLY CALLED THE LOCAL DEFENCE VOLUNTEERS (LDV), INITIALS WHICH, WITH WRY HUMOUR, THEY MAINTAINED STOOD FOR 'LOOK, DUCK AND VANISH'.

BELOW: ARMY MOTORCYCLISTS PATROLLING THE SUSSEX DOWNS FOR SIGNS OF GERMAN PARATROOPS. ANTI-INVASION PATROLS WERE ACTIVE THROUGHOUT THE SUMMER.

Thus wartime Britain is today seen in a remarkably nostalgic light, but above all, the population as a whole is seen as having enjoyed an intense unity of purpose, combined with a great moral strength. Like all great legends, this view has its basis in reality, though the truth is more complex, and it is necessary to preface any description of 'the people at war' with this cautionary explanation.

There was heroism, of course, and there was nobility, selflessness, and public spiritedness. Huge swathes of the population volunteered for military service rather than wait for the call-up, while others gave up their well-paid peacetime jobs to do valuable war work. People volunteered for service in the Local Defence Volunteers, or as auxiliary firemen, policemen, or as fire-watchers or air raid wardens. There was a great response to appeals for scrap metal and aluminium saucepans and there were amazing examples of volunteers participating in war production. Stamped-out metal seats for Spitfires were 'lipped' in school workshops by schoolboys wielding hide-faced hammers, and Women's Institute Groups filed the rough edges from forged aircraft components.

When Eden appealed for volunteers for the Local Defence Volunteers (later renamed the Home Guard) on 13 May, a quarter of a million people responded within one week, and one million had joined by August. And despite being poorly equipped and poorly armed, the Home

Guard were eager to fight, pleased to take on essential guard and patrol activities and proud to free up frontline troops for other duties. The eagerness of the Home Guard was reflected by the ingenuity with which they armed themselves. One Essex platoon was armed only with cutlasses, while the Mid Devon Hunt formed a mounted troop on Dartmoor. Alongside the makeshift Home Guard, with their shotguns, swords, clubs and home-made petrol bombs, there was also a top-secret resistance. Three battalions of Auxiliary Units were formed, well armed and well trained, with ingenious hides accommodating sections or even platoons. In the event of invasion they would have gone to ground and then emerged in the enemy's rear to perform observation and sabotage missions.

There were a number of other organisations which those not called up into the Forces could join to help the war effort and the nation's defence. An Air Raid Warden service was

established in 1937, tasked with advising the public, supervising shelters, issuing gas masks and checking the 'Blackout' (the obscuration of lighting at night to frustrate German navigation). Some 60,000 Auxiliary Fire Service volunteers augmented the 6000 professional firemen, while the Auxiliary Police Corps also fulfilled an invaluable role supporting the regular Police, guarding PoWs, directing rescues, enforcing Air Raid Precautions regulations and helping downed RAF airmen get back to their bases.

Arguably the most valuable of the volunteer services during the Battle of Britain was the Observer Corps. While radar was able to look out to sea, providing early warning of incoming raids, it was virtually blind to its rear, looking back over the land. The Observer Corps was responsible for tracking and reporting the movement of aircraft overland. The success of the Observer Corps was attributed to the enthusiasm of its members, many of whom were aviation enthusiasts and early aeroplane spotters, who regarded their work as an extension of their hobby. The system was based on that used during the Great War, when Police Constables reported enemy aircraft movements to the Admiralty, and later to General Ashmore at the War Office.

Ashmore was on the 1924 committee which set up the first peacetime experiments in observing enemy aircraft

AMERICA AND THE BATTLE OF BRITAIN

Faced with a German invasion, Britain's armed forces (and crucially also those of its Empire and Dominions) were virtually the only obstacles standing in the way of total victory for Nazi Germany in Western Europe. In 1940, the alliance which eventually saw Germany's defeat (Britain, Russia and the USA) was inconceivable. Russia was still formally allied with Germany, and though some in the USA were vehemently anti-Nazi (including President Roosevelt himself), the country was generally reluctant to get involved in what was seen as a European war.

Despite his sympathy, Roosevelt was initially unwilling to do much to help. Britain's first appeal for the loan of 40–50 old destroyers and for the supply of aircraft, anti-aircraft guns and ammunition were politely stalled. Some Americans resented that Great War debts had still not been fully repaid, while others believed that if Germany were to win, any military support for Britain would turn out against American interests.

The Ford Motor Company refused to manufacture Merlin aero-engines under licence, because it did not want to 'be involved in the war', though fortunately fellow car-makers Packard did accept a contract. Prominent figures (including Charles Lindbergh) campaigned actively to maintain US neutrality, some through dislike of Britain's colonial power, some through disgust at appeasement, some through self interest and some through sympathy for the Nazi cause. The US ambassador in London, Joseph Kennedy, predicted that 'democracy is finished in England' and urged a policy of non-intervention. However, some Americans (most notably those on the General and Naval Staffs) recognised that a British defeat would render America more vulnerable to both economic warfare and even direct attack, particularly if the British Fleet were to fall into German hands.

But even those who favoured helping Britain realised that the USA was in no position to intervene directly, and would not be for many months. In short, Britain was alone in its resistance of the Nazi war machine. Yet US interventionists gained influence rapidly, and in return for naval basing agreements in Newfoundland, Bermuda, the Bahamas, Jamaica, St. Lucia, Trinidad and British Guiana, and for a guarantee that the Royal Navy would not be handed over to Germany in the event of a British defeat, America finally agreed to supply 50 surplus destroyers, and limited numbers of aircraft. But this agreement was not reached until August, and was too late to affect the course of the Battle of Britain. In the end, Britain had to survive the Battle of Britain on its own, and after it did so, the foundations of the Anglo-American alliance were laid.

> In many quarters the fall of France was quietly welcomed, with a widespread feeling that the French had let Britain down again and again. Such attitudes went to the top of British society. The King remarked that 'Personally I feel happier now that we have no Allies to be polite to and pamper', while Churchill welcomed the fact that Britain's destiny was now in its own hands.

movements, and established nine trial posts between Tonbridge and the Romney Marshes, with a control centre at Cranbrook. The first Observers were recruited as Special Constables (unpaid volunteers trained to act as police officers), echoing the system first used in World War I. These experiments were extremely successful, and led to the establishment of two Observer Corps zones to cover Kent and Sussex, headquartered in Maidstone and Horsham.

The Observer Corps participated in the 1925 Air Exercises with conspicuous success, and as a result the organisation was expanded, with new zones in the eastern counties and Hampshire. By the end of 1925, there were 100 observer posts, with four Group headquarters. Each of these was attached to a Fighter Command sector aerodrome, thus No.1 Group at Maidstone was attached to Biggin Hill, No.2 Group at Horsham to Kenley, No.3 Group at Winchester to Tangmere and No.18 Group at Colchester to North Weald. The Royal Air Force took over control of the Observer Corps in 1929, placing a retired Air Commodore in charge of the organisation. The Observer Corps underwent a steady expansion throughout the 1930s, until there were five Observer Corps Areas, 16 Groups, and a Corps Headquarters co-located with that of Fighter Command itself at Bentley Priory.

The Observers made their observations with binoculars and telescopes, and used extraordinary makeshift devices and procedures to determine the bearing and estimate the height of enemy formations. These details, together with the aircraft type, strength and position within a series of 2km (1.2-mile) map squares, were passed by telephone landline to the Group Headquarters. Each Group HQ had some 12 plotters arranged around a gridded map table on which the progress of the formations was watched and updated, with each plotter being connected to two or three posts. Tellers sat on a raised dais, and passed their 'air picture' on to RAF sector, Group and Command Operations rooms, receiving back updates from the Chain Home and Chain Home Low radar stations.

The Observer Corps was mobilised en masse in 1938 following the Munich crisis, and the whole system was tested during the 1939 Air Exercises. Its posts were then permanently manned for six unbroken years from 24 August 1939 until the end of the war. The Observer Corps (granted the prefix Royal in 1941, in recognition of its invaluable contribution to the defence of the British Isles in the Battle of Britain) was, like the other civilian organisations, a justifiable source of national pride.

RIGHT AND BELOW:
MEMBERS OF THE
OBSERVER (LATER ROYAL
OBSERVER) CORPS PLAYED
A VITAL PART IN THE
BATTLE OF BRITAIN BY
SUPPLEMENTING RADAR
PLOTS WITH ADDITIONAL
ESTIMATES OF RAID
ALTITUDES AND STRENGTH.

OPPOSITE PAGE: ROCKET
BATTERIES FORMED AN
IMPORTANT ASPECT OF
BRITAIN'S AIR DEFENCES.
ONE SUCH BATTERY COULD
FIRE A SALVO OF 128
MISSILES ON ITS OWN.

But alongside the pride of Britain's civilian efforts, there are some less palatable facts. Food rationing, for example, provided a business opportunity for racketeers and black marketeers, and to those who thought nothing of using money to buy their way out of discomfort, and who saw no reason why the burden of war should be shared equally. And there were other human failings. When Lady Balfour found herself trapped in the rubble after the Luftwaffe knocked out the Café de Paris, she felt what she had thought were rescuers slipping the rings from her fingers. And after hours of tending to the wounded, the cabby she hailed to take her home refused to let her into his taxi, telling her he didn't want blood in his cab. And on more than one occasion, the first rescue workers or policemen on the scene of a bombing arrested looters whose pockets were full of jewellery and wallets taken from the dead and dying. The problem of looting was extremely widespread, to the extent that even the Auxiliary Fire Service initially gained a reputation for looting the buildings they saved.

Although British society did not collapse in the face of the German bombing campaign, things did look very ugly in the early days, when the working class East Enders felt that they were shouldering the burden alone. 'Fortunately', the threat of serious disorder diminished when the West End and fashionable Kensington and Chelsea began to experience the effect of the bombing. Yet when East Enders were evacuated from their

bombed out homes, some of them had to sleep outdoors in Epping Forest because the locals would not take them into their homes.

Britain's perception of its traditional 'fair play' to the down-trodden also took a knock during the Battle of Britain. Having given sanctuary to fleeing Jews and opponents of the Nazis, British plans to intern only those enemy aliens assessed as being likely to support their own countries did not last. Such plans soon gave way to a less discerning round-up, which sometimes saw Jews and those with impeccable anti-Nazi credentials interned side-by-side with PoWs or rabid Nazis, and often in the most disgraceful conditions. This shameful episode was a direct result of public pressure, which quite quickly amounted to hysteria, fuelled by fear of fifth columnists and by an indiscriminate hatred of all things German.

Having given sanctuary to fleeing Jews and opponents of the Nazis, British plans to intern only those enemy aliens assessed as being likely to support their own countries did not last. Such plans soon gave way to a less discerning round-up, which sometimes saw Jews and those with impeccable anti-Nazi credentials interned side-by-side with PoWs or rabid Nazis, and often in the most disgraceful conditions.

RIGHT: A GUN BATTERY ON THE SOUTH COAST OF ENGLAND. COASTAL ARTILLERY COULD THREATEN CONVOYS AND SHIPPING AS WELL AS AIRCRAFT.

However, despite the instances of social division and less-than-admirable behaviour among the population, the British do seem to have worked together remarkably well. In his book *Hitler on the Doorstep*, Egbert Kieser gently mocked the over-enthusiastic and sometimes disproportionate response of the Home Guard to the threat of invasion, and the general paranoia surrounding the risk of invasion. But he summed up Britain's response to the Nazi threat thus:

> In such a mood, the British even gave up hallowed privileges, sacrifices that they made on the altar of the mother country: they willingly let themselves be registered in lists (something they normally never did), obeyed orders from above without complaining and even carried a personal identity card, a thing that every Briton hates, with them all the time. They dug trenches and dugouts right through the centres of their beloved flowerbeds and carefully tended lawns. They donated their aluminium cooking pots for aircraft production, took down the iron railings protecting their front gardens and painted over the bumpers of their cars with white paint. It was soon to become apparent, however, that the British were not only play-acting. When the curtain actually rose on this sinister drama, they were at least morally prepared. Even the German intelligence service reported with indignation on 1 June: 'The English are not even considering defeat!'

ABOVE: A BOMB AIMER IN TRAINING AT AN RAF BOMBING SCHOOL. BOMB AIMING WAS LITERALLY A HIT-OR-MISS AFFAIR IN THE EARLY DAYS OF THE WAR; MOST BOMBS MISSED THEIR TARGETS, BUT THE BOMBING EFFORT HELPED BRITISH MORALE.

CHAPTER 4

Kanalkampf: 1 July – 7 August

LEFT: LINE-UP OF JUNKERS JU 87 STUKAS. THESE DIVE-BOMBERS WERE PROMINENT IN THE INITIAL ATTACKS ON BRITISH COASTAL CONVOYS, AND WERE HEAVILY ESCORTED BY MESSERSCHMITTS.

ABOVE: A SUPERMARINE
SPITFIRE OF NO 92 EAST
INDIA SQUADRON, WHICH
BECAME OPERATIONAL ON
9 MAY 1940.

BELOW: A WARSHIP
ESCORTING A CHANNEL
CONVOY MAKING SMOKE
TO SHIELD THE VESSELS
FROM THE EYES OF
ATTACKING BOMBER CREWS.
SMOKESCREENS WERE A
VERY EFFECTIVE MEANS OF
DEFENCE AGAINST BOTH AIR
AND SURFACE ATTACKERS.

The Battle of Britain began quietly, with what amounted to little more than skirmishing as the Luftwaffe probed at Britain's air defences, primarily by attacking convoys. This put Fighter Command in a difficult situation, since it would suffer attrition if it responded, and shipping losses would be prohibitive if it did not. And yet, in July 1940, many believed that Fighter Command could not afford to suffer attrition, and that it had to be conserved in case of a full-scale attack. Some twelve convoys went through the Channel every day, and about one third of these came under fire. More of the cargo they carried could and should have gone by rail, and Dowding pressed for more shipping to be sent on a longer route via the north of Scotland. But Churchill was happy for the convoys to be used as bait, and for them to distract some of the Luftwaffe's attention away from ports, port approaches, and coastal targets. In Britain, the Battle of Britain is usually timed as beginning on 10 July, though that day was little different from the days which went before it, and there had, by then, already been more than twelve raids by more than 50 aircraft, and the RAF had already lost 18 fighters and 13 pilots.

On the other side of the Channel, Oberst Johannes Fink, the Geschwaderkommodore of KG 2 at Arras, was appointed Kanalkampführer (Channel Battle Commander), and was tasked with clearing the Straits of Dover of British activity. He was to use his three Gruppen of Do 17s, together with two Gruppen of Ju 87 Stukas, and the fighters of JG 26 and JG 53. This was a tiny force for such an ambitious undertaking (and would soon undergo a dramatic expansion), but Fink knew how to obey orders and set about his task. He based himself in a bus near Bleriot's statue at Cap Blanc Nez, as close as he could get to the scene of the action.

On 1 July, the Luftwaffe attacked the east coast ports of Hull and Wick, and made a set-piece attack on convoy 'Jumbo', as well as flying a number of reconnaissance missions. In doing so they lost eleven or twelve aircraft to British fighters and anti-aircraft guns (the twelfth may have suffered an engine failure), while one RAF Blenheim crashed that night after its pilot was blinded by searchlights – the crew were killed when the wreckage was bombed by enemy aircraft. These German losses were good news for the RAF, although the day also gave some indication of future problems. For example, nine RAF fighters finally downed a solo Dornier Do 17Z after a chase of more than 80.5km (50 miles), conducting largely ineffective 'Fighting Area Attacks' all the way. Another Do 17 escaped after being attacked by three Spitfires, none of which had loaded guns, having taken off for a training sortie! Fighter Command shot down a single Do 215 on 2 July, and accounted for four enemy aircraft on 3 July, losing only a single aircraft which was struck by lightning. This was a reasonable return from the 570 sorties mounted that day, although the Luftwaffe enjoyed some other successes. During a raid by a Do 17 on No.13 EFTS at White Waltham, for example, six Tiger Moths were destroyed on the ground, and one airman was killed. By now, KG 2 had been joined by KG 54 and KG 77, and by KG 26 and KG 30 operating from Norwegian bases. But up until that day the bulk of the German losses were of reconnaissance aircraft, usually operating singly.

The Kanalkampf stepped up a gear on 4 July, when the Luftwaffe began to mount more, better coordinated, and larger attacks. The day also marked the beginning of 'Free Chase' sorties by Messerschmitt Bf 109s, which were intended to catch the 'Standing Patrols'

which the Luftwaffe were convinced the RAF was maintaining. They still failed to realise that Fighter Command's success in intercepting raids was due to early warning (by radar) and rapid reaction, and not by maintaining massive numbers of aircraft in the air waiting for the enemy. The significance of the coastal radar stations had yet to dawn on the Luftwaffe.

The Germans mounted two major attacks on 4 July, the first, by 33 Ju 87s against Portland naval base, and the second against a convoy in the Straits of Dover. At Portland, the attackers vanished before the RAF could intervene, though anti-aircraft fire accounted for one Stuka and damaged another. One of the gunners, Acting Seaman Jack Foreman, even won a posthumous VC for his bravery. The convoy attack was timed with great precision and hit as the ships were without an air escort. The bombers lingered at the scene, however, and were caught by eight Hurricanes from No.79 Squadron. These were, in turn, attacked by the Do 17s 30 Bf 109 escorts, and one Hurricane was shot down.

During the early evening, No.32 Squadron was scrambled to intercept an incoming raid, but the nine Hurricanes met what proved to be a 36-strong force of Bf 109Es, and two were forced down, both pilots surviving their forced landings. One of the Bf 109Es was also shot down, and another crashed on landing due to combat damage. The Germans also lost an He 111 that day, this falling to three No.92 Squadron Spitfires near Wincanton.

Although it was summer, unsettled weather still exerted a huge influence on the day-to-day course of the Battle. After the hectic pace of Thursday 4 July, Friday dawned with heavy cloud and some mist. A number of German formations lumbered into the air, and were detected by Chain Home, but only small numbers of aircraft actually crossed the Channel. A single Heinkel He 111H was shot down into the Channel off Dover after being intercepted by the nine Spitfires of No.65 Squadron at 0630, and a three-aircraft section of No.64 Squadron engaged the enemy when it undertook an evening reconnaissance over

the Pas de Calais. One Spitfire was shot down, and one had a forced-landing at Hawkinge with combat damage, and the third made it safely back to Kenley. But the mission was symptomatic of the cross-Channel fighter recce sorties, in that it achieved little (the pilots being too busy to provide worthwhile information on enemy ground dispositions), cost aircraft, and confused the radar picture. Fortunately for the RAF's score-keepers, No.611 Squadron had earlier caused such damage to an LG 1 Bf 109E off Spurn Head that it was completely written off after crashing at Limoges.

Even before the Battle, Fighter Command had started to prepare itself for an attack from French airfields, establishing No.10 Group and building a satellite aerodrome at Warmwell. On Saturday 6 July, Dowding moved No.609 Squadron from Northolt to Middle Wallop, and No.87 Squadron from Church Fenton to Exeter, while a Blenheim night-fighter unit, No.236 Squadron, was moved to Thorney Island to provide a night defence for Portsmouth and Southampton. With poor weather in the south of England, most of the action took place in the north. The RAF suffered no combat losses but shot down a reconnaissance Bf 110 over the North Sea, 161km (100 miles) east-north-east of Aberdeen, while a recce Do 17P force-landed in Sweden and was interned. Despite the poor weather, the Luftwaffe mounted a number of night raids, and bombs fell on Aldershot, Farnborough, Godalming, and Haslemere, killing 62 people and temporarily blocking four railways. All this was before the Battle of Britain had officially even started. The intended military targets of the bombers were unharmed.

During the morning of Sunday 7 July, Fighter Command downed three Do 17Ps as they attempted to shadow an eastbound convoy, a convoy which generated 215 Fighter Command sorties, and which enjoyed a nine-aircraft escort for the whole of its passage through the Channel. Free Chases by large numbers of Bf 109Es bore fruit only once, when No.54 Squadron lost two of its Spitfires. These fell as B Flight positioned itself

ABOVE: PILOTS HAD TO COMPLETE COMBAT REPORTS AFTER SORTIES. THE AUTHOR OF THIS REPORT WAS FLT LT 'SAILOR' MALAN, WHO WENT ON TO BECOME ONE OF THE RAF'S LEADING ACES.

TOP: THIS HEINKEL HE 111 OF KG4 WAS SHOT DOWN BY A BLENHEIM OF No 23 SQUADRON JUST OFF CLEY NEXT THE SEA, NORFOLK, ON 19 JUNE 1940. THE WRECK LAY IN THE WATER UNTIL 1969, WHEN IT WAS DESTROYED AS A NAVIGATION HAZARD.

ABOVE: THE GERMANS USED THE HEINKEL HE 59 FLOATPLANE FOR AIR/SEA RESCUE DUTIES. SUSPICION THAT THEY WERE BEING USED FOR CLANDESTINE ACTIVITIES LED TO ORDERS TO SHOOT THEM DOWN.

to make a Fighting Area Attack on a single He 111, only to find themselves under fire from at least one Staffel of Bf 109s.

As the convoy reached a position abeam Dover, it came under heavy attack by some four Staffeln of Do 17s (45 bombers from KG 2). These sank one ship and damaged three more, but despite good warning from Chain Home, the RAF was slow to react. No.65 Squadron lost three pilots to a well-timed Bf 109 sweep as six of its aircraft climbed out from Hornchurch. One of the survivors, Flt Sgt Franklyn, chased a Bf 109 to the French coast, where he finally shot it down, and then flew towards the convoy, where he destroyed another. No.64 Squadron did better, falling on the Dorniers just as they regained the French coast, severely damaging two of the raiders.

There were further convoy battles on 8 July, and these proved costly to Fighter Command, which lost two No.79 Squadron Hurricanes shot down in flames and one No.610 Squadron Spitfire. All three pilots died. No.610 Squadron partially balanced the score by downing a Bf 110 and damaging a Dornier, and more stragglers were shot down by Flt Sgt 'Sammy' Allard of No.85 Squadron (already one of the Command's top-scorers) and by Nos 41 and 249 Squadrons in Yorkshire. More importantly, Fighter Command could feel happy that it

GERMAN LOSSES

The whole subject of German losses during the Battle of Britain is confusing. Some units did not report their losses through the normal channels (this especially applying to certain reconnaissance, weather reconnaissance, minelaying and air sea rescue units) and other records have simply been lost, many of them in the confusion of Germany's defeat in 1945. As a result, kills confirmed by post-war examination of official German records (and used by us) do not include some aircraft whose destruction was confirmed by the recovery of wreckage and sometimes even by the capture of surviving crew-members. It thus seems likely that Fighter Command was somewhat more successful than the figures given in this book might otherwise suggest.

was getting to grips with the menace posed by Free Chasing Bf 109s. Despite inevitably being outnumbered (the Free Chases were usually in Gruppe strength) No.54 Squadron downed two Bf 109s near Dover, and No.74 downed another, although No.65 Squadron's CO, Squadron Leader Cooke, was shot down and killed.

The first few days of the Kanalkampf pleased both sides. The RAF had taken a steady toll on the Luftwaffe, and had enjoyed some success in protecting the convoys. On the other side, the Luftwaffe's fighters had inflicted relatively heavy casualties on Fighter Command (and this seemed particularly so at the time, listening to the Bf 109E pilots' inflated claims) for relatively light losses. In fact, the RAF had all but held its own even in fighter-versus-fighter combat, and the toll of aircrew killed in the various Ju 88s, He 111s and Dorniers shot down by Fighter Command should have been a serious cause for concern.

9 July began with low cloud and rain, and although one of the overnight raiders was caught by a dawn patrol from No.257 Squadron, their victim regained enemy territory, though it crash-landed near Antwerp with a dead crew member aboard.

The first major engagement of the day came when six No.151 Squadron Hurricanes (one flown by North Weald's Station Commander, Group Captain Victor Beamish) intercepted a force estimated at 100 enemy bombers and fighters as they began to attack a convoy. One Hurricane was shot down, but the pilot baled out safely, while another pilot was wounded, but the small force managed to break up the enemy bombers and prevent any damage to the ships. In addition to this, the Hurricanes downed a Bf 110 of III./ZG 26 and claimed two Bf 109s shot down. III./ZG 26 had already lost two more Bf 110s during a diversionary

ABOVE: AN AVRO ANSON OF NO 504 'COUNTY OF ULSTER' SQUADRON, RAF COASTAL COMMAND, OVERFLYING A CONVOY. IN THE EARLY STAGES OF THE BATTLE, CONVOYS WERE KEY TARGETS FOR THE LUFTWAFFE.

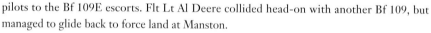

raid near Folkestone, but had damaged one of the attacking Hurricanes, and wounded the pilot, Squadron Leader Lott of No.43 Squadron. The Luftwaffe brought another attack to bear on the convoy later that afternoon, but ran into nine Spitfires from No.65 Squadron which shot down one Bf 109. Bad weather and other interceptions caused the raid to break up again, and one Heinkel eventually fell before the guns of No.17 Squadron. Its attackers fired 2000 rounds, some from as little as 45m (148ft), demonstrating the inadequacy of the 7.69mm (0.303in) machine gun, and the state of gunnery in Fighter Command.

After its losses, Luftflotte 2 sent out a number of He 59 floatplanes on a search and rescue mission. One of these was forced down by No.54 Squadron, who lost two pilots to the Bf 109E escorts. Flt Lt Al Deere collided head-on with another Bf 109, but managed to glide back to force land at Manston.

A final mass attack was launched by the Ju 87s of I./StG 77, which attacked Portland. No.609 Squadron took off from nearby Warmwell to intervene, and shot down one of the attackers, but lost one of their own Spitfires to the heavy escort of Bf 109s. The day ended with the RAF having lost seven aircraft, and the Luftwaffe ten, though only six of these were fighters. Most worryingly for the Luftwaffe, this tally included four of the much-vaunted Bf 110s, which had been deployed in strength for the first time that day, and which had proved easy targets even for the RAF's Hurricanes.

The Battle of Britain officially began on Wednesday 10 July, though with only two losses to enemy action (and with four aircraft being damaged), it was a quieter day for Fighter Command than many of those that had gone before. With nine enemy aircraft shot down (and with five more severely damaged in combat) it was also a more successful day than some. This was perhaps just as well, since some units were already beginning to show signs of strain. No.54 Squadron, for example, had been reduced to eight aircraft (from 12) and 13 pilots (from 18), while No.79 Squadron's pilots were in such a poor state that they were ordered north for a rest. Historian Francis Mason said of them that

FORMATIONS AND TACTICS

Before the war, RAF Fighters had operated in v-shaped formations ('vics') of three aircraft, with the leader stepped in front of two wingmen. The leader of the vic was able to keep a lookout, while his wingmen (tucked in very close) concentrated on keeping station. When flying in squadron strength, four vics flew one behind the other, giving a formation that was easy to control, and very manoeuvrable. But the drawback was that only one pair of eyes was available to look for the enemy, with everyone else concentrating on keeping formation.

In Spain, the pilots of the Condor Legion developed a looser four-aircraft formation (a Schwarm) broadly in line abreast, but well separated, with each pilot able to check the tails of his neighbours. The Battle of France soon showed that the RAF's standard formation was not ideal, and from an early stage, squadrons began stationing the rearmost vic higher, weaving above and behind the formation. This was an improvement, but only just, and served mainly to make the 'weavers' even more vulnerable.

By the time of the Battle of Britain, the strictly regimented and choreographed 'Fighting Area Attacks' had been discredited, and the raison d'être of the tight, easily controllable squadron formation began to disappear as more flexible tactics were developed. By July, many units were experimenting with new formations. No.54 Squadron's successes on 8 July were interesting, since the unit was widely believed to be suffering from combat fatigue (as was No.79 Squadron) and heavy losses had prompted it to swap from flying in two 'vics' of three to using 'pairs' as the standard tactical formation. Credit for the adoption of the German-style 'Finger Four' is hard to place with any degree of confidence, since No.152 Squadron, under Squadron Leader Peter Devitt, also began using flights of three 'pairs' (and occasionally single 'fours') during mid-July. In No.74 Squadron, 'Sailor' Malan retained the vic of three, but used a vic of three flight leaders, each of whom had three aircraft in line astern behind him. When the formation broke, it broke into three lines of four aircraft, though these were in line astern, not line abreast.

In time, of course, the RAF simply 'stole' the German Schwarm, re-naming it as the 'Finger Four' because of its supposed resemblance to the outstretched fingers of a human hand.

they had 'reached the stage of physical and mental exhaustion at which they were of minimal value to the defence, and represented a distinct danger to themselves.' Unfortunately, No.79 Squadron's place in the frontline was taken by the Defiants of No.141 Squadron, which were not destined to be any more successful.

The 10 July broke with thick cloud and thundery rain, and with eight convoys at sea in British coastal waters. The largest of these was 'Bread', which set off from the Thames Estuary with the morning tide, rounding the North Foreland soon after 1000. About three quarters of an hour later, six No.74 Squadron Spitfires intercepted a solitary reconnaissance Do 17P – and its escort of an entire Gruppe of JG 51 Bf 109Es. The escorts did their job well, and prevented all but a couple of attacks. The Dornier limped home (with dead and wounded crew), and two of the Spitfires had to force land at Manston. A covering Free Chase over Kent drew up No.610 Squadron, one of whose Spitfires was shot down.

With the return of the reconnaissance Do 17, the Luftwaffe began planning a major attack, and although six No.32 Squadron Hurricanes were over the convoy as the raid struck, they required reinforcement. As a result, the 26 Do 17Zs of I./KG 2, and the escort of five Staffeln of Bf 110s and Bf 109s, were met by seven Hurricanes from No.56 Squadron, nine from No.111, and by eight No.74 Squadron Spitfires, as well as the six original Hurricanes. With some 60 enemy fighters and 30 RAF fighters, the odds were more even than was often the case, and a massive mêlée developed. This opened with a head-on attack against the enemy formation by Nos 32 and 111 Squadrons in line-

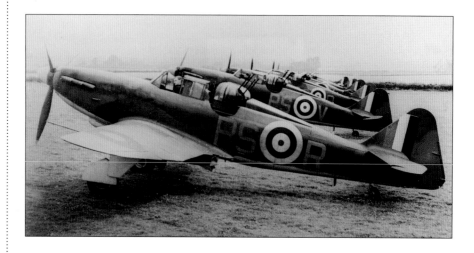

abreast, which distracted the enemy bomb aimers sufficiently to ensure that only one hit was scored of 150 bombs dropped. German morale was not dented, however, and when they returned to base, the jubilant bomb-aimers claimed four merchant ships sunk, plus a heavy cruiser, together with 11 of the attacking RAF fighters! Before the fight was over, six No.64 Squadron Spitfires joined the fray, and these harassed the retreating Bf 110s back to the French coast, severely damaging one. The other RAF fighters involved in the action downed three and damaged several enemy aircraft without loss to themselves, bringing the day's score to nine enemy aircraft destroyed.

A mass raid by 63 Luftflotte 3 Ju 88s against Falmouth and Swansea escaped interception but fortunately did little damage. No.92 Squadron at Pembrey were scrambled too late to intercept. The raid was, however, intercepted by Wing Commander Ira Jones, a First World War veteran serving as Wing Commander (Flying) at Stormy Down. He took off in an unarmed Hawker Henley and loosed off his Verey signal pistol at a Ju 88 'with considerably more feeling than effect.'

The 10 July ended with about 20 enemy bombers roaming over southern England, aiming at any 'chinks' in the blackout. This was pointless and unproductive, and served no real purpose other than to stoke up anti-German feeling in Britain. Hitler had yet to issue his final 'appeal to reason', and may not have realised that Britain's civilian population was being targeted.

The poor weather continued on 11 July, but the Luftwaffe sustained an impressive tempo of operations. Many reconnaissance sorties were mounted, resulting in the loss of two Do 17Ps, one downed by the legless ace Douglas Bader, recently appointed CO of No.242 Squadron. A third Do 17P was

attacked by Squadron Leader Peter Townsend, but accurate return fire knocked out Townsend's engine, and he was forced to bale out. The fact that an ace of Townsend's calibre could be shot down by a Do 17 demonstrates only to clearly that these aircraft presented their attackers with quite a challenge, and engagements were far from being a foregone conclusion. Fortunately, Townsend was picked up by a naval launch after 20 minutes in the water. This was something else which couldn't be taken for granted, and a scarcely credible number of downed aircrew were left to drown or die of exposure only a short distance from the coast, such were the inadequacies of Britain's air sea rescue organisation. On that very day Sergeant F.J.P. Dixon of No.510 Squadron drowned off Portland after baling out successfully.

The 11 July was a day of unexpected outcomes. Sperrle committed ten Ju 87s to attack a convoy at 0700, and these sunk the armed yacht 'Warrior', while their escorts (out-numbering No.609 Squadron by ten-to-one) accounted for two Spitfires. Reports of two He 59 floatplanes on the water prompted the navy to send out two destroyers from Plymouth, with air cover provided by three Blenheims. The destroyers were attacked by a Ju 88 which was in turn shot down by the Blenheims, which also chased off an He 111. One of the He 59s was scuttled, and its crew were rescued by the other, which flew off before the RN force could reach the area. A second 24-aircraft Stuka raid was sent out against Portland, with an escort of 40 Bf 110s. They arrived as the Warmwell squadrons were refuelling, and six No.601 Squadron Hurricanes were scrambled from Tangmere, arriving too late to prevent the bombing, but finding the Ju 87s still at low level, with their

ABOVE: HAWKER HURRICANES OF NO 111 SQUADRON, THE FIRST UNIT TO RECEIVE THE FIGHTER IN JANUARY 1938. NO 111 SQUADRON WAS BASED CROYDON FOR MOST OF THE BATTLE OF BRITAIN, AND WAS IN THE THICK OF THE FIGHTING.

LEFT: A BOULTON-PAUL DEFIANT OF NO. 262 SQUADRON. THE HEAVY REAR TURRET MEANT THAT THE FIGHTER COULD NOT CARRY FORWARD-FACING ARMAMENT, AS ITS PERFORMANCE WAS SEVERELY AFFECTED.

escorts too high to interfere with their first deadly attack. Three Ju 87s were shot down, and two more were badly damaged, while two Bf 110s also fell. No.601 Squadron returned to Tangmere unscathed. During the whole course of the day the RAF lost six fighters, but German losses were significantly higher, at fifteen, including four Bf 110s.

Both flights of No.601 Squadron were scrambled to counter the next major raid, by 12 He 111s and a similar number of Bf 110s. This developed into a running fight which continued over Portsmouth, where the Heinkels unloaded their bombs. Portsmouth's anti-aircraft gunners joined in, shooting down a Hurricane (the pilot baling out with burns and shrapnel wounds). One Heinkel was damaged, and another was forced to swerve into its wingman, destroying both aircraft. A Bf 110 was also shot down, crashing near Lymington. One of its crew was captured, but the aircraft does not appear in German loss returns.

After a night of quite heavy raids, Friday 12 July continued the pattern of low cloud and rain. Interestingly, German bombers had flown over a blazing warehouse in Camberwell during the night, but had not attacked it, such was the strictness of their orders not to bomb London. The day was mainly one of nuisance raiders and small formation attacks, several of which were detected and intercepted. There was one major raid, against convoy 'Booty', by two Staffeln of II./KG 2's Do 17Zs and two Staffeln of III./KG 53. The raid was intercepted by Nos 17, 85 and 151 Squadrons, all of which scored successes, though two aircraft were lost (with their pilots). By the end of the day, Fighter Command had lost three Hurricanes in combat, but destroyed eight enemy bombers, five of them He 111s. One of the latter fell before the guns of three No.74 Squadron pilots – Malan, Mould and Stephenson.

The pattern of the Battle continued unchanged on 13 July, with solo reconnaissance aircraft and mass raids against convoys stretching the defences. German reconnaissance was effective enough to allow accurate planning of attacks, but one convoy confounded both its

ABOVE: NOSE-MOUNTED MG17 MACHINE GUN INSTALLATION IN A MESSERSCHMITT BF 110.

LEFT: FASTER THAN MOST CONTEMPORARY FIGHTERS WHEN IT FIRST APPEARED IN THE 1930S, THE BRISTOL BLENHEIM MK I LIGHT BOMBER WAS SOON OUTCLASSED. IT WAS USED AS AN INTERIM MEASURE IN THE BATTLE.

RIGHT: JUNKERS JU 88 OF KG30, SHOT DOWN OVER THE NORTHEAST COAST OF ENGLAND DURING THE ATTACK ON 5 AUGUST 1940. KG30 WAS BASED AT AALBORG IN DENMARK.

BELOW: LUFTWAFFE BOMBER CREWS BEING BRIEFED FOR THE MAJOR ATTACK ON LONDON, 7 SEPTEMBER 1940. THE GERMAN DECISION TO SWITCH THE MAIN ATTACKS FROM THE RAF AIRFIELDS TO LONDON WAS A FATAL MISTAKE.

escort and their attackers by arriving late. An air battle ensued without any attacks on the ships, which sailed on unscathed. The day marked the debut of Lehrgeschwader 1, a mixed wing of dive bombers, bombers and Zerstörers manned by highly experienced former instructors and test pilots, which also functioned as an operational evaluation unit. Another debut of sorts was that of New Zealander Colin Grey of No.54 Squadron, who scored the first of 14 victories against a fleeing JG 51 Bf 109. Over the course of the day, Fighter Command downed five enemy aircraft (another falling to AA fire) for three combat losses, though a fourth Hurricane was destroyed in a fatal landing accident after combat.

Although several He 59 floatplanes had already been shot down by Fighter Command (despite their red cross markings), it was not until 14 July that an order was circulated to all pilots ordering them to shoot down such aircraft, which were perceived as being used for 'purposes not consistent with the privileges generally accorded to the Red Cross'. Very poor weather afforded British convoys useful protection, and only a small number of sorties were flown. The only major attack of the day was by three Staffeln of Stukas, escorted by about 30 Bf 109Es. 16 Hurricanes from Nos 151 and 615 Squadrons intercepted the raid, along with twelve Spitfires from No.610. One Hurricane pilot was shot down, while the Luftwaffe lost one Ju 87 and one Bf 109.

Low cloud again hampered operations on 15 July. No.56 Squadron failed to hit any of the 15 Do 17Zs which attacked a convoy, but operating under a 61m (200ft) cloudbase,

the Do 17s were no more accurate in bombing their targets. A raid by LG 1 against Westland was no more successful, though Fighter Command's tally for the day did include a Ju 88A and an He 111H, for the loss of one Hurricane, this probably falling to friendly AA fire near Dartmouth. Fortunately the pilot survived.

On 16 July, Hitler promulgated his Führerdirektiv 16, which announced his decision to 'prepare and if necessary carry out' an invasion with the aim of eliminating England as a base for war against Germany. The priority accorded to the Royal Navy and coastal defences as targets was re-stated, and an intensive mining campaign began in the Firth of Forth, and in the Humber and Thames estuaries. The rest of the target list drawn up soon proved to be out-of-date and ill researched. Areas of operation were allocated to the three Luftflotten facing England, with Luftflotte 5 taking targets north of a line running from the Humber to Carlisle, and with Luftflotte 3 taking the area west of a line running from the eastern edge of the Isle of Wight up to Carlisle. Luftflotte 2 took the rest of the country. But while 16 July was a big day from an administrative point of view, poor weather ensured that it was relatively quiet. Fighter Command suffered no combat (or non-combat losses) but Flying Officer W.H. Rhodes-Moorhouse (son of the Great War Victoria Cross winner) managed to shoot down a Ju 88A of KG 54.

Continuing poor weather on 17 July again prevented both sides from mounting intensive operations. The biggest raid was one by six He 111s from Norway-based KG 26, which attacked the ICI factory at Ardeer, Ayrshire. One bomber was shot down by No.603 Squadron Spitfires on its return journey. The only other RAF kill was scored by No.92 Squadron, who downed a KG 51 Ju 88A near Bristol at about 1925. Fighter Command also lost two aircraft, a No.603 Squadron Spitfire going missing from a patrol, and a No.64 Squadron aircraft falling to a Free Chase by Bf 109Es which attacked the squadron near Beachy Head and disappeared before any of the surviving Spitfire pilots could catch sight of them.

THE FIRST OF THE EAGLES

Before the USA entered the war, small numbers of American citizens decided that they would fight. Some were driven by a hatred of Nazism, others by a simple desire for adventure. Some reached Britain via Canada, others came direct. Some were already experienced pilots, others were tyros. Eventually Fighter Command would include three Eagle Squadrons of American volunteers, but during the Battle of Britain there were only seven Americans in Fighter Command, six of whom were destined to give their lives for Britain, fighting in RAF uniform. The first of the seven to reach the front line was Pilot Officer W.M.L. 'Billy' Fiske, who joined No.601 Squadron at Tangmere on 15 July. Fiske was shot up on 16 August, but landed successfully at Tangmere despite this. Unfortunately, Tangmere was under attack, and Fiske's aircraft was strafed, and burst into flames. Groundcrew managed to get Fiske out, but unfortunately he died of wounds the next day, on 17 August 1940. The seven American pilots scored only three shared victories, but their contribution was far more important than this total would suggest. Of large character, they were popular members of their squadrons, making an invaluable contribution to morale and setting a fine example for the US citizens who followed them into the RAF. Apart from Fiske, the American Battle of Britain pilots were Pilot Officer A.G. Donahue who flew with No.64 Squadron, Pilot Officer J.K. Haviland (the only survivor) of No.151 Squadron, Pilot Officers V.C. 'Shorty' Keough, Andy Mamedoff and E.Q. 'Red' Tobin who served with No.609 Squadron and Pilot Officer P.H. Leckrone of No.616 Squadron.

Although the weather was no better on 18 July, air operations were more hectic, and RAF losses were heavy. In fact, the RAF's losses were heavier than those suffered by the Luftwaffe, though exaggerated claims meant that few people realised this at the time. Three Spitfires were shot down (two by Ju 88s), and three Blenheims failed to return. German combat losses amounted to only five aircraft. Luftflotte 5 was particularly busy, mounting a number of small-scale attacks. Kesselring's Luftflotte 2 mounted a more imaginative attack. Finally, Kesselring realised that the British were using radar to detect his aircraft even as they formed up over France for their attacks. He therefore deliberately assembled a raid to coincide with a passing convoy, but when it emerged from cloud near the target, No.610 Squadron found to their surprise that the raid consisted solely of Bf 109Es, which made a single slashing attack through the British formation, shooting down one Spitfire.

Adolf Hitler made his famous 'appeal for reason' on 19 July, genuinely hoping that Britain might accept an 'honourable peace'. During his speech he said that 'If this struggle continues, it can only end in the annihilation of one of us. Mr Churchill thinks it will be Germany. I know it will be Britain. I am not the vanquished begging for mercy. I speak as a victor. I see no reason why this war should go on. We would like to avert the sacrifices which must claim millions.' He took the opportunity to elevate Göring to the unique new rank of Reichsmarschall.

The same day also saw the combat debut of the Defiants of No.141 Squadron, which had arrived in the south of England only a week before. Nine Defiants were assaulted by about two dozen Bf 109Es from II./JG 2. Four Defiants were shot down immediately, and of the crews only one pilot survived, baling out wounded into the sea. Another Defiant was shot down moments later, and though the gunner baled out, he drowned. Of the surviving aircraft, one lost its engine shortly before landing, and crashed. The gunner had successfully baled out, and the pilot survived the crash. Another aircraft was written off after landing, such was the extent of its damage. Its gunner had also baled out on

the pilot's orders, but was never seen again. Had the Hurricanes of No.111 Squadron not intervened, the entire formation would have been lost.

Apart from the loss of seven Defiants, Fighter Command lost five Hurricanes, whereas the Luftwaffe lost only four aircraft in combat. Fighter Command's own claims only totalled 13 enemy aircraft, which would have represented a very narrow victory. Even at the time, 19 July seemed like a black day however you looked at it.

Fortunately, just when the RAF needed a victory, 20 July brought one, and one which had a remarkably small cost. The RAF downed 14 enemy aircraft, including five of the deadly and much-feared Bf 109Es. These were among 50 enemy fighters escorting a Stuka raid against a convoy, and against whom 24 RAF fighters were sent. Despite the odds, only two RAF fighters were shot down in this battle, but accounted for five Bf 109s and a Ju 87, and damaged five more Stukas. During the whole day two Spitfires were shot down, together with four Hurricanes and a single Blenheim. Only one of the pilots of these aircraft survived and

the losses included two pilots who drowned after successfully baling out.

Sunday 21 July was relatively quiet, and learning from the previous day's experience, Fighter Command provided the convoys with strong escorts. Thunderstorms in the afternoon did little to help Fighter Command, and did a great deal to damage the strength of Balloon Command, one of whose detachments lost six balloons in a single 30-minute period that day. Fighter Command lost one

ABOVE: A FORMATION OF HEINKEL HE 111 BOMBERS BOUND FOR ENGLAND. HEINKELS EQUIPPED A SPECIALLY-FORMED 'PATHFINDER' GROUP, KGR100, WHOSE TASK WAS TO LEAD NIGHT ATTACKS ON BRITISH TARGETS.

LEFT: THE MESSERSCHMITT 109 SHOWS OFF ITS ANGULAR LINES. THE FIGHTER WAS CONSTANTLY MODIFIED THROUGHOUT THE WAR, BECOMING HEAVIER AND LESS MANOEUVRABLE. NEVERTHELESS, IT REMAINED FORMIDABLE.

Hurricane in combat, and two more were damaged, but shot down six enemy aircraft. Göring called Milch and his three Luftflotte commanders to Karinhall, where he outlined his instructions for the air campaign which would prepare the way for Hitler's invasion of Britain, re-emphasising the need to attack the Royal Navy and seal up its ports (including Plymouth, Portland, Portsmouth and Dover) by mining, and thus preventing the navy from interfering with the progress of the German invasion fleet.

The British Government finally responded to Hitler's 19 July appeal on 22 July, in a speech by Lord Halifax, the Foreign Secretary. It was a remarkable speech, which usefully summed up the general attitude in the country at large to Hitler at this stage of the war.

Many of you will have read two days ago the speech in which Herr Hitler summoned Great Britain to capitulate to his will. I will not waste your time by dealing with his distortion of almost every main event since the War began. He says he has no desire to destroy the British Empire, but there was in his speech no suggestion that peace must be based on justice, no word of recognition that the other nations of Europe had any right to self-determination, the principle which he has so often invoked for Germans. His only appeal was to the base instinct of fear, and his only arguments were threats. Hitler has now made it plain that he is preparing to direct the whole weight of German might against this country. That is why in every part of Britain there is only one spirit, a spirit of indomitable resolution. Nor has anyone any doubt that if Hitler were to succeed it would be the end, for many beside ourselves, of all those things which make life living. We realise that the struggle may cost us everything, but just because the things we are defending are worth any sacrifice it is a noble privilege to be the defenders of things so precious. We never wanted the War; certainly no-one here wants the War to go on for a day longer than is necessary. But we shall not stop fighting until freedom, for ourselves and others, is secure.

After Göring's Karinhall conference on 21 July, the 22 July saw a marked reduction in enemy daylight air activity. A KG 30 Ju 88 dropped its bombs on a cemetery at Leith, ironically demolishing the graves of German airmen killed in the Great War. Otherwise, the highlight of the day occurred off Selsey Bill, where three No.145 Squadron Hurricanes shot down a prowling Do 17P. Once darkness fell, the Luftwaffe flew more than 100 mining sorties. The night did see one historic event, when Flying Officer Glynn Ashfield destroyed a Do 17, guided to his target by Sergeant Reginald Leyland and his new AI Mk III radar

set, after being talked towards the enemy aircraft by the FIU's CO, Wing Commander George Chamberlain, using a track provided by the Poling Chain Home station.

The next day saw the RAF mount near-continuous convoy patrols, but there were no attacks, and Fighter Command downed only a pair of reconnaissance aircraft. Having withdrawn No.141 Squadron to Prestwick on 22 July, Dowding continued to withdraw exhausted units from the frontline. No.43 Squadron (which had lost six pilots in three weeks) moved from Tangmere to Northolt, and was replaced by No.1 Squadron, while No.247 Squadron from Sumburgh moved to Exeter (and later Roborough) to provide fighter defence for Plymouth. No.247 Squadron was equipped with Gladiator biplanes, the first appearance of these anachronisms in the Battle.

On 24 July, Fighter Command enjoyed another good day, shooting down eight enemy aircraft for only two combat losses. Better yet, a major convoy battle resulted in 27 Spitfires of Nos 54, 65, and 610 Squadrons intercepting a raid of 18 Do 17Zs and about 40 Bf 109s. The Do 17s maintained a tight formation, and put up a heavy and accurate barrage of fire, and escaped without loss, but III./JG 26 lost three Bf 109s (shooting down one No.54 Squadron aircraft and damaging another) in the action. As JG 26 withdrew, III./JG 52 swept in over Kent to cover the retreat, but ran straight into No.610 Squadron's nine Spitfires, who promptly shot down two of the Bf 109Es. JG 52 lost another Bf 109E (again to No.610 Squadron) later that day. Fighter Command was beginning to learn that if a single squadron of Spitfires or Hurricanes ran up against a 40-strong Gruppe of Bf 109s (three or four-to-one odds), it would suffer heavy losses, but odds of two-to-one in the Germans' favour would produce a British victory. This was remarkable, but partly reflected the tremendous disadvantage suffered by the Bf 109Es, which had to turn and run for home after a short time in combat, or risk running out of fuel.

German attacks intensified on 25 July. Luftflotte 2 concentrated on convoy attacks, but Luftflotte 3 mounted several attacks on Portland. A large westbound convoy was the focus of most of the day's air combat, as the Luftwaffe attempted to exhaust the British escorts,

No.65 Squadron's Spitfires were the first to engage the enemy. Flight Sergeant Franklin scoring a rare 'manoeuvre kill' by making sudden evasive turns (known as 'jinking') at low level and forcing his pursuer (in a JG 52 Bf 109E) to fly into the sea.

LEFT: A HEINKEL APPROACHING ITS TARGET. THE HE 111 WAS A VERY RELIABLE AIRCRAFT AND A STABLE BOMBING PLATFORM. TOWARDS THE END OF THE WAR IT WAS USED TO AIR-LAUNCH V-1 FLYING BOMBS AGAINST BRITAIN.

BELOW: 'SAILOR' MALAN, SO NICKNAMED BECAUSE HE HAD SERVED IN THE MERCHANT NAVY BEFORE BECOMING A PILOT.

sending them home early and then sending in heavy bomber strikes while the RAF aircraft were rearming and refuelling. It was a reasonable plan, but Fighter Command foiled it by keeping only a light escort with the convoy, reinforcing it when necessary.

No.65 Squadron's Spitfires were the first to engage the enemy, Flight Sergeant Franklin scoring a rare 'manoeuvre kill' by making sudden evasive turns (known as 'jinking') at low level and forcing his pursuer (in a JG 52 Bf 109E) to fly into the sea. 20 Hurricanes from Nos 32 and 615 Squadrons had an inconclusive tussle with some 40 Bf 109Es soon afterwards, before both sides returned to base, short of fuel. In the absence of an escort, 60 Ju 87s attacked, and when nine No.54 Squadron Spitfires raced to the scene they were faced by dozens of Bf 109Es, losing two of their number. The German fighters escaped without loss.

The next attack (by 30 Ju 88s of KG 4, escorted by about 50 Bf 109Es) threatened to overwhelm the convoy's escort of only eight No.64 Squadron Spitfires. Three remaining No.64 Squadron aircraft scrambled to join the fray, along with the twelve Hurricanes of Squadron Leader John Thompson's No.111 Squadron. 'Treble One' entered the battle with a head-on line abreast charge, and the Ju 88As broke off and ran for home, followed by their escorts.

As the convoy passed abeam Folkestone, it came under attack by 60 Stukas, which hit several ships, sinking five and damaging four more, including the destroyers *Boreas* and *Brilliant*. Nine Hurricanes of No.56 squadron arrived as the Stukas continued their assault, and turned them

away. Nine German E-boats attacked the convoy at about the same time, but were beaten off. 10 Spitfires of No.54 Squadron, and three from No.64 entered the fray, but the screen of Bf 109Es was too strong, and one of the No.64 Squadron Spitfires was shot down before the engagement concluded. A final attack on the convoy at about 1830 resulted in the destruction of a pair of Bf 109Es by No.610 Squadron. The day's action cost Fighter Command six Spitfires and four dead pilots, but Luftwaffe combat losses amounted to twelve aircraft, including five Bf 109Es. One loss (believed to have been to AA fire near Harwich) was a Bf 110C of Erprobungsgruppe 210, which made its Battle of Britain debut that day. The unit was a special fighter-bomber wing tasked with developing and practising Pathfinder techniques.

On Friday 26 July, Fighter Command lost a single Hurricane to enemy action, and another to Dover's AA guns. Both pilots were killed. The Luftwaffe also suffered two combat losses, one a Bf 109E, the other a Do 17Z downed at night, over the Bristol Channel, by Pilot Officer John Cock of No.87 Squadron. The pace of operations was generally slow, with small groups of shipping attracting only small-scale attacks. No.54

Squadron was finally sent north to Catterick, and its place at Hornchurch was taken by No.41 Squadron.

Although Fighter Command got the better of the Luftwaffe on 27 July, with one loss to five kills (including one to AA fire), Kesselring's tactics finally paid off and won him a significant victory. After the sinking of the destroyers *Wren* (off Aldeburgh) and *Codrington* (in Dover Harbour) the Royal Navy abandoned Dover as a base for anti-invasion ships, and re-deployed its destroyers to Harwich and Sheerness. The Channel was becoming an increasingly dangerous place for British warships. The lesson of concentrating forces to meet convoy attacks was evidently forgotten on 27 July, which saw three Hurricanes scrambled from Middle Wallop to protect a convoy being attacked by 30 Stukas of I./StG 77 with a Gruppe of JG 27 acting as escorts. Despite odds of about 20-to-one, the Hurricanes escaped unharmed after shooting down one Stuka.

Six Spitfires and three Hurricanes fared less well against the next raid, losing one of the No.609 Squadron Spitfires without inflicting any casualties on the enemy. The close escort of Bf 109Es succeeded brilliantly in preventing the RAF fighters from exploiting the Stuka's vulnerability.

Sunday 28 July saw two of the greatest pilots of the Battle duel for the first time, during a day which cost Fighter Command four

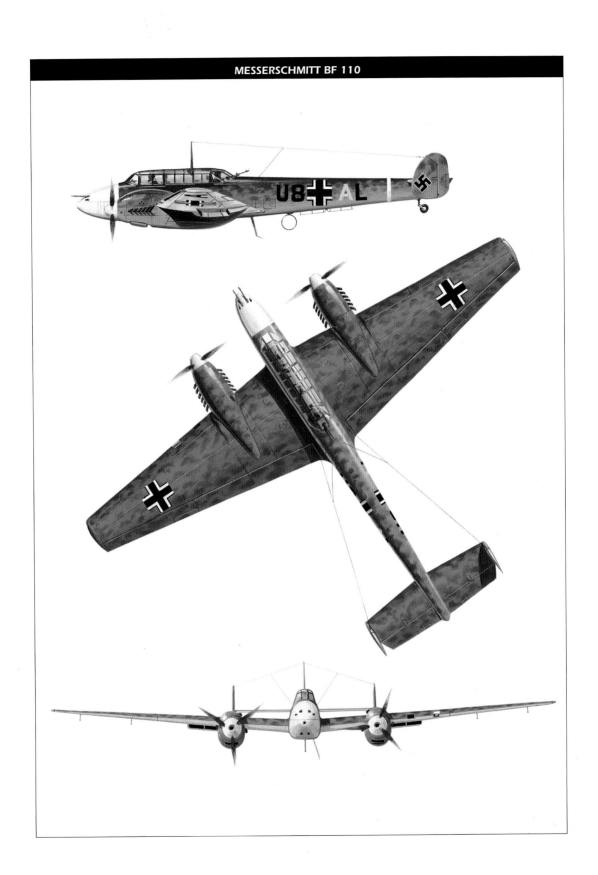

aircraft, and the Luftwaffe eight aircraft, including four Bf 109Es. Another Bf 109E was badly damaged when its engine failed after being hit in the same combat. For a change, that Sunday dawned bright and clear, and Fighter Command moved eight squadrons forward to advanced landing grounds. To counter a large raid approaching Dover, Fighter Command scrambled the Spitfires of No.74 Squadron (led by 'Sailor' Malan) from Manston, and a squadron of Hurricanes from Hawkinge. The Hurricanes were under orders to attack the enemy bombers, leaving the Bf 109Es to No.74. The enemy bombers turned back without dropping their bombs, and Malan found himself leading his dozen Spitfires against more than 40 Bf 109Es from I./ and II./JG 51, led by Major Werner Mölders. Malan downed one of the 109s in the leading Kette, and then raked another from spinner to rudder post. This aircraft dropped out of the fight and limped back to Wissant, where it crash-landed. Its pilot, Mölders himself, was lightly wounded, and had to leave the unit to recuperate. No.74 Squadron downed three of the Bf 109Es, and seriously damaged three more, for the loss of two of its own Spitfires.

Monday 29 July was another fine day, and one in which there was further fierce, bloody action. The day saw Fighter Command lose two Spitfires and a Hurricane, with several more landing with severe damage. On the other hand, the defences accounted for eleven enemy aircraft, although not one of these was a fighter. The biggest attack of the day was targeted at Dover, where 48 Ju 87s from IV (Stuka)/LG 1, II./StG 1 and II./StG 4 attacked, escorted by 80 Bf 109Es. The defence sent up 11 No.41 Squadron Spitfires and 12 No.501 Squadron Hurricanes from Manston and Hawkinge, but their task was made more difficult by heavy anti-aircraft fire. One No.41 Squadron Spitfire was shot down (with its pilot) and four more force-landed with combat damage, but the two RAF Squadrons shot down four Ju 87s and damaged a fifth.

The same day saw a convoy attacked by a low-level force of KG 76 Ju 88As, but one of these flew into a balloon cable and was lost, and another was shot down by AA fire. The aircraft had swept in under the radar and Fighter Command did not respond until the ships were under attack. The second convoy (in the Thames estuary) was attacked by Erprobungsgruppe 210, escorted by ZG 26. These were intercepted by No.501 Squadron, but although both sides claimed kills, all aircraft struggled back to base, some with heavy

ABOVE: RAF PILOTS AT READINESS BESIDE THEIR HURRICANES. AT THE HEIGHT OF THE BATTLE SQUADRONS IN THE FOREFRONT WERE FLYING THREE OR FOUR SORTIES A DAY, AND THE STRAIN OF COMBAT WAS BEGINNING TO HAVE ITS EFFECT.

LEFT: THE MESSERSCHMITT BF 110 WAS NOT AS SUCCESS AS A FIGHTER, LACKING THE MANOEUVRABILITY OF SINGLE-ENGINED FIGHTERS.

OPPOSITE PAGE: THE SWIRLING VORTEX OF INVISIBLE BATTLE...' VAPOUR TRAILS OVER LONDON ON 7 SEPTEMBER 1940. CURIOUSLY ENOUGH, NO ONE AT THIS STAGE KNEW EXACTLY WHAT CAUSED THESE TRAILS.

damage. The second convoy had been spotted by a Dornier, which was chased back to the Belgian coast by Flying Officer Patrick Woods-Scawen of No.85 Squadron, who fired all his ammunition and damaged the aircraft (which crash landed at St. Inglevert) but could not down it. Proof that the Channel was becoming progressively less safe for the Royal Navy was provided when a small raid sank the destroyer *Delight* near Portland.

Low cloud and steady rain limited operations on 30 July, which ended with no RAF combat losses, and with the destruction of only three Luftwaffe aircraft, one by AA fire. Haze similarly limited operations on the last day of the month, though there was more activity. Fighter Command lost two No.74 Squadron Spitfires (with their pilots) over Dover, when the squadron climbed to tackle two Staffeln of JG 2 – the famous Richthofen Geschwader. The Bf 109Es were driven off, one with such severe damage that it was classed

RIGHT: ENEMY BOMBS FALLING AMONG THE SHIPS OF A BRITISH CHANNEL CONVOY. CONVOY ATTACKS WERE DESIGNED TO TEMPT FIGHTER COMMAND TO BATTLE, BUT THE RAF's COMMANDERS WISELY REFUSED TO COMMIT LARGE NUMBERS OF THEIR PRECIOUS AIRCRAFT.

as a 100 per cent loss after force-landing at Fécamp.

By 31 July, Hitler was beginning to realise that a decisive victory against Britain would not be easy, and some advisers were already pointing out that even if it could be achieved, the loss of her empire would primarily benefit Japan and the USA. Hitler was reported to have started saying that Russia's destruction 'must be made part of the struggle against England; with Russia smashed, England's hope would be shattered.'

Although the RAF certainly matched the Luftwaffe during July, its success carried with it a heavy price. 80 regular RAF Squadron and Flight Commanders had been killed or wounded, and most tactical formations were now being led by officers whose experience of handling formations was brief, and limited. Even pre-war officers like 'Sailor' Malan who were newly qualified as Flight Leaders (Malan just before the war), would soon be Squadron or even Wing Leaders. Men and machines were relatively easy to replace – by the end of July, Dowding was able to establish his squadrons at 20 aircraft each (plus two 'Command Reserves') and the Command's pilot strength was 214 higher on 31 July than it had been on the first day of the month. Dowding increased the established number of pilots (generating an immediate on-paper shortage), but the actual number of pilots never dropped as low as it had been as the Battle started. But experience could not be replaced, and the best of the new boys inevitably needed time and training before they could handle their aircraft (let alone an entire formation) with the ease that the pre-war, peacetime-trained pilots took for granted.

On the German side, July provided mixed messages. There is no doubt that (like the RAF) the Luftwaffe over-estimated the casualties it had inflicted, but even so it was shaken by the extent of its losses. It should have learned the lesson that it was better to mount many small hit-and-run raids to 'soak up' the defences rather than to amass large raids which Fighter Command could usually get to in time to inflict losses, even if not always in time to prevent the target from being hit. Nor did the Luftwaffe learn the lesson that when used in fighter-only Free Chase operations, the Bf 109s usually inflicted heavy casualties, but when tied to close escort their kills were often matched by much smaller numbers of RAF fighters. The first warning had been given that the Ju 87 and Bf 110 were hopelessly vulnerable, and were likely to suffer heavy losses unless they were closely escorted. Yet if German claims were anything like accurate, it was assumed that Fighter Command must be near defeat, and the German commanders re-grouped ready for the planned massive attack which would herald the invasion. Thus the first week of August was relatively quiet, following the pattern set on the less busy days of July. Raids and convoy attacks continued sporadically, but losses were light. On 1 August, the RAF lost

RIGHT: THE JUNKERS JU 88, ONE OF THE FINEST BOMBERS PRODUCED DURING WORLD WAR II. IT TOOK PART IN THE FIRST RAID ON BRITAIN IN 1939 AND ALSO THE LAST, AN ATTACK ON NORTHERN ENGLAND ON 3 MARCH 1945.

RIGHT: THE JUNKERS JU
88, ONE OF THE FINEST
BOMBERS PRODUCED
DURING WORLD WAR
II. IT TOOK PART IN THE
FIRST RAID ON BRITAIN IN
1939 AND ALSO THE LAST,
AN ATTACK ON NORTHERN
ENGLAND ON 3 MARCH
1945.

BELOW: ARMOURERS
CHECKING THE BROWNING
.303 MACHINE GUNS IN
A HURRICANE. THESE
MACHINE GUNS WERE
EVENTUALLY REPLACED BY
20MM HISPANO CANNON
IN BOTH THE HURRICANE
AND SPITFIRE.

a Hurricane, while the Luftwaffe lost five aircraft. On 2 August, the RAF suffered no combat losses, while the Luftwaffe suffered three. Fighter Command again escaped losses on 3 and 4 August, with the Luftwaffe losing two aircraft on the first day, one to a Blenheim, and losing a Bf 109E to a Blenheim on 4 August.

Despite superb weather and fat convoy targets, the Luftwaffe mounted few attacks on 5 August, with a Free Chase by Bf 109s in the morning, and a Ju 88/Bf 109 convoy attack in the afternoon. A No.41 Squadron Spitfire crashed on take off at Manston, and two No.64 Squadron Spitfires were shot down by the Free Chasing Bf 109s. One Bf 109 was shot down, and another landed with heavy damage. The next day was quieter, with a handful of enemy reconnaissance aircraft venturing near the British coast. One Do 17Z was shot down by No.85 Squadron's Hurricanes, but it was the only combat casualty of the day. On 7 August, there were some nuisance raids, and one Ju 88 went missing, though no RAF pilot claimed it. But

the highlight of the day was provided by Bomber Command, who struck IV./JG 54 at Haamstede just as the unit was due to return to the line at Guines. Three Bf 109s were destroyed as they taxied, their pilots all being killed, and five more aircraft were damaged. The squadron finally returned to Guines two weeks later.

Meanwhile, Herman Göring had held a final conference at Karinhall on 6 August, provisionally setting a date (10 August) for Adler Tag (Eagle Day). Some date the Battle of Britain as beginning on this day, while others date it from 8 August, when the scale and ferocity of the fighting picked up. But the 8 August did not mark the start of the mass attacks which characterised Göring's Adlerangriff (Attack of Eagles), but rather a more serious prosecution of the ongoing Kanalkampf. Adlerangriff really began in earnest on 11 August.

RAF AIR ORDER OF BATTLE (FIGHTER COMMAND UNITS) 7 JULY 1940

NO. 11 GROUP

Headquartered at Uxbridge, No.11 Group was commanded by Air Marshal Keith Park. Its area of responsibility stretched from Essex clockwise around to South Wales. Its Sector Stations were North Weald, Hornchurch, Biggin Hill, Kenley, Tangmere, Middle Wallop and Filton. Middle Wallop and Filton were transferred to the No.10 Group, headquartered at Box, on 18 July. No.10 Group formed to cover the western part of the No.11 Group area, from just west of the Isle of Wight.

North Weald Sector

No.56 Squadron	RAF North Weald	Hurricane
No.85 Squadron	RAF North Weald	Hurricane
No.151 Squadron	RAF North Weald	Hurricane
No.25 Squadron	RAF Martlesham Heath	Blenheim

Hornchurch Sector

No.65 Squadron	RAF Hornchurch	Spitfire
No.74 Squadron	RAF Hornchurch	Spitfire
No.54 Squadron	RAF Rochford	Spitfire

Biggin Hill Sector

No.32 Squadron	RAF Biggin Hill	Hurricane
No.600 Squadron	RAF Biggin Hill (Manston)	Blenheim
No.610 Squadron	RAF Biggin Hill (Gravesend)	Spitfire
No.79 Squadron	RAF Hawkinge	Hurricane
No.604 Squadron	RAF Gravesend	Blenheim

Kenley Sector

No.64 Squadron	RAF Kenley	Spitfire
No.615 Squadron	RAF Kenley	Hurricane
No.111 Squadron	Croydon	Hurricane

Northolt Sector

No.1 (F) Squadron	RAF Northolt	Hurricane
No.257 Squadron	RAF Northolt (Hendon)	Hurricane

Tangmere Sector

No.43 Squadron	RAF Tangmere	Hurricane
No.145 Squadron	RAF Tangmere	Hurricane
No.601 Squadron	RAF Tangmere	Hurricane
FIU	RAF Tangmere	Blenheim

Middle Wallop Sector

No.236 Squadron	RAF Middle Wallop	Blenheim
No.238 Squadron	RAF Middle Wallop	Hurricane
No.501 Squadron	RAF Middle Wallop	Hurricane
No.609 Squadron	RAF Warmwell	Spitfire

Filton Sector

No.87 Squadron	Exeter	Hurricane
No.213 Squadron	Exeter	Hurricane
No.92 Squadron	RAF Pembrey	Spitfire
No.234 Squadron	RAF St Eval	Spitfire

NO.12 GROUP

Under the Command of Air Marshal Trafford Leigh-Mallory, No.12 Group stretched from Essex to North Yorkshire, with Sector Stations at Debden, Duxford, Coltishall, Wittering, Digby, and Kirton in Lindsey.

Kirton in Lindsey Sector

No.222 Squadron	RAF Kirton in Lindsey	Spitfire
No.253 Squadron	RAF Kirton in Lindsey	Hurricane

Digby Sector

No.29 Squadron	RAF Digby	Blenheim
No.46 Squadron	RAF Digby	Hurricane
No.266 Squadron	RAF Digby	Spitfire
No.611 Squadron	RAF Digby	Spitfire

Wittering Sector

No.23 Squadron	RAF Wittering (Collyweston)	Blenheim
No.229 Squadron	RAF Wittering	Hurricane

Duxford Sector

No.19 Squadron	RAF Duxford	Spitfire
No.264 Squadron	RAF Duxford	Defiant

Coltishall Sector

No.66 Squadron	RAF Coltishall	Spitfire
No.242 Squadron	RAF Coltishall	Hurricane

Debden Sector

No.17 Squadron	RAF Debden	Hurricane
No.85 Squadron	RAF Debden & Martlesham	Hurricane

NO.13 GROUP

Commanded by Air Marshal Saul, No.13 Group was headquarterd at Newcastle and covered northern England and Scotland. It had Sector Stations at Church Fenton, Catterick, Usworth, Turnhouse, Dyce and Wick.

Wick Sector

No.3 Squadron	RAF Wick	Hurricane
No.504 Squadron	RAF Castletown	Hurricane

Dyce Sector

No.263 Squadron	RAF Dyce	Hurricane
No.603 Squadron	RAF Dyce (A Flight)	Spitfire
No.603 Squadron	RAF Montrose (B Flight)	Spitfire

Turnhouse Sector

No.141 Squadron	RAF Turnhouse	Defiant
No.245 Squadron	RAF Turnhouse	Hurricane
No.253 Squadron	RAF Turnhouse	Hurricane
No.602 Squadron	RAF Drem	Spitfire
No.605 Squadron	RAF Drem	Hurricane

Usworth Sector

No.72 Squadron	RAF Acklington	Spitfire
No.152 Squadron	RAF Acklington	Spitfire
No.607 Squadron	RAF Usworth	Hurricane

Catterick Sector

No.41 Squadron	RAF Catterick	Spitfire
No.219 Squadron	RAF Catterick	Blenheim

Church Fenton Sector

No.73 Squadron	RAF Church Fenton	Hurricane
No.87 Squadron	RAF Church Fenton	Hurricane
No.249 Squadron	RAF Church Fenton	Hurricane
No.616 Squadron	RAF Leconfield	Spitfire

CHAPTER 5

A Duel of Eagles: 8 August – 6 September

LEFT: A PILOT OF NO 85 SQUADRON PICTURED AFTER A SORTIE DURING THE BATTLE OF BRITAIN. APART FROM A SPELL AT CROYDON IN AUGUST 1940, THE SQUADRON SPENT MOST OF THE PERIOD IN THE 12 GROUP AREA.

ABOVE: GROUND CREW
REMOVING TARPAULINS
FROM THE ENGINES OF A
HEINKEL HE 111 PRIOR
TO A SORTIE FROM A
FRENCH AIRFIELD IN THE
SUMMER OF 1940.

OPPOSITE BELOW: JUNKERS
JU 87 STUKAS DIVING ON
THEIR TARGET. NOTE THE
VERY LARGE FLAP AREA,
WHICH ENABLED THE STUKA
TO MAINTAIN A STEEP
ANGLE OF DIVE WITHOUT
EXCEEDING ITS CRITICAL
SPEED.

Historians have selected the 8 August as the first day of the Battle of Britain 'proper' (or of the Battle's 'Second Phase') so often that this date has become almost universally accepted. Certainly the day was marked by intensive air operations and heavy fighting, with correspondingly heavy losses, although these operations were still, in the main, centred around convoy attacks. There would then be something of a lull until 11 August, when the very nature of the German air offensive changed profoundly.

Convoy Peewit (CW9) consisted of 20 merchant ships and nine escorts, and sailed from the Medway Ports on the evening tide on 7 August. Detected by the new German 'Freya' sea-surveillance radar near Calais, the convoy was engaged by E-boats as it attempted to pass through the Straits of Dover. Three ships were sunk, and three more were damaged. Sporadic attacks by small formations of dive-bombers were ineffective, thanks partly to the convoy's own balloon barrage. A massive attack was therefore planned for 8 August to hit the convoy as it passed the Isle of Wight, involving 57 Stukas from StG 2, 3 and 77, and with escort provided by 20 Bf 110s of V./LG 1 and 30 Bf 109Es drawn from II./ and III./ JG 27. The Chain Home station at Ventnor gave sufficient warning for the raid to be met by 18 Hurricanes and a squadron of Spitfires, though the Bf 109E escort managed to keep the British fighters off the Stukas until they had made their attacks. The convoy scattered, negating the effectiveness of its balloon barrage, and four more merchant vessels were sunk. But the Luftwaffe lost three Ju 87s, one Bf 110 and three Bf 109s shot down, with eight more aircraft badly damaged, at a cost to Fighter Command of five Hurricanes.

The remnants of Convoy Peewit struggled on, only to come under attack again that afternoon, this time from 82 Ju 87s and 68 escorts. The raid was again met by two squadrons of Hurricanes, and fierce fighting ensued. Peewit suffered less harshly, though when it finally limped into Swanage, only four of the ships remained untouched, seven had been sunk, and six had been forced to seek sanctuary or repair in various ports along the route. Total Fighter Command losses for the day totalled 14 Hurricanes, three Spitfires and a Blenheim, but it had accounted for 20 enemy aircraft, including 10 Bf 109Es. Many more Luftwaffe aircraft limped home (or close to home) with major damage, many so severely that they were scrapped, others so badly mauled that they played no further part in the Battle.

BELOW: HURRICANES OF NO 85 SQUADRON IN TYPICAL FORMATION. THE RAF CONTINUED TO USE SUCH TIGHT COMBAT FORMATIONS UNTIL 1941, THEN ADOPTED THE MUCH MORE SENSIBLE AND FLUID PATTERN USED BY THE LUFTWAFFE.

After the ferocity of the previous day, 9 August was relatively calm. The Luftwaffe did send out several hundred scattered sorties, and some of these were intercepted. Official loss figures show one He 111 shot down by AA fire in the Humber estuary, one by No.79 squadron, and a Ju 88 shot down by Nos 234 and 601 Squadrons. JG 51 went balloon-busting at Dover, but were turned back by No.64 Squadron, though not before Dover's AA defences had downed one of their own balloons!

Many remember the summer of 1940 as having been one of glorious weather, but while there were some lovely days, there were many that were not. Saturday 10 August was so bad that

ABOVE: GERMAN PILOTS RELAXING BETWEEN SORTIES. THE WAITING, MOST ADMITTED, WAS THE WORST PART; ONCE AIRBORNE AND HEADING FOR ACTION, FEW PILOTS HAD TIME TO FEEL FEAR OR APPREHENSION.

RIGHT: A WOMEN'S AUXILIARY AIR FORCE AIRWOMAN MONITORS A CATHODE RAY TUBE DISPLAY AT AN RDF (RADIO DIRECTION FINDING) STATION. THE NAME RADAR WAS NOT ADOPTED UNTIL LATER IN THE WAR.

Göring's planned Adler Tag was postponed, and the day passed with neither side suffering a combat loss. There were some small-scale raids, but low cloud prevented the Germans from hitting their targets, and the British from intercepting the raiders.

With the benefit of hindsight, many now see Sunday 11 August as having provided the Luftwaffe with a dress rehearsal for Adler Tag. Whitaker's Almanac even dated it as the first day of the Battle! The day began with a series of Free Chase attacks by Bf 109s, and by a balloon strafing attack on Dover by Erprobungsgruppe 210. The first three Free Chases resulted in the loss of one No.74 Squadron Spitfire (whose pilot baled out) and two Bf 109Es. Kesselring then launched a series of Staffel-strength raids to try and saturate the British defences, but Park refused to be drawn, and most of the Bf 109Es enjoyed a fruitless dash around the Kent countryside before going home to refuel. There were isolated combats, but with little result.

A major attack by 54 Ju 88s from I./ and II./KG 54 and 27 KG 27 He 111s was launched against Portland, with an escort of 61 Bf 110s from ZG 2 and 30 Bf 109s from III./JG 2, led by a Great War veteran, Dr Erich Mix. Fighter Command launched 74 fighters in response, drawn from Nos 1, 87, 145, 152, 213, 238, 601 and 609 Squadrons. No.609 arrived first, and charged straight across the Bf 110's defensive circle, shooting down five of the enemy fighters. Most of the Fighter Command aircraft became tangled with the German fighters, leaving only about 10 aircraft to go through to attack the

enemy bombers. More Bf 109s (from JG 27) arrived to cover their comrades' withdrawal, but the Luftwaffe returned without six Bf 109s, six Bf 110s, five Ju 88s and a single He 111. The enemy personnel lost included three Gruppenkommandeurs, and several other senior officers. For these 18 aircraft losses, they destroyed 16 Hurricanes (with 13 pilots killed) and a single Spitfire (whose pilot drowned after successfully baling out). Search and rescue operations in the wake of the battle drew further action, but the other major air battle of the day centred around Convoy Booty off Harwich, attacked by the Bf 110s of Erprobungsgruppe 210 and the Do 17s of 9./KG 2. The Bf 110s were led, as usual, by their flamboyant Swiss commander, Hauptmann Walter Rubensdörffer, a veteran of the Spanish Civil War, and arguably the Luftwaffe's greatest fighter-bomber exponent. The raid was intercepted by Nos 17, 74, and 85 Squadrons, but completed its attack. At least four Bf 110s fell to the guns of No.17 Squadron's Hurricanes.

No.74 Squadron was in action again soon after, this time scrambled with 'Sailor' Malan leading. The 'Tigers' were joined by more Spitfires from No.54 Squadron and the

ABOVE: SPLENDID SHOT OF A MESSERSCHMITT BF 109, SHOWING THE MOTTLED BLUE-GREY FUSELAGE CAMOUFLAGE PATTERN CHARACTERISTIC OF GERMAN FIGHTERS DURING THE BATTLE OF BRITAIN.

RIGHT: THEY ALSO
SERVED... AN ORDERLY
SPEAKS TO A COLLEAGUE
AT A BARRAGE BALLOON
STATION SOMEWHERE
IN ENGLAND. BARRAGE
BALLOONS CAUSED A
NUMBER OF ENEMY LOSSES,
AND CERTAINLY HAD A
DETERRENT EFFECT. NOTE
THE EARLY HOUR.

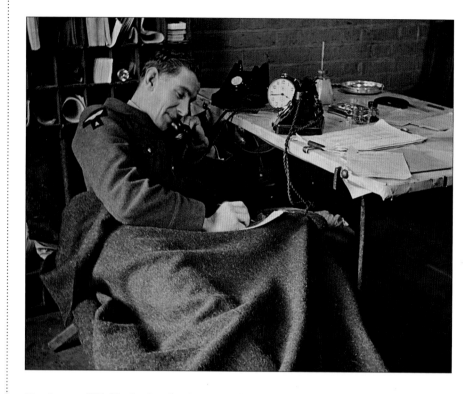

Hurricanes of 'Treble One' as they intercepted a raid by 45 Do 17s, a Staffel of Stukas and a strong escort, aimed against another convoy in the mouth of the Thames. Operations then petered out as the weather deteriorated, bringing a welcome respite to both sides. Over the course of the day, Fighter Command lost 24 Hurricanes (with 20 pilots) and six Spitfires (with four pilots) but shot down 13 Bf 109s, 10 Bf 110s, five Ju 88s, two Ju 87s, two He 59s and single examples of the Do 17 and Heinkel 111.

The heavy losses suffered on 11 August at last left the Luftwaffe in no doubt that British radar was giving Fighter Command considerable warning of incoming raids, and after strong pleading from General Martini (the Luftwaffe's signals chief), it was finally decided that all known radar stations should be put out of action before Adlerangriff, which was scheduled to start on Tuesday 13 August. This left only a day for the bombers to achieve the objective.

Despite the massive size of Chain Home's antenna masts, the radar stations were small, pinpoint targets, and the attacks against them were entrusted to Rubensdörffer's Erprobungsgruppe 210. Six of the unit's Bf 110s made a brilliant series of near-simultaneous attacks on the stations at Dover, Rye, Pevensey, and Dunkirk, but only managed to put the first station off the air for a matter of hours. With radar coverage degraded, however, the Luftwaffe was able to make unopposed attacks against Lympne and Hawkinge, and one dive-bombing attack against a convoy was detected too late to be prevented. Rye had reported the initial enemy formation as hostile bombers, but the Fighter Command Filter Room at Bentley Priory assigned it an X-code (doubtful status) As the enemy aircraft swept in, Bentley Priory phoned the Rye Chain Home station to ask what was happening. 'Your

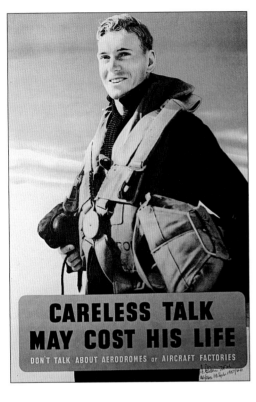

CARELESS TALK MAY COST HIS LIFE

DON'T TALK ABOUT AERODROMES or AIRCRAFT FACTORIES

X-Plot is bombing us!', came back the legendary reply.

Radar did provide warning of a raid by almost 100 Ju 88s of KG 51, backed up by 120 Bf 110s from ZG 2 and ZG 76 and escorted by 25 JG 53 Bf 109s. This huge armada swept towards Brighton, then veered westwards towards the Isle of Wight. Park and Brand reacted by throwing up 48 Hurricanes and 10 Spitfires. The enemy fighters formed a massive circle high above as the bombers split into two groups. The smaller group, of perhaps 15 aircraft, attacked Ventnor's Chain Home station, demolishing every building in the compound and damaging the antenna. It would be out of action for three days, restored to operation only by the use of mobile generators and truck-mounted operations rooms. The RAF had already practised the use of mobile transmitters, hooking them up to the transmitter masts, which were extremely difficult to damage, and the ability to bring stations back into function helped persuade the Luftwaffe that the fixed radar sites were actually harder to knock out than was really the case.

Ironically, these attacks on the RAF's radar stations were controversial within the Luftwaffe, some senior officers believing radar to be useful to the Luftwaffe, since it could be exploited to coax British fighters into the air where they could then be destroyed most easily. This incredible attitude had its roots in an acceptance of the Luftwaffe's over-ambitious and optimistic kill claims, which fostered the belief that when Fighter Command was drawn up into the air, it always suffered catastrophic losses.

The remainder of the Ju 88s swept over Portsmouth naval base, attacking targets for about 15 minutes, where two were brought down by AA fire. As they emerged from the ring of barrage balloons, RAF fighters fell on them, but always in numbers too small to tempt down the enemy fighters from their lofty perch. KG 51 lost 10 Ju 88s while the fighters waited, and the Bf 109s only came screaming down as the Ventnor raiders faced imminent annihilation. The Bf 109 Free Chase sent in to cover the withdrawal had been anticipated, and ran straight into No.615 Squadron's 12 Hurricanes, which downed two German fighters in rapid succession.

LEFT: WITH BRITAIN UNDER SIEGE, FEARS OF ENEMY AGENTS WERE RIFE. IN FACT, THE GERMAN INTELLIGENCE NETWORK IN BRITAIN WAS SURPRISINGLY POOR, AS WAS THEIR TARGET INTELLIGENCE.

BELOW: A HEINKEL HE 111 RELEASING ITS BOMB LOAD. THE MISSILES WERE STACKED VERTICALLY IN THE AIRCRAFT'S BOMB BAY, PRODUCING THE RATHER ODD 'TUMBLING' EFFECT SEEN HERE ON RELEASE.

ABOVE: A FORMATION OF
JUNKERS JU 87 STUKAS.
THE WORD 'STUKA' –
AN ABBREVIATION OF
STURZKAMPFFLUGZEUG –
WAS IN FACT APPLIED TO
ALL GERMAN DIVE
BOMBERS, BUT WAS
COMMONLY ASSOCIATED
WITH THE JU 87.

As the nearest Fighter Command airfield to the enemy, Manston was a tempting target, and was destined to be hit again and again throughout the Battle. Of all the Battle of Britain stations, Manston's ordeal would be the worst, and would eventually undermine morale to a worrying degree. After the attacks on the irrelevant Lympne and the heavy attack on Hawkinge (where two hangars, the maintenance workshops and four Spitfires had been destroyed), the Luftwaffe turned its attention to Manston. Erprobungsgruppe 210 swept in to strafe the airfield, which was also heavily bombed by 18 Do 17s from KG 2. The airfield workshops were gutted and two hangars were hit, but only one of the based Blenheims was destroyed, and No.65 Squadron's detached Spitfires were not seriously damaged. The airfield was re-opened within 24 hours. But 150 high explosive and fragmentation bombs were dropped on the airfield, sending a mushroom cloud thousands of feet into the air. The noise, smoke, dust and destruction must have been terrifying, and even after the raid was over, some groundcrew refused to come out from their shelters.

The day ended with Fighter Command counting the loss of 11 more Hurricanes and 10 more Spitfires, and of eight and three pilots, respectively. But on the credit side, the Luftwaffe had lost 28 aircraft, including 11 Bf 109Es.

The next day marked the first day of the Luftwaffe's planned air campaign, known as Adler Tag, though it began farcically, with a postponement order from Göring delaying the operation until the afternoon reaching only some of the participating units. Thus Fink's 74 Do 17s of KG 2 took off at 0500 for an attack on the Isle of Sheppey. His formation's escort (a massive gaggle of Bf 110s, led by the one-legged Great War veteran Joachim Huth), received a recall message, but couldn't communicate with the bombers – which had the wrong crystals in their radios.

Huth flew in front of the bomber formation and manoeuvred energetically, but this was taken as high spirits, and the Do 17s pressed on without their escort, subsequently losing five of their number to the RAF. They were lucky not to lose more, this luck manifesting itself in the fact that only Malan's No.74 Squadron reached the bombers before they hit Sheppey and the airfield at Eastchurch. Their tormentors also included No.151 Squadron, including the RAF's only cannon-armed Hurricane (L1750), flown that day by Flight Lieutenant Roderick Smith, who claimed a kill before his windscreen shattered.

Another unit which failed to receive the postponement and recall orders was KG 54, whose Ju 88As set off to attack the RAF at Farnborough and the Army Cooperation Command aerodrome at Odiham. Heavy clouds and marauding RAF fighters prompted the formation leader to turn his men round after they were only about 16km (10 miles) over England, and they fled almost without loss. Almost, because one crew was ordered to bale out (at the very sight of Spitfires according to some sources, or because the engines were failing according to others) and the Flight Engineer did so before the pilot regained control of the situation and flew home. A Free Chase mounted by I./JG 2 to cover this raid did go ahead as planned, and shot down a Hurricane.

A full three hours later, I./ZG 2 (still unaware of the postponement) took off to escort KG 54 on an attack against Portland. The Ju 88As didn't show up at the rendezvous and the Bf 110s pressed on alone, losing one aircraft to No.238 Squadron before turning for home.

Adlerangriff was launched properly in the middle of the afternoon, opening with a massive 300-aircraft attack against No.10 Group. II./JG 53 provided 30 Bf 109Es (led by Günther, Freiherr (Baron) von Maltzahn) which swept ahead of the main force, which was more closely escorted by 30 Bf 110s of V./LG 1 and 30 Bf 109s from JG 27. The bombers consisted of 40 Ju 88s from I./, II./ and III./LG 1 and about 79 Ju 87 Stukas from StG 77 and StG 2.

The most important task of JG 53's sweep was to decoy Fighter Command out to the west, but it failed to do this, merely bringing

BELOW: A 'CHAIN HOME' (CH) RADAR STATION ON THE ENGLISH COAST. BY THE OUTBREAK OF WAR 20 CH STATIONS WERE OPERATIONAL, STRETCHING FROM SOUTHAMPTON TO NEWCASTLE-UPON-TYNE.

LEFT: CONTROLLERS AT A CHAIN HOME STATION. FOR SECURITY REASONS, CH STATIONS WERE KNOWN AS AMES (AIR MINISTRY EXPERIMENTAL STATIONS), A TITLE THAT DID NOT FOOL THE GERMANS.

RIGHT: OBSERVER CORPS PERSONNEL KEEPING TRACK OF INCOMING PLOTS. THIS PHOTOGRAPH WAS TAKEN AFTER THE BATTLE OF BRITAIN; THE TITLE 'ROYAL' (SEE SHOULDER FLASHES) WAS NOT BESTOWED ON THE CORPS UNTIL LATER IN THE WAR.

BELOW: A GERMAN FIGHTER PILOT FROM JAGDGESCHWADER 26. THE UNIT'S MESSERSCHMITT BF 109s WERE HEAVILY INVOLVED IN THE BATTLE.

most of the fighters to a higher state of readiness, and tempting others into the air, where they were ready to meet the main attack when it fell. By the time the Stukas and Ju 88s crossed the coast, some 77 RAF fighters were scrambling.

Ju 88s penetrated to Southampton and bombed it heavily, but the Ju 87s were less successful in their attack on Middle Wallop. Their escort had already turned for home, short of fuel, and six of the attackers were shot down by No.609 Squadron's Spitfires. More Ju 88s were supposed to bomb Middle Wallop airfield, but some failed to find it and bombed Andover instead, and one aircraft dropped its bombs on Middle Wallop village. The remaining Stukas similarly failed to find Warmwell, and scattered their bombs around the countryside before fleeing.

On the other flank, Luftflotte II launched its dive-bombers soon after 1700. The main thrust was turned back by No.56 Squadron's Hurricanes, and the bombers scattered their bombs randomly as they fled. But the other major element of the attack in the east fared better. IV(St)/LG 1's 40 Ju 87s attacked Detling (not a Fighter Command station) with great success, killing 67 and destroying 22 aircraft. A well-timed Free Chase by JG 26 was led by Major Gotthardt Handrick (Gold Medallist in the Modern Pentathlon in the 1936 Berlin Olympics) and ensured that none of the attackers were lost.

Adlerangriff continued into the night, when 15 He 111s of Kampfgruppe 100 attacked the Short Brothers factory at Belfast, destroying five Stirlings. Nine more of the unit's He 111s were less successful in attacking Castle Bromwich, only four crews finding the target, and inflicting only trivial damage and not affecting Spitfire production. Other bombers were also unsuccessful, although 100 people were killed, and some railway lines damaged.

As British bombers returned to their bases after an epic Trans-Alpine bombing raid on the northern industrial cities of Milan and Turin, they dropped their remaining

THE BATTLE OF BRITAIN

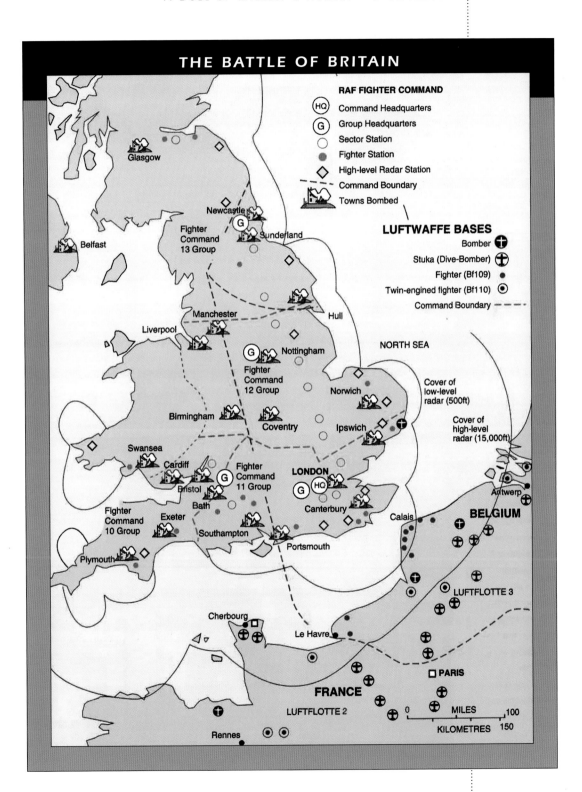

RAF FIGHTER COMMAND

- (HQ) Command Headquarters
- (G) Group Headquarters
- ○ Sector Station
- ● Fighter Station
- ◇ High-level Radar Station
- — · — Command Boundary
- Towns Bombed

LUFTWAFFE BASES

- ✚ Bomber
- ⊕ Stuka (Dive-Bomber)
- ● Fighter (Bf109)
- ⊙ Twin-engined fighter (Bf110)
- – – – Command Boundary

Glasgow

Belfast

Newcastle
Fighter Command 13 Group
Sunderland

Manchester

Liverpool

Hull

NORTH SEA

Nottingham
Fighter Command 12 Group

Norwich

Cover of low-level radar (500ft)

Cover of high-level radar (15,000ft)

Birmingham
Coventry
Ipswich

Swansea
Cardiff
Fighter Command 11 Group
LONDON

Bristol
Bath
Canterbury

Fighter Command 10 Group
Exeter
Southampton
Portsmouth

Calais

Antwerp

BELGIUM

Plymouth

Cherbourg

Le Havre

LUFTFLOTTE 3

□ PARIS

FRANCE

LUFTFLOTTE 2

0   MILES   100

KILOMETRES   150

Rennes

bombs (as was their customary practice) on a bombing range at Charlton-on-Otmoor, near Abingdon. Seeing the explosions, several He 111s of KG 55 raced to the scene and unloaded their bombs, resulting in a heavy raid on what was no more than an isolated patch of Oxfordshire countryside!

Both sides over-claimed heavily, with the RAF crediting its pilots with the destruction of 64 enemy aircraft (they actually accounted for 37) and the Luftwaffe even more imaginatively claiming 84 (the real figure being 13). But the RAF did lose 47 aircraft on the ground, one of them a fighter, and while Fighter Command could be pleased with even its real tally of enemy aircraft, only poor intelligence and even poorer navigation had prevented Adler Tag from inflicting serious damage on Fighter Command.

TOP: THE STUKA'S
REPUTATION SUFFERED
GREATLY IN THE BATTLE, AS
THE LACK OF GERMAN AIR
SUPERIORITY MEANT THAT
IT WAS OFTEN CAUGHT BY
BRITISH FIGHTERS.

RIGHT: A GERMAN BOMB
IS EXPLODED NEAR THE
OPERATIONS BLOCK AT
RAF KENLEY.
IF THE LUFTWAFFE HAD
KEPT ON ATTACKING BRITISH
AIRFIELDS FOR JUST A
FEW MORE DAYS, FIGHTER
COMMAND WOULD HAVE
BEEN IN DIRE STRAITS.

In many ways, the Luftwaffe enjoyed greater success on 14 August, though the pace of operations was slower. The most successful operation of the day was the attack on Dover by the Stukas of II./StG 1 and IV(Stuka)/LG 1, which attacked the Kent harbour and sank the Goodwin Lightship, while their escort (about 90 Bf 109Es from JG 26) protected them from the RAF fighters. One Gruppe stayed close to the dive bombers, but the other two (led by Hauptmann Fischer and Adolf Galland) fought it out with 42 Spitfires and Hurricanes of Nos 32, 65, 610 and 615 Squadrons, which arrived in a trickle, ensuring that all were heavily outnumbered. Things were relaxed enough for JG 26 that one of its Staffeln left the fight to go balloon-busting, downing eight of Dover's barrage balloons. Despite the German numerical superiority, only three RAF fighters were shot down, and one more was totally destroyed in a forced-landing after the battle, and its pilot was wounded.

Erprobungsgruppe 210 attacked Manston (again) setting four hangars on fire and destroying three more Blenheims on the ground. No.600 Squadron took its revenge, however, its personnel downing one of the raiders with a newly-rigged 20mm cannon. The airfield's 'proper' Royal Artillery defenders shot down another with their 40mm Bofors guns. Elsewhere, the Luftwaffe offensive took the form of small groups of raiders attacking a wide range of targets along a 160km (100-mile) front. Three He 111s attacked Middle Wallop, though the lead aircraft was shot down by Spitfires whose squadron hangar had just been damaged.

ABOVE: THIS FAKED PHOTOGRAPH PURPORTS TO SHOW A SPITFIRE ATTACKING A DORNIER 17 'SOMEWHERE OVER ENGLAND'. THE SPITFIRE IS A CAPTURED AIRCRAFT; ITS ORIGINAL ROUNDELS HAVE BEEN REPAINTED – IN THE WRONG PLACE.

Even in the north of England, German bombers found themselves under attack. Near Chester an He 111 of KG 27 was shot down by three staff instructors from No.7 OTU at Hawarden.

The day also marked a further rearrangement of No.11 Group's order of battle, with No.145 Squadron being rotated north to Drem, in Scotland, No.74 to Wittering (where it would continue to play a part in the Battle) and No.238 to St. Eval. Incoming units included No.266 at Hornchurch and No.249 at Boscombe Down.

Total RAF losses for the day totalled five, while the Luftwaffe lost 18 aircraft to RAF fighters, and two to ground fire, plus several more in landing accidents following the stress of combat. The German losses included five Bf 109s shot down in fighter-versus-fighter combat, making 14 August one of the first days in which the RAF managed to down as many single-engined fighters as it lost. In retrospect, it was a good omen for the day that followed.

Referred to throughout the Luftwaffe as 'Black Thursday', 15 August saw a major setback for the German air offensive. Bad weather promised to hinder operations, so Göring summoned his Luftflotte commanders to Karinhall for what would amount to a recriminatory post-mortem on Adler Tag.

As the weather cleared, the decision to launch the day's planned operations was finally taken. Interestingly, these were focused against Fighter Command's airfields,

ABOVE: THIS MG15 MACHINE GUN WAS SALVAGED FROM A HEINKEL AND USED BY A COMPANY OF THE SOMERSET LIGHT INFANTRY. IT WAS CLAIMED TO HAVE BROUGHT DOWN A ME 109 – A SOMEWHAT UNLIKELY TALE.

RIGHT: THIS BF 109E CRASH-LANDED AT NORTHDOWN, MARGATE, ON 24 JULY 1940 AFTER BEING ATTACKED BY A SPITFIRE. ITS PILOT, OBLT BARTELS, WAS SEVERELY WOUNDED AND TAKEN PRISONER.

A BIG DAY FOR LUFTFLOTTE V

Before 15 August, Luftflotte V's contribution to the Battle of Britain was limited to a handful of attacks by single aircraft or small formations. The difficulty facing the Luftflotte V commander was that while his Norwegian- and Danish-based bombers could reach Britain, they could not do so with a single-seat fighter escort. Yet German intelligence was certain that the only way the RAF could have mounted such a fierce resistance in the south was by stripping the north of its fighter and anti-aircraft defences.

It thus made perfect sense that Luftflotte V should participate in Adler Tag and Adlerangriff. Accordingly, Stumpff launched 18 Heinkel He 115 seaplanes in a feint against Dundee, with 63 He 111s of I./ and III./KG 26 flying in on a slightly more southerly course (towards Edinburgh) before turning south towards Newcastle. The Heinkels aimed to attack the RAF airfields at Dishforth and Usworth, with secondary targets in Sunderland and Middlesborough. These aircraft struggled into the air with 6000kg (13,228lb) bombloads, and were accompanied by 21 Bf 110Ds of I./ZG 76, long-range Zerstörers fitted with the Dackelbäuche – a plywood fairing which covered an auxiliary fuel tank. Unfortunately, the tracks of the He 115 feint and the main raid were too close together, and what should have been a decoy only served to increase Fighter Command's anxiety that a single major raid was inbound.

With a vital convoy sailing from Hull, no chance could be taken, while every fighter squadron in No.13 Group 'itched' to have a crack against the enemy. No.72 Squadron from Acklington was the first to get to the enemy formation, blowing apart two Bf 110s (whose empty but vapour-filled Dackelbäuchen exploded like bombs). No.605 Squadron from Drem were the next on the scene, followed by No.41 Squadron from Catterick and No.79 Squadron from Acklington. Seven Heinkels and seven Bf 110Ds were shot down before the survivors dumped their bombs and fled for home. As they straggled home, one ran into an anti-shipping strike composed of Blenheims from No.235 Squadron at Bircham Newton, and was promptly shot down.

As the Heinkels had flown south along the coast, No.13 Group scrambled the Defiants of No.264 Squadron to protect the convoy which had now left Hull. Even as the Heinkels fled, Chain Home detected another raid, of 50 bombers, flying in towards Driffield. At 1307, No.13 Group

scrambled 12 Spitfires from No.616 Squadron and six Hurricanes of No.73 Squadron's 'B' Flight to intercept the raiders. These turned out to be a mix of Ju 88A bombers and Ju 88C Zerstöreren from KG 30, which had set out from Aalborg in Denmark. The Ju 88s raced for the Bomber Command airfield at Driffield, where a Station Defence Exercise was fortuitously already underway, with all guns manned and most personnel already in their slit trenches. The Ju 88s destroyed some 10 Whitley bombers, and badly damaged six more, and many airfield buildings were wrecked or damaged. But the fighters and AA fire downed seven of the attacking aircraft (two bombers and five Ju 88Cs) and three more crashed in Holland on their journey home. The mission proved beyond any doubt that unescorted bomber raids ran the risk of very heavy losses, even over the supposedly undefended north of England.

as the decision had already been taken that attacks against Chain Home would 'not cause lasting damage'. This was a grave mistake, and demonstrated the German lack of understanding of how seriously they had damaged the radar stations they had attacked, nor how makeshift were the repairs. Of course, when it is said that the Luftwaffe targeted Fighter Command airfields, it would be more accurate to say that they targeted what they believed to be Fighter Command airfields. On 15 August, for example, the

BELOW RIGHT: LUFTWAFFE
MECHANICS AT WORK
ON THE ENGINES OF A
DORNIER DO 17. THE
DORNIER WAS ORIGINALLY
TO HAVE BEEN POWERED
BY DB600A ENGINES
DEVELOPING 1000HP, BUT
BECAUSE THESE WERE IN
SHORT SUPPLY THE 900HP
BRAMO 323A-1 WAS USED
INSTEAD.

target list included Driffield (a Yorkshire bomber base), Worthy Down (primarily a storage site) and Eastchurch (an unimportant forward operating base).

A major Stuka attack against Hawkinge did great damage, though fortunately the based fighters had been scrambled, shooting down two of the attackers, though four were lost to Bf 109Es. Quite apart from the damage to Hawkinge's infrastructure, the raid knocked out power to the Chain Home stations at Dover and Rye, and the Chain Home Low station at Foreness. Lympne was hit even harder, and II./ZG 76's Bf 110s made a strafing and bombing attack on Manston.

Before 15 August, Luftflotte 5 in Scandinavia had played little part in the Luftwaffe's air campaign, providing light raids by small groups of aircraft. Convinced that the north had been stripped of its fighter and AA defences, the Luftwaffe finally committed Luftflotte 5 in

One Hurricane pilot (Squadron Leader John Dewar of No.213 Squadron) found his cockpit full of smoke and fumes, and flew home half in and half out of the cockpit, using the stick but not rudder, and ducking back into the smoke-filled cockpit to lower flaps and undercarriage, landing successfully!

LEFT: PILOTS AND AIR GUNNERS OF A BOULTON PAUL DEFIANT SQUADRON WHILING AWAY THE TIME AT READINESS. THE DEFIANT WAS A DISASTER AS A DAY FIGHTER, BUT WENT ON TO SCORE VICTORIES AT NIGHT.

BELOW: AN RAF PILOT SAYS GOODBYE TO HIS PET BEFORE TAKE-OFF. SUCH PETS HELPED ALLEVIATE THE BOREDOM OF WAITING FOR THE CALL TO SCRAMBLE.

full strength, virtually without fighter escort. The result was to be catastrophic, as described on page 161.

Back in the south, Rubensdörffer's Erprobungsgruppe 210 mounted a devastating attack on Martlesham Heath, which knocked it out for two days. Three defending fighters were downed by the Bf 109E escort and the German force escaped without loss. A much larger raid (by some 88 Do 17Zs from KG 3, escorted by 130 Bf 109Es from JG 51, JG 53 and JG 54, and coordinated with a Free Chase by 60 JG 26 Bf 109Es) was equally successful. Even though the RAF vectored 36 fighters towards the raid, these were unable to penetrate the enemy fighter screen, and only two bombers were shot down, though the RAF fighters were cut to pieces in their attempts to stop the raid. The Dorniers attacked the Short Brothers factory at Rochester (disrupting Stirling production) and Eastchurch.

Heavily-escorted Staffel-strength attacks by KG 1 and KG 2 further stretched Fighter Command, but when 60 LG 1 Ju 88s (escorted by 40 of ZG 2's Bf 110s) attacked Southampton, Middle Wallop, Worthy Down and Odiham,

LEFT: A GREAT MANY PILOTS ON BOTH SIDES ENJOYED THE COMPANY OF PET DOGS. THIS PHOTOGRAPH SHOWS GERMAN ACE ADOLF GALLAND WITH HIS PARTICULAR FAITHFUL FRIEND.

As the two Hurricane pilots descended in their chutes, they were fired upon by the Home Guard. Nicholson was peppered by shotgun pellets, but his comrade was less lucky, his shroud lines parting and letting him fall to his death. This incident won Nicholson Fighter Command's only Victoria Cross of the war.

RIGHT: A STICK OF GERMAN BOMBS FALLING TOWARDS WORCESTER AERODROME. WORCESTER WAS NOT EVEN A MILITARY AIRFIELD, LET ALONG A FIGHTER COMMAND ONE – ANOTHER EXAMPLE OF FAULTY GERMAN INTELLIGENCE.

BELOW: FLIGHT LIEUTENANT JAMES NICHOLSON, VC.

they were hit hard by four Fighter Command squadrons, losing large numbers of aircraft. Things went less well when three squadrons (Nos 87, 213 and 234) tried to stop 40 Stukas attacking Portland. The escort of 60 Bf 109s (of JG 27 and JG 53) and 20 Bf 110s inflicted heavy casualties. One Hurricane pilot (Squadron Leader John Dewar of No.213 Squadron) found his cockpit full of smoke and fumes, and flew home half in and half out of the cockpit, using the stick but not rudder, and ducking back into the smoke-filled cockpit to lower flaps and undercarriage, landing successfully!

The final wave of attacks included another raid by the remarkable Rubensdörffer's Erprobungsgruppe 210 against Kenley, planned to coincide with an attack against Biggin Hill by Dorniers. The Bf 110s missed their rendezvous with their fighter escort, and then attacked Croydon instead of Kenley. They caused great damage, but were set upon by No.111 Squadron, while No.32 Squadron arrived in time to deal with the late-arriving Bf 109s. Rubensdörffer himself was shot down and killed, along with several of his most experienced aircrews. The Dorniers also missed their target, hitting the almost empty West Malling. Luftwaffe target recognition and navigation was exceptionally poor, and the aircraft which attacked Odiham earlier in the day returned to base convinced that their target had been Andover.

By the time the day's operations were over, thanks to the disastrous attacks in the north, German losses exceeded 71 aircraft (and missing loss returns may account for another 30 losses), including 32 Bf 110s and Bf 109Es. The RAF lost 18 Hurricanes and 11 Spitfires. Senior Luftwaffe commanders must have begun to wonder whether they would be able to destroy the RAF in four days, as they'd planned, and if they could, what sort of Luftwaffe they'd be left with.

Despite its heavy losses, the Luftwaffe continued to sustain frequent and heavy attacks the next day. Attacks included a damaging raid on Tangmere destroying many buildings and aircraft, and a Stuka raid against Ventnor's Chain Home station (surprisingly, in view of Göring's instruction to stop such attacks the previous day). There were also a number of heavy attacks by Do 17s and Ju 88s. One of these was intercepted by the Hurricanes of No.249 Squadron, which were attacked by Bf 109s from above. One section, led by Flight Lieutenant James Nicholson, was particularly badly hit. One aircraft dropped out of the formation heavily damaged, struggling back to Boscombe Down, and another was shot down in flames, its pilot baling out. Nicholson's aircraft was set ablaze, but he pressed his attack despite this, only baling out (hideously burned) after completing his attack. As the two Hurricane pilots descended in their chutes, they were fired upon by the Home Guard. Nicholson was peppered by shotgun pellets, but his comrade was less lucky, his shroud lines parting and letting him fall to his death. This incident won Nicholson Fighter Command's only Victoria Cross of the war.

One of the most successful Luftwaffe attacks was made by two Ju 88s, which joined the circuit at Brize Norton with their gear down, appearing out of the haze as though they were a pair of Blenheims. But as they crossed the perimeter fence they raised their wheels and dropped 32 bombs, destroying one hangar and 46 aircraft, including 11 stored Hurricanes. Things could have been even worse. A 250kg (550lb) bomb hit the ammunition store and failed to explode. The two Ju 88s escaped unscathed.

ABOVE: THE CREW OF A STUKA PREPARING FOR A SORTIE. THE JU 87 WAS WITHDRAWN FROM THE BATTLE OF BRITAIN AFTER SUFFERING HEAVY LOSSES AT THE HANDS OF THE RAF'S SPITFIRES AND HURRICANES.

LEFT: A SPITFIRE OF NO 92 SQUADRON IN A RATHER BENT STATE AFTER A FORCED LANDING. DAMAGED FIGHTERS WERE SALVAGED AND RETURNED TO THE FRONT-LINE SQUADRONS AS QUICKLY AS POSSIBLE.

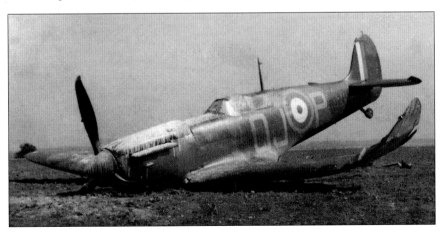

Generally, the Bf 109Es began flying closer escort, reducing bomber casualties, but imposing a higher cost on the fighters themselves. The policy of close-escort would subsequently be applied even more rigidly, with serious consequences. The Luftwaffe's tactics on 16 August (when it reached a peak of 1715 sorties) cost it 44 aircraft, including 18 Bf 109s, while the RAF lost only 23 fighters.

After two days of very heavy fighting, Saturday 17 August was much quieter, and the only combat loss on either side was an Arado Ar 196 which flew too close to a Royal Navy trawler, which shot it down. Early the next morning a single He 111 was destroyed by a No.29 Squadron Blenheim, 25 miles off Spurn Head.

But the respite was brief, and 18 August has gone down in the history books as 'The Hardest Day'. During its course, Fighter Command lost 30 Hurricanes and seven Spitfires, but shot down 61 enemy aircraft, including 16 Bf 109Es. But the most decisive defeat of the day was that of the Stukagruppen, which lost 17 aircraft (adding to 39 lost during the previous two weeks).

After sending over a wave of high flying recce aircraft, Kesselring launched a major raid against Biggin Hill. Planned as a coordinated attack, the raid became two separate raids, the first by Do 17s, the second by Ju 88s. Two of the Do 17s were shot down immediately, and two more crashed in the Channel, while three more force-landed in France. One of the two aircraft which regained its base did so with a dead pilot, the young flight engineer taking over to fly back to his base and make a normal wheels-down landing. Feldwebel Wilhelm-

BELOW: RAF KENLEY UNDER ATTACK ON 18 AUGUST 1940, SEEN FROM A DO 17 OF KG76. KG76 LOST SIX AIRCRAFT THAT DAY, AND EIGHT MORE STAGGERED BACK TO FRANCE WITH DEAD OR WOUNDED CREW MEMBERS.

LEFT: GERMAN
MESSERSCHMITT BF 109S
FLYING LOW NEAR THE
FRENCH COAST, IN TYPICAL
FORMATION. STAYING LOW
HID THE AIRCRAFT FROM
RADAR, BUT GAVE THEM A
TACTICAL DISADVANTAGE.

Friedrich Illg won a well-deserved Knight's Cross for his achievement. The wave of Ju 88s also lost two aircraft shot down. An attack on Kenley was more successful, though two of the raiders were destroyed by parachute-and-cable anti-aircraft devices. Some 12 personnel were killed, and 10 Hurricanes and a pair of Blenheims were destroyed in the bombing. Five more Hurricanes were shot down by Bf 109Es, which swept in to cover the withdrawal of the bombers. The Sector Operations Room was damaged, and a replacement was put into operation in a local shop. Disruption to telephone lines made it difficult for Sector Operations Centres to report to Fighter Command HQ, and this prompted an immediate revision of the emergency communications procedures.

A wave of attacks hit the airfields at Ford, Gosport and Thorney Island, and the Chain Home station at Poling, where Hurricanes and Spitfires massacred the attacking Stukas, shooting down 16, plus eight of their escorts, for six losses. Further waves of attacks followed, but none were particularly effective.

The Luftwaffe had lost 228 aircraft in the previous week, including 52 Bf 109s, while Fighter Command's losses had totalled only 105 aircraft. Moreover, Luftwaffe losses had included a Geschwaderkommodore, several Gruppenkommandeur and several Staffelkapitans, experienced officers who were impossible to replace. But on the credit side, it believed that it had destroyed 664 RAF aircraft, and that it had permanently destroyed 11 of the 44 aerodromes it had attacked (Driffield, Eastchurch, Gosport, Hawkinge, Lee on Solent, Lympne, Manston, Martlesham Heath, Portsmouth, Rochester and Tangmere). Furthermore, it was estimated that Fighter Command had no more than 300 fighters left (and not 700) and so the Battle continued without much respite. On 19 August, however, things were quieter. Fighter Command lost three Spitfires (all shot down by Ju 88s or He 111s) and a Coastal Command Blenheim failed to return from a Norwegian reconnaissance.

ABOVE: PHOTOGRAPH
PURPORTING TO SHOW A
SPITFIRE BREAKING AWAY
FROM AN ATTACK ON A
MESSERSCHMITT 110.
IT LOOKS GENUINE, BUT
IN FACT IS A GERMAN
PROPAGANDA SHOT.

RIGHT: COCKPIT OF A
MESSERSCHMITT 109.
THE 109'S COCKPIT WAS
CRAMPED, BUT IT WAS LAID
OUT WELL AND ALL THE
NECESSARY KNOBS AND
LEVERS WERE EASILY WITHIN
THE PILOT'S REACH.

Later, a Hurricane was lost after colliding with a balloon cable. The Luftwaffe lost four aircraft to Fighter Command, and five more were lost or badly damaged after running out of fuel when they returned to France.

That day Göring ordered an end to Free Chase tactics by the Bf 109Es, and ordered Luftflotte 3's fighters forward to the Pas de Calais to extend their reach. Bf 109 units in Luftflotte 5 were transferred to the Channel front and in an effort to stem the loss of officers ordered that multi-crew aircraft would have only one commissioned officer in their crews. Refusing to acknowledge his own responsibility, Göring undertook a major reshuffle of his fighter commanders, dismissing the 'Old Guard' and promoting younger men in their place.

Fighter Command also took the opportunity to consider how its tactics should develop in the light of operational experience. Issuing new instructions, Dowding implicitly acknowledged the disastrous inefficiency of his search and rescue organisation by discouraging the despatch of fighters to intercept even small formations of enemy aircraft which were not 'over land or within gliding distance of the coast'. He also stressed again the importance of sending the minimum number of squadrons to engage enemy fighters, and to continue to prioritise Luftwaffe bombers.

Things remained fairly quiet on Tuesday 20 August, thanks mainly to poor weather. Fighter Command lost only two aircraft, but shot down at least seven enemy aircraft. In the House of Commons, Churchill famously rose to celebrate Fighter Command's achievements. 'The gratitude of every home in our Island, in our Empire and indeed throughout the world, except in the abodes of the guilty, goes out to British airmen who, undaunted by odds, unwearied in their constant challenge and mortal danger, are turning the tide of world war by their prowess and devotion. Never in the field of human conflict was so much owed by so many to so few.' Many Fighter Command pilots jokingly wondered whether Churchill was referring to their mess bills!

Continuing poor weather limited operations again on 21 August, and only one Fighter Command Hurricane was shot down. The Luftwaffe despatched numerous three-aircraft nuisance raids, but these proved vulnerable. Twelve Ju 88s and Do 17s were shot down by Fighter Command, and another fell to AA fire. The 22 and 23 August were busier, but losses remained light. The RAF lost four fighters on 22 August, and the Luftwaffe lost two aircraft on each day, with others damaged or crashing on landing.

Many historians have described 24 August as having marked the start of the supposed 'Third Phase' of the Battle, in which Fighter Command was more deliberately targeted. Certainly, the pressure on Fighter Command increased, but in truth, the strategic direction of the air campaign remained the same, it was just that the Luftwaffe prosecuted its attacks with greater skill and better tactics. But Fighter Command airfields had been targeted for weeks, and had been subject to heavy attack, while drawing the Spitfires and Hurricanes into the air had also been a long-standing Luftwaffe priority.

The weather changed on Saturday 24 August, which dawned bright and clear, and by 0830 Chain Home was reporting the assembly of a massive force. This raid consisted of 40 Do 17s, escorted by some 66 Bf 109Es. Fighter Command scrambled twelve squadrons (about 72 aircraft) to meet the raid, but found the dense fighter screen all but impenetrable. One of the RAF units despatched was No.264, with its Defiants, though the type was quite unsuitable for scrambles (with its ponderous boarding procedure) and was quite unable to cope with modern fighter opposition. Remarkably the Defiants returned from their first mission unscathed, but had more success and less luck on their second mission, losing three aircraft, although four Ju 88As were downed by the Defiants flown by Banham, Garvin, Whitley and Thorn, while Barwell and his gunner, Martin, shot down a Bf 109 which promptly collided with another. Later, two Defiants collided on the ground, and another was shot down by Bf 109s.

ABOVE: THE BULLDOG BREED: WINSTON CHURCHILL, SOON TO BECOME PRIME MINISTER, SEEN AT DOWNING STREET WITH HIS SECRETARY, BRENDAN BRACKEN, THE DAY AFTER THE GERMAN INVASION OF BELGIUM AND HOLLAND.

RIGHT: THE HORNET
EMBLEM ON THE NOSE OF
THIS HURRICANE DENOTES
THAT IT BELONGS TO NO
213 SQUADRON, WHICH
WAS BASED AT TANGMERE
DURING THE CLIMAX OF THE
BATTLE OF BRITAIN.

BELOW: CREW MEMBERS IN
THE COCKPIT OF A GERMAN
BOMBER. IT WAS COMMON
PRACTICE FOR PILOTS TO
GIVE RUDIMENTARY FLYING
LESSONS TO OTHER CREW
MEMBERS IN CASE THE
LATTER HAD TO FLY THE
AIRCRAFT HOME – WHICH
THEY SOMETIMES DID.

Manston was attacked again, with great ferocity, reducing it to little more than an emergency landing and refuelling station, and Hornchurch and North Weald also came under attack. The North Weald attack was met by three squadrons, and many of the bombers were turned back without attacking. Only the Bf 110 Zerstörers prevented a massacre, since the Bf 109Es had already withdrawn, short of fuel. As the attacks intensified, Park called upon the commander of the neighbouring No.12 Group to provide urgent fighter cover for his airfields. Leigh-Mallory attempted to assemble his squadrons into a huge wing over Duxford, and as a result, apart from six No.19 Squadron Spitfires, the No.12 Group fighters failed to get to North Weald on time. The Spitfires were the cannon-armed Mk IBs, though unfortunately the four were plagued by gun stoppages. Despite this they shot down three Bf 110s.

The other big raid on 24 August was by the Ju 88s of LG 1, and hit Portsmouth hard, causing 104 civilian deaths and 237 serious injuries. The Ventnor radar was still having trouble providing range information, and No.609 Squadron's Spitfires were positioned too low. They found themselves 1524m (5000ft) below LG 1's Ju 88s, down sun and in the middle of an anti-aircraft barrage. The unit was lucky to escape without loss.

The night of 24 August saw the first night raids on the capital, with bombs falling in the City, Bethnal Green, East Ham, Finsbury and Stepney, causing serious fires. These had not been authorised by Göring, who had demanded personal control of when and whether to attack the great cities of London and Liverpool, and he was accordingly furious to find out that he had been disobeyed. When the day's raids finally finished, the RAF had lost

LEFT: GERMAN PILOTS STANDING BY THE MESSERSCHMITT 109S AWAITING THE ORDER TO TAKE OFF ON A SORTIE OVER SOUTHEAST ENGLAND. THE BF 109 HAD A RELATIVELY SHORT RADIUS OF ACTION.

BELOW LEFT: THE ROBUST, WORKMANLIKE HURRICANE WAS LESS IN THE PUBLIC EYE THAN THE GLAMOROUS SPITFIRE, BUT IT WAS MORE NUMEROUS AND DESTROYED MORE ENEMY AIRCRAFT. IN ALL, 565 HURRICANES WERE LOST IN THE BATTLE OF BRITAIN.

24 aircraft, at least one to friendly AA fire, one Blenheim to RCAF Hurricanes, and with the total also including five Defiants. The Luftwaffe fared even worse, with the loss of more than 30 aircraft, including 16 Bf 109Es.

Taking off shortly after midnight, Flight Lieutenant James Sanders of No.615 Squadron found, stalked and shot down an He 111, all without radar assistance! Such 'Cat's Eye' patrols became an increasingly important part of the RAF's response to Luftwaffe night bombing. Despite fine weather, Sunday 25 August began slowly, and Kesselring initially confined himself to sending Staffel-strength formations up and down the Channel, ready to turn north to attack at any point, but keeping the defences guessing. This went on until about 1600, when Ventnor's Chain Home station reported a 100-plus raid forming up west of the Cherbourg Peninsula, though this would subsequently prove to be something of an underestimation. As the raid approached Weymouth, the RAF scrambled squadrons from Exeter, Middle Wallop, Tangmere and Warmwell. The German bombers (from II./KG 51 and II./KG 54) and Zerstörers (from I./ and II./ZG 2 and V./LG 1) split into three groups (of about 70 aircraft each) to attack Portland, Weymouth and Warmwell, just as a Gruppe of Bf 109Es from JG 53 swept in as escorts. The outnumbered RAF fighters turned back

Following the Luftwaffe bombing of London, Bomber Command visited Berlin on the night of 25/26 August. This attack so angered the Nazi hierarchy that it would eventually provoke retaliation, swinging the Luftwaffe away from its main goal (of destroying Fighter Command) into ultimately ineffective bombing raids on London. This switch of targets has been attributed by many as being the turning point in the Battle.

ABOVE: SPITFIRES IN
ECHELON FORMATION
'PEELING OFF' FOR THE
BENEFIT OF THE AIR
MINISTRY CAMERAMAN. OF
A TOTAL OF 747 SPITFIRES
DELIVERED TO FIGHTER
COMMAND FROM JULY TO
OCTOBER 1940 INCLUSIVE,
361 WERE LOST.

most of the bombers, and none of the targets were badly hit. Another raid (against Kent) was similarly turned back, the defenders including No.32 Squadron. This hard-worked unit lost a pilot, reducing its strength to only eight, and was accordingly withdrawn for rest and reformation at Acklington. RAF losses that day totalled 18, with the Luftwaffe losing 20, including seven Bf 109Es.

Following the Luftwaffe bombing of London, Bomber Command visited Berlin on the night of 25/26 August. This attack so angered the Nazi hierarchy that it would eventually provoke retaliation, swinging the Luftwaffe away from its main goal (of destroying Fighter Command) into ultimately ineffective bombing raids on London. This switch of targets has been attributed by many as being the turning point in the Battle. It did not occur immediately, however, although Luftflotte 3 switched to night bombing of the industrial Midlands for the next three weeks, making its last daylight attack on 26 August, thereafter diluting the effort against Fighter Command.

The pattern of operations on 26 August was much as it had been the previous day, though this time the main No.11 Group Sector Stations at Biggin Hill and Kenley came under attack. Scrambling from Kenley in two groups, No.616 Squadron had a particularly hard time, losing six aircraft as they ran into a force of 80 Bf 109Es. No.264 Squadron's Defiants were also engaged, losing three of their number, though all three pilots and one of the gunners lived to fight another day. The squadron claimed six Do 17s, however (and

THE BIG WING

Throughout the Battle of Britain, RAF fighter pilots often found themselves outnumbered. This was hardly surprising – the Luftwaffe mostly operated in Gruppe strength (between 30 and 40 aircraft) while the RAF operated in Squadrons (between nine and 12 aircraft) or even in six-aircraft Flights.

Increasing the number of aircraft committed to an engagement could merely increase the losses. Dowding and Park realised that they therefore had to play a careful game, using fighters to stop the enemy bombers from hitting their targets, while avoiding fighter-versus-fighter combat. Thus Park drip-fed his fighters into battle, attempting to minimise losses while maximising the return, and avoiding the Bf 109Es wherever possible. Park was not dogmatically opposed to using fighters in large numbers. However, he felt that intercepting the enemy quickly with a small force was usually better than slowly gathering a whole Wing which arrived too late – experience showed that it could take twice as long to assemble a three-squadron Wing than a formation of only two squadrons.

The Battle of Britain was fought largely in the skies over No.11 Group's area, but the No.11 Group commander, Keith Park, called upon neighbouring Groups for extra fighters when needed. No.10 Group's AOC, Brand, sent whatever Park asked for, but when Park asked Leigh-Mallory, the AOC of No.12 Group, it was never quite so simple.

Leigh-Mallory has often been presented as resenting the way in which Park sometimes seemed to view the Battle as a purely No.11 Group affair. The 'Big Wing' offered Leigh-Mallory the best chance of raising the profile of his Group. Leigh-Mallory wanted to use a whole Wing to deliver local air superiority and shoot down the enemy in the largest possible numbers. But geography dictated that the Battle was primarily a No.11 Group affair, and Park had every right to expect that his counterparts in neighbouring Groups would support him when necessary.

This Leigh-Mallory and No.12 Group signally failed to do. On numerous occasions, Park asked for one or two squadrons to protect his airfields against an impending raid, only for Leigh-Mallory to laboriously scramble his Big Wing, which would inevitably arrive too late, or sometimes not at all. When it did arrive, it caused huge amounts of confusion, with the Observer Corps reporting the unexpected formation, and with No.11 Group occasionally scrambling its own fighters to investigate.

Park was eventually moved to set out five points for No.12 Group.

1) Send squadrons where and at the height requested.
2) Send fighters only when requested.
3) Control should be informed as to the whereabouts of No.12 Group's squadrons.
4) Squadrons should not alter their patrol lines without informing their controllers.
5) They should not waste time forming a five squadron Wing if asked for two squadrons.

The Big Wing's defenders complained that Park seldom gave sufficient warning and claimed that the Wing achieved great success. In fact, many of the Big Wing squadrons proved weak when used individually, with poor gunnery skills, navigation and tactics – though their pilots did tend to be very good indeed at formation flying! The successes claimed by the Big Wing's supporters have often been based on the Wing's own claims, which were at times shockingly inflated.

RIGHT: PILOTS OF NO 1 SQUADRON PICTURED IN FRANCE EARLY IN 1940. NO 1 SQUADRON WAS ONE OF THE RAF UNITS THAT FORMED THE FIGHTER ELEMENT OF THE RAF'S ADVANCED AIR STRIKING FORCE, THE OTHER BEING NO 73.

post-war research confirms that they definitely destroyed at least three of these), and one crew (pilot Sergeant Edward Thorn, gunner Sergeant Frederick Barker) also downed a Bf 109E which attacked as they prepared to force-land, having accounted for two Dorniers.

A raid aimed against Debden and Hornchurch ran into even more trouble. Canewdon radar had believed the attack involved much larger numbers of aircraft than was the case, and Fighter Command scrambled all available fighters. The escorting Bf 109Es were operating at the limit of their range and had to avoid combat and turn back, while the bombers ran straight into Colchester's flak, so that only six Dorniers pressed their attacks on Debden. The remainder then ran up against some seven squadrons of Spitfires and Hurricanes and were forced to turn tail and flee, abandoning their planned attack on Hornchurch altogether. The only major problem for the RAF was that when No.11 Group had requested No.12 Group cover for its airfields, it again failed to materialise, and Debden was left without fighter protection.

LEFT: NO.12 GROUP
FIGHTERS ASSEMBLE INTO A
'BIG WING', A TACTIC OF
DUBIOUS VALUE WHEN TIME
WAS OF THE ESSENCE.

BELOW: JUNKERS
JU 88 OF KG30
'EAGLE' GESCHWADER,
BROUGHT DOWN NEAR
NORTHAMPTON. KG30
SUFFERED HEAVILY IN THE
LUFTFLOTTE 5 ATTACK ON
NORTHERN ENGLAND, 15
AUGUST 1940.

Both the Canadians of No.1 Squadron (RCAF) and the Czechs of No.310 Squadron were now committed to the fight, each unit losing three aircraft, though the Czechs evened the score by downing three enemy aircraft. During the course of that Monday, the RAF lost 28 aircraft, while the Luftwaffe lost 33, including 14 Bf 109Es.

Things were quieter on 27 August, thanks to low cloud and drizzly rain, and both sides took the opportunity to assess their tactics. Dowding finally withdrew the exhausted No.65 Squadron from the line to rest and re-train at Church Fenton. Fighter Command lost a single Spitfire in combat (shot down by a Ju 88) but inflicted three kills on the Luftwaffe.

With the withdrawal of Luftflotte 3's bombers from the fray, the weight of the Luftwaffe attacks fell almost entirely on the No.11 Group area. 28 August was a day of intensive action for Fighter Command, with several unusual features. No.264 Squadron suffered the loss of four of its 12 Defiants (and five more were unserviceable on landing, due to battle damage), one of their gunners being shot dead as he descended in his parachute. Later the same day, the Luftwaffe made a brief return to Free Chase tactics, and a small group of RAF fighters found themselves vectored onto a huge gathering of about 60 Bf 110s and 80 Bf 109Es. The defenders lost five aircraft, but shot down six of the attackers. Fighter-versus-fighter combat was just what Fighter Command was trying to avoid, however, and the destruction of 14

Bf 109Es among the 18 Luftwaffe aircraft shot down that day was little compensation for the loss of 18 RAF fighters (13 of them Spitfires and Hurricanes).

On the night of 28/29 August, all three Luftflotten stepped up their night raids, usually operating behind the dedicated Pathfinders of Kampfgruppe 100, and against which Fighter Command could do little. Birmingham, Bournemouth, Bristol, Coventry, Derby, Liverpool, Manchester and Sheffield all came under attack, with widespread damage and relatively heavy casualties. The Blenheim night fighters did not get a single contact with the enemy. The next day was quiet, allowing Dowding to withdraw Nos 264 and 615 Squadrons from the fray, bringing in Nos 222 and 253 to replace them. Kesselring attempted to decoy RAF fighters into the air without much success, then launched two Free Chase operations in the evening. The RAF lost nine fighters on 29 August, but shot down 10 of the enemy's aircraft, eight of them Bf 109Es.

In terms of its intensity, the Battle of Britain did enter a new phase on 30 August, as the Luftwaffe launched an all-out effort to destroy Fighter Command in the run-up for the invasion they were told would follow. After a number of light probing attacks, Kesselring unleashed a massive three-wave attack on Kent. The RAF ignored the first wave of 60 Bf 109Es, but scrambled on the second wave, which consisted of 70 bombers, 30 Zerstörers and another 60 Bf 109Es. By 1145 all of Park's squadrons were airborne, and 10 were in

ABOVE: BOULTON PAUL DEFIANTS OF NO 264 SQUADRON. THIS UNIT ACHIEVED SOME SUCCESS OVER DUNKIRK IN MAY 1940, BUT IT WAS DECIMATED IN DAYLIGHT OPERATIONS DURING THE BATTLE OF BRITAIN.

RIGHT: A GERMAN BOMBER PILOT'S VIEW FROM THE COCKPIT OF A DORNIER DO 17. GLAZED NOSES GAVE EXCELLENT VISIBILITY, BUT MADE AIRCREWS VULNERABLE TO HEAD-ON ATTACKS.

action, and he called upon No.12 Group to cover his airfields. Amazingly, Leigh-Mallory responded in time, though the No.12 Group fighters tasked with defending Biggin Hill did not even see the small group of Ju 88s which attacked the airfield under their noses.

The early actions that day showed up some deficiencies in the newly arrived 'replacement' squadrons, which did not seem to be using the revised tactics adopted by more experienced units. No.222 Squadron went into battle in tight formation, with a weaver behind, who was promptly shot down, and the squadron lost eight Spitfires (but only one pilot) during the course of the day. Park had already complained (on 26 August) about the variable quality of the units sent to him as replacements. He felt that No.13 Group always appreciated the heavy fighting in the south of England and sent its best units, while he felt that Leigh-Mallory preferred to hang onto No.12 Group's top pilots. He pointed out that two squadrons sent by No.13 Group had destroyed 43 enemy aircraft for only four losses, while three from No.12 Group had shot down 17 enemy aircraft for the loss of 13 of their own aircraft.

He was particularly disappointed by the performance of No.616 squadron, which Kenley's Sector Commander recommended should be returned to No.12 Group due to its 'low fighting efficiency'. Park requested that he be sent another squadron from No.10 or No.13 Group, 'if No.12 Group is unable to spare an experienced squadron.'

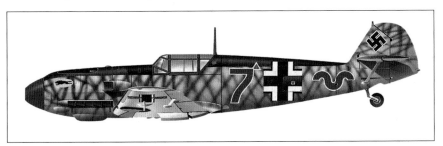

ABOVE: SPITFIRES OF
NO 19 SQUADRON AT
DUXFORD, 1940. THE
SQUADRON SPENT MUCH OF
ITS TIME AT ITS DISPERSAL
AIRFIELD OF FOWLMERE,
FROM WHERE IT DESTROYED
A NUMBER OF RAIDERS IN
AUGUST 1940.

Fighter Command was given little respite before the next wave of attacks, and thanks to a lucky hit on the main electricity grid that morning, the Chain Home and Chain Home Low stations at Beachy Head, Dover, Fairlight, Foreness, Pevensey, Rye and Whitstable were all out of action and only five of Dowding's squadrons engaged the enemy. Kesselring's third wave of attacks swept in as the second wave finally withdrew, powering on to attack Fighter Command's airfields at Biggin Hill, Kenley and North Weald, and factories at Luton, Oxford, Radlett (Handley Page) and Slough. Biggin Hill was badly damaged, and control of its sector passed to Hornchurch.

Luftflotte 3 continued the onslaught by night, though with lighter opposition, and mounted a 130-aircraft raid on Liverpool. During that day, Fighter Command flew 1054 sorties (a record for the Battle), and lost 21 aircraft in combat, but destroyed 36 enemy aircraft, including 16 Bf 109s.

Despite its heavy losses, the Luftwaffe launched another day of heavy attacks on 31 August, forcing Fighter Command to mount 978 sorties in response (the third highest tally of the Battle). In doing so, Fighter Command suffered 38 combat losses, though now that most combat was overland, the proportion of pilots killed had dropped dramatically. Nevertheless, the Command lost eight pilots killed. For the second day in a row, one of these was shot while hanging beneath his parachute. But the Luftwaffe suffered similarly heavy casualties, losing 38 aircraft in combat, including 21 Bf 109Es and 12 of their single-seat fighter pilots killed or missing.

The day began with a Free Chase by Bf 109Es, who fell upon No.1 Squadron, RCAF, before it could respond to a recall order. Three of the inexperienced Canadians were shot down in short order. The Bf 109Es found no further fighter opposition, and returned home via Dover, where they destroyed every single one of the town's barrage balloons. A second raid attacked North Weald, its escort bettering the Fighter Command squadrons sent against it. Another formation of Do 17s and Bf 109Es ran into Treble One, however,

who opened the fight with their trademark line-abreast head on attack, at which the enemy bombers jettisoned their bombs and fled.

The Luftwaffe attacked various airfields, including Croydon, Debden, Detling, Eastchurch, Hornchurch and Biggin Hill (whose telephone system, just repaired after the previous day's attacks, was knocked out). Erprobungsgruppe 210 made a return to its specialised pinpoint attacks, targeting Chain Home and Chain Home Low stations

in Kent and Sussex. Several were damaged, but all were back on air by the end of the day. These attacks should have been followed up, and a week of attacks on Chain Home stations could have blinded Fighter Command, but capitalising on successful attacks was never a Luftwaffe strength, whose bombing campaign was always somewhat random in its targeting.

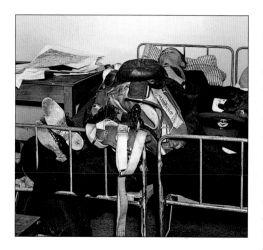

By the end of August, Fighter Command had lost 11 of its 46 Squadron Commanders killed or seriously wounded, together with 39 of its 96 Flight Commanders. Others had been rotated out of the frontline with their exhausted and battle-fatigued squadrons. Two more units, No.56 Squadron (down to seven aircraft) and No.151 Squadron (down to 10 aircraft and 12 pilots), both without a CO, were transferred out of the line on Sunday 1 September. Dowding would have transferred out more had he not needed to keep some experienced units in the line. Some of the remaining units were dangerously diminished, and half a dozen stayed only to be effectively destroyed during the following week – No.85 Squadron, which had lost nine aircraft in four days, lost six more on 1 September.

Biggin Hill was attacked again (twice) on 1 September, the second attack destroying the Sector Operations Room and cutting telephone and electricity lines once more. The Electricity Board and Post Office engineers succeeded in connecting up a temporary operations room in a local village shop. The day ended with Fighter Command having suffered 13 combat losses (Luftwaffe losses are difficult to estimate, due to incomplete records). The Luftwaffe issued its 'Operations Staff 1A Order', calling for an all-out assault on Britain's aircraft factories, to prevent the frontline units receiving replacement aircraft.

Finally present in France (rather than at his Karinhall HQ in East Prussia), Göring took direct charge of the Luftwaffe's air campaign, alternately berating and lavishly praising

his subordinates, sometimes shaking with anger, and sometimes full of benevolent good humour. During a meeting with his fighter commanders, Göring's attitude seemed almost schizophrenic – showing fury at their failure to protect 'his' bombers, then jollying them along and showing care and concern for their needs. But the meeting ended on a sour note, when Adolf Galland, having been asked if there was anything he needed, replied that he would like 'a squadron of Spitfires!'

The Luftwaffe launched just short of 1000 sorties against England on 2 September, in what was basically a four-phase attack. The first raid was targeted against Biggin Hill, Eastchurch, North Weald and Rochford, and was intercepted by relatively small numbers of fighters, due to Fighter Command's tactic of keeping standing patrols over the sector airfields. Dover was the target of the second phase of attacks, which was broken up by the defenders. The last two phases again hit Fighter Command's airfields, and especially Biggin Hill, Brooklands (with the raiders aiming at Hawker's assembly sheds, and not the nearby Vickers factory), Detling, and Kenley. The German formations started including extra escorts very much higher, and these aircraft frequently set traps for unwary RAF fighters. 'Beware the Hun in the Sun' became an ever more relevant cautionary watchword. By the end of the day, Fighter Command had lost 18 fighters in combat (and more through accidents or being bombed on the ground) while the day's operations cost the Luftwaffe 27 aircraft, including 15 Bf 109Es.

Tuesday 3 September saw more changes to Fighter Command's order of battle. No.85 Squadron (down to eight aircraft and 11 pilots) was finally withdrawn, while Nos 504 and 616 Squadrons returned to the north, replaced by Nos 41 and 66 Squadrons from

LEFT: A DORNIER **17** ON ITS LAST PLUNGE TO EARTH ON **18 AUGUST 1940.**

BELOW: A GROUP OF RAF FIGHTER PILOTS DISPLAYING A SOUVENIR CUT FROM THE WRECK OF AN ENEMY BOMBER. BOTH SIDES TOOK GREAT PRIDE IN ACQUIRING PIECES OF SHOT-DOWN AIRCRAFT FOR DISPLAY IN THEIR CREW ROOMS.

Catterick and Kenley, and Treble One moved from Debden to Croydon. When it became clear that Tuesday's first attack consisted entirely of fighters, the three squadrons scrambled were ordered to avoid combat, and disengaged to the north. A second wave of German aircraft bombed North Weald, which was left unguarded despite requests to No.12 Group. RAF fighters (from Nos 1, 17, 46, 249, 257, 310 and 603 Squadrons) reached the scene as the bombers and their escorts withdrew, and engaged in bitter fighting, most notably with the Bf 110s, which gave a surprisingly good account of themselves. No.19 Squadron also entered the fight with eight of its cannon-armed Spitfires, but when six of them suffered gun stoppages, the squadron was forced to withdraw. Things also went badly for No.25 Squadron, who lost two aircraft to No.46 Squadron, who mistook the returning Blenheims for Ju 88s. But things got very much better for No.25 in the evening, albeit after a false start. One aircraft was hit by return fire as it attacked an enemy bomber, but managed to limp home, but another, flown by Pilot Officer Michael Herrick (with gunner Sergeant John Pugh) shot down two more raiders. This was an amazing achievement, since the Blenheim's AI radar was unreliable and temperamental. Fighter Command's combat losses that Tuesday totalled 18 aircraft (including the Blenheims), but their planes had shot down 14 enemy aircraft, three of them Bf 109Es.

Wednesday 4 September began with the usual assault on Kent airfields, with the main blows falling on Lympne and Eastchurch. The second phase of attacks involved a formation of 70 or so He 111s and Do 17s, with an escort of more than 200 Bf 109Es. These attacked a number of targets principally to draw attention away from a raid by 20 Bf 110s from V(Z)/LG 1, which attacked Brooklands. After losing six aircraft to Hurricanes en route to the target, the survivors directed their bombs against the Vickers works and not Hawker's

The German formations started including extra escorts very much higher, and these aircraft frequently set traps for unwary RAF fighters. 'Beware the Hun in the Sun' became an ever more relevant cautionary watchword.

factory, which escaped unscathed. Fighter Command suffered 16 combat losses (one to 'friendly' AA fire, and one of the pilots who baled out was shot dead in his parachute). The Luftwaffe lost 20 aircraft in combat, including four Bf 109Es.

There was no real pattern to the air fighting on 5 September. Kesselring unleashed some 22 separate attacks over the space of eight hours. The day marked the combat debut of a four-cannon Hurricane (flown by No.46 Squadron's Alexander Rabagliati), which proved devastatingly effective, clearly pointing to the best way forward for fighter armament. That night, the FIU flew its first operational patrol with the new Beaufighter, though its AI radar failed, and it landed without any kills. The Luftwaffe's bombers managed to set the fuel storage tanks at Thameshaven ablaze, marking a highly visible success against a critically important target. The Luftwaffe shot down 22 RAF fighters on 5 September, though these accounted for 20 Luftwaffe aircraft, including 16 Bf 109Es.

Attacks continued in much the same pattern on 6 September, with a large German force attacking Thameshaven by deliberately approaching at 3658m (12,000ft), actually within the pall of smoke from the fires caused by the previous day's attacks. The raid even included a single Stuka Staffel, which escaped unscathed, though two Ju 87s were claimed by Victor Beamish, North Weald's Station Commander, as 'probables'. During the day, the RAF's losses ran to 25 fighters shot down, though 13 Luftwaffe bombers and Zerstörers fell to AA and fighters and Fighter Command downed 20 Bf 109Es. The Poles suffered particularly heavily, with the loss of five aircraft and two pilots wounded.

As the fighter-versus-fighter battle continued, losses on both sides reached the critical point. The RAF was beginning to find it hard to replace its personnel losses, and was probably suffering worse (or less bearable) attrition than the Luftwaffe. Some believed that

No.11 Group needed to be completely rotated out of the Battle area, to be replaced en masse by fresher units, and some even began to talk of withdrawing from the airfields south of London altogether. On the other hand, the Luftwaffe's fighter pilots were finally realising that their claims had been over-optimistic, and that there was still a great deal of fight left in their opponents. Meanwhile, German losses were increasing, robbing the Jagdwaffe of some of its star pilots, while the less favoured parts of the Luftwaffe (the Zerstörer and Stuka Gruppen, for example) were clearly at crisis point.

RAF AIR ORDER OF BATTLE (FIGHTER COMMAND UNITS) 1 AUGUST 1940

NO.10 GROUP

Middle Wallop Sector

No.238 Squadron	RAF Middle Wallop	Hurricane
No.604 Squadron	RAF Middle Wallop	Blenheim
No.609 Squadron	RAF Middle Wallop	Spitfire
No.152 Squadron	RAF Warmwell	Spitfire

Filton Sector

No.87 Squadron	Exeter	Hurricane
No.213 Squadron	Exeter	Hurricane
No.92 Squadron	RAF Pembrey	Spitfire
No.234 Squadron	RAF St. Eval	Spitfire

NO.11 GROUP

North Weald Sector

No.56 Squadron	RAF North Weald	Hurricane
No.151 Squadron	RAF North Weald	Hurricane
No.25 Squadron	RAF Martlesham Heath	Blenheim
No.85 Squadron	RAF Martlesham Heath	Hurricane

Hornchurch Sector

No.41 Squadron	RAF Hornchurch	Spitfire
No.65 Squadron	RAF Hornchurch	Spitfire
No.74 Squadron	RAF Hornchurch	Spitfire

Biggin Hill Sector

No.32 Squadron	RAF Biggin Hill	Hurricane
No.600 Squadron	RAF Biggin Hill (Manston)	Blenheim
No. 610 Squadron	RAF Biggin Hill	Spitfire
No.501 Squadron	RAF Gravesend	Hurricane

Kenley Sector

No.64 Squadron	RAF Kenley	Spitfire
No.615 Squadron	RAF Kenley	Hurricane
No.111 Squadron	Croydon	Hurricane

Northolt Sector

No.43 Squadron	RAF Northolt	Hurricane
No.257 Squadron	RAF Northolt (Hendon)	Hurricane

Tangmere Sector

No.1(F) Squadron	RAF Tangmere	Hurricane
No.266 Squadron	RAF Tangmere	Spitfire
No.601 Squadron	RAF Tangmere	Hurricane
FIU	RAF Tangmere	Blenheim
No.145 Squadron	RAF Westhampnett	Hurricane

Debden Sector

No.17 Squadron	RAF Debden	Hurricane

NO.12 GROUP

Kirton in Lindsey Sector

No.222 Squadron	RAF Kirton in Lindsey	Spitfire
No.264 Squadron	RAF Kirton in Lindsey	Defiant

Digby Sector

No.29 Squadron	RAF Digby	Blenheim
No.46 Squadron	RAF Digby	Hurricane
No.611 Squadron	RAF Digby	Spitfire

Wittering Sector

No.23 Squadron	RAF Wittering (Collyweston)	Blenheim
No.229 Squadron	RAF Wittering	Hurricane

Duxford Sector

No.19 Squadron	RAF Duxford (Fowlmere)	Spitfire

Coltishall Sector

No.66 Squadron	RAF Coltishall	Spitfire
No.242 Squadron	RAF Coltishall	Hurricane

NO.13 GROUP

Wick Sector

No.3 Squadron	RAF Wick	Hurricane
No.804 Squadron, FAA	RAF Wick	Gladiator
No.232 Squadron	RAF Sumburgh	Hurricane
No.504 Squadron	RAF Castletown	Hurricane
No.808 Squadron, FAA	RAF Castletown	Fulmar
No.141 Squadron	RAF Prestwick	Defiant

Dyce Sector

No.263 Squadron	RAF Grangemouth	Hurricane

Turnhouse Sector

No.253 Squadron	RAF Turnhouse	Hurricane
No.603 Squadron	RAF Turnhouse	Spitfire
No.602 Squadron	RAF Drem	Spitfire
No.605 Squadron	RAF Drem	Hurricane

Usworth Sector

No.72 Squadron	RAF Acklington	Spitfire
No.79 Squadron	RAF Acklington	Hurricane
No.607 Squadron	RAF Usworth	Hurricane

Catterick Sector

No.54 Squadron	RAF Catterick	Spitfire
No.219 Squadron	RAF Leeming	Blenheim

Church Fenton Sector

No.73 Squadron	RAF Church Fenton	Hurricane
No.249 Squadron	RAF Church Fenton	Hurricane
No.616 Squadron	RAF Leconfield	Spitfire

LUFTWAFFE AIR ORDER OF BATTLE (BATTLE OF BRITAIN UNITS) 13 AUGUST 1940

OBERBEFEHLSHABER DER LUFTWAFFE

Under the direct command of Reichsmarshal Göring from Berlin.

1(F)/Aufkl.Gr.OkL	Berlin	Various
2(F)/Aufkl.Gr.OkL		Do 215, He 111H
Westa 1 ObdL	Oldenburg	Do 17Z, He 111H
Westa 2 ObdL	Brest/Lanveoc-Poulmic	He 111H
Westa 26 ObdL	Brussels-Grimberghen	Do 17, He 111, Bf110

LUFTFLOTTE 2

Air Fleet 2 was headquartered at Brussels, under the command of Field Marshal Kesselring, and included 23 whole Kampfgruppen, two Stukagruppen, four Zerstörergruppen, 13 Jagdgruppen and miscellaneous reconnaissance units. It also included a Nachtjäger (night-fighter) division, but this played no part in the battle, and is here omitted.

I Fliegerkorps

Fliegerkorps I was headquartered at Beauvais, under the command of Colonel-General Grauert, and consisted principally of three bomber wings.

Stab KG 1	Rosieres en Santerre	He 111H
I./KG 1	Montdidier	He 111H
II./KG 1	Montdidier	He 111H-1, 2?
III./KG 1	Rosieres en Santerre	He 111H-2
Stab KG 76	Cormeilles en Vexin	Do 17Z
I./KG 76	Beauvais/Tille	Do 17Z-1
II./KG 76	Creil	Ju 88A-1
III./KG 76	Cormeilles en Vexin	Do 17Z-2,-3
Stab KG 77	Laon	Ju 88A-1
I./KG 77	Laon	Ju 88A-1
II./KG 77	Asch	Ju 88A-1,5
III./KG 77	Laon	Ju 88A-1
5(F)/122	Haute Fontaine	Do17P, He111H,
Ju88A		

II Fliegerkorps

Fliegerkorps II was headquartered at Ghent, under the command of General Loerzer, and consisted principally of three bomber wings, together with the experimental fighter bombers of Erpr.Gr.210.

Stab KG 2	Saint Leger	Do 17Z-2
I./KG 2	Cambrai	Do 17Z-2,-3
II./KG 2	Saint Leger	Do 17Z-2,-3
III./KG 2	Cambrai	Do 17Z-2
Stab KG 3	Le Culot	Do 17Z-2
I./KG 3	Le Culot	Do 17Z-2
II./KG 3	Antwerp/Deurne	Do 17Z-2,-3
III./KG 3	Saint-Trond	Do 17Z-2
Stab KG 53	Lille-Nord	He 111H-2
I./KG 53	Lille-Nord	He 111H-2
II./KG 53	Lille-Nord	He 111H-2,3
III./KG 53	Lille-Nord	He 111H-2,3,4
II./StG 1	Pas de Calais	Ju 87B
IV(St)/LG 1	Tramecourt	Ju 87B-2
Erprobungsgr. 210	Calais Marck	Bf 109E, 110C,D

9 Fliegerdivision

9 Fliegerdivision was headquartered at Soesterberg, under the command of Lieutenant-General Coeler, and consisted principally of three bomber wings, though these consisted of only five full Kampfgruppen rather than the usual nine.

Stab KG 4	Soesterberg	He 111P
I./KG 4	Soesterberg	He 111H-4
II./KG 4	Eindhoven	He 111P-2
III./KG 4	Schipol	He 111P
Stab KG 40	Brest-Guipavas	Ju 88A-1
I./KG 40	Brest-Guipavas	Fw 200C
Kampfgrüppe 100	Vannes-Meucon	He 111H-1,2,3
Kampfgrüppe 126	Marx	He 111H
3(F)/122	Eindhoven	He111H, Ju88A

Jafu 2

Fighter support for Luftflotte 2 came from Jagdfliegerführer 2 headquartered at Wissant, under the command of Colonel von Döring, and which consisted principally of 13 day-fighter Gruppen in five wings, together with one wing of Bf 110 Zerstörers.

Stab JG 3	Wierre au Bois	Bf 109E
I./JG 3	Grandvilliers	Bf 109E
II./JG 3	Samer	Bf 109E
III./JG 3	Desvres u Le Touquet	Bf 109E
Stab JG 26	Audembert	Bf 109E
I./JG 26	Audembert	Bf 109E
II./JG 26	Marquise-Ost	Bf 109E
III./JG 26	Caffiers	Bf 109E
Stab JG 51	Wissant	Bf 109E
I./JG 51	Pihen bei Calais	Bf 109E
II./JG 51	Marquise-Ouest	Bf 109E
III./JG 51	St.Omer-Clairmarais	Bf 109E
Stab JG 52	Coquelles	Bf 109E
I./JG 52	Coquelles	Bf 109E
II./JG 52	Peuplingues	Bf 109E
III./JG 52	Zerbst	Bf 109E
Stab JG 54	Campagne-les-Guines	Bf 109E
I./JG 54	Guines-en-Calaises	Bf 109E
II./JG 54	Hermelingen	Bf 109E
III./JG 54	Guines-en-Calaises	Bf 109E
Stab/ZG 26	Lille	Bf 110C
I./ZG 26	Yvrench-St Omer	Bf 110C/D
II./ZG 26	Crécy-St Omer	Bf 110C
III./ZG 26	Barly-Arques	Bf 110C-2,4

LUFTWAFFE AIR ORDER OF BATTLE (BATTLE OF BRITAIN UNITS) 13 AUGUST 1940

LUFTFLOTTE 3

Air Fleet 3 was headquartered in Paris, under the command of Field Marshal Sperrle, and included 15 Kampfgruppen, seven Stukagruppen, one Schlachtgruppe, four Zerstörergruppen, nine Jagdgruppen and miscellaneous reconnaissance and support units.

VIII Fliegerkorps

Fliegerkorps VIII was headquartered at Deauville, under the command of General Richthofen, and consisted principally of three Stuka wings, with some fighter-bomber, Zerstörer, and reconnaissance units.

Stab/StG 1	Angers	Ju 87B
I./StG 1	Angers	Ju 87R
III./StG 1	Angers	Ju 87B-2
Stab/StG 2	St. Malo	Ju 87B
I./StG 2	St. Malo	Ju 87B
II./StG 2	Lannion	Ju 87R-1,B?
Stab/StG 77	Caen	Ju 87B
I./StG 77	Caen	Ju 87B
II./StG 77	Caen	Ju 87B
III./StG 77	Caen	Ju 87B
II(S)/LG 2	Böblingen	Bf 109E-7
V(Z)/LG 1	Caen	Bf 110C,D
2(F)/11	Raum Bernay	Do17P, Bf 110
2(F)/123		Do17P

V Fliegerkorps

Fliegerkorps V was headquartered at Villacoublay, under the command of General Ritter von Greim, and consisted principally of three bomber wings, (with a total of eight Kampfgruppen) together with two reconnaissance units.

Stab KG 51	Orly	Ju 88A-1
I./KG 51	Melun	Ju 88A-1
II./KG 51	Orly	Ju 88A-1
III./KG 51	Étampes	Ju 88A-1
Stab KG 54	Evreux	Ju 88A-1
I./KG 54	Evreux	Ju 88A-1
II./KG 54	St. André	Ju 88A-1
Stab KG 55	Villacoublay	He 111P-2
I./KG 55	Dreux	He 111H, P
II./KG 55	Chartres	He 111H-3, P
III./KG 55	Villacoublay	He 111P-2
4(F)/14	Raum Cherbourg	Do17M,P, Bf 110
4(F)/121	Villacoublay	Do17P, Ju 88A

IV Fliegerkorps

Fliegerkorps IV was headquartered at Dinard, under the command of Major General Pflugbeil, and consisted principally of two bomber wings, together with an independent Kampfgruppe, the remnants of a Stuka wing's staff flight, and a reconnaissance unit.

Stab LG 1	Orléans-Bricy	Ju 88A
I(K)/LG 1	Orléans-Bricy	Ju 88A-5
II(K)/LG 1	Orléans-Bricy	Ju 88A-1
III(K)/LG 1	Chateaudun	Ju 88A-5
Stab KG 27	Tours	He 111P
I./KG 27	Tours	He 111P
II./KG 27	Tours	He 111P, H-3
III./KG 27	Tours	He 111P
Kampfgrüppe 806	Nantes, Caen	Ju 88A
Stab/StG 3	Bretigny	Ju 87B, He 111H
		Do 17M,Z
3(F)/31	St. Brieux	Do17P, Bf 110

Jafu 3

Fighter support for Luftflotte 3 came from Jagdfliegerführer 3 headquartered at Wissant, under the command of Colonel von Massow, and consisted principally of nine day-fighter Gruppen in three wings, together with one two-Gruppen wing of Bf 110 Zerstörers.

Stab JG 2	Beaumont le Roger	Bf 109E
I./JG 2	Beaumont le Roger	Bf 109E
II./JG 2	Beaumont le Roger	Bf 109E
III./JG 2	Le Havre	Bf 109E
Stab JG 27	Cherbourg-Ouest	Bf 109E
I./JG27	Plumetôt	Bf 109E
II./JG 27	Crépon	Bf 109E
III./JG 27	Arcques	Bf 109E
Stab JG 53	Cherbourg	Bf 109E
I./JG 53	Rennes	Bf 109E
II./JG 53	Dinan	Bf 109E
III./JG 53	Brest	Bf 109E
Stab ZG 2	Toussus-le-Noble	Bf 110C
I./ZG 2	Caen-Carpiquet	Bf 110D
II./ZG 2	Guyancourt	Bf 110C-2,5,D

LUFTFLOTTE 5

The tiny Air Fleet 5 was headquartered at Stavanger, under the command of Colonel-General Stumpff.

X Fliegerkorps

Fliegerkorps X was headquartered at Stavanger, under the command of General Geiseler, and consisted principally of two bomber wings (four Gruppen), one Zerstörergruppe, and two fighter gruppen, together with reconnaissance and support elements.

Stab KG 26	Stavanger	He 111P
I./KG 26	Stavanger	He 111H-3,4
III./KG 26	Stavanger	He 111H-3,4
Stab KG 30	Aalborg	Ju 88A-1
I./KG 30	Aalborg	Ju 88C
III./KG 30	Aalborg	Ju 88C-2
I./ZG 76	Stavanger-Forus	
Stab JG 77		Bf 109E
I./JG 77		Bf 109E
II./JG 77	Stavanger Trondheim	Bf 109E
Stab/KüFlGr 506	Stavanger	He 115
1./KüFlGr 506	Stavanger	He 115
2./KüFlGr 506	Stavanger	He 115
3./KüFlGr 506	Stavanger	He 115
3(F)/Aufkl.Gr.OkL	Stavanger	Do 215, He 111H
		Bf 110C
1(F)/120	Stavanger	Do 17P, He 111H
1(F)/121	Stavanger/Aalborg	He 111H, Ju 88A
2(F)/22	Stavanger	Do 17P/M
3(F)/22	Stavanger	Do 17P/M
Westa Kette X Flk	Stavanger	He 111H

CHAPTER 6

The Blitz: 7 September – 31 October

LEFT: FIREMEN AT WORK IN EASTCHEAP, LONDON, DURING THE 'BLITZ'. OVER 13,000 LONDONERS LOST THEIR LIVES BETWEEN 7 SEPTEMBER AND 31 DECEMBER 1940, WHEN THE MAIN FOCUS FOR THE LUFTWAFFE'S BOMBERS WAS BRITAIN'S CAPITAL.

Most historians agree that the very nature of the Battle of Britain changed on 7 September, with a shift away from the direct attack on Fighter Command's airfields and the factories which produced its aircraft. The change in targeting was driven by Göring and supported by Kesselring, who felt that the anti-airfield campaign had run its course, and that Fighter Command was finished. But Sperrle protested strongly, believing that Fighter Command probably still had a thousand aircraft left, and wished to continue to scourge the No.11 Group airfields. He was overruled.

But it would be a mistake to see the targeting of London as necessarily marking a fundamental change in direction by the Luftwaffe. The aim was still the destruction of Fighter Command, and the targeting of London merely represented a switch to a target which the Germans felt was most likely to draw the RAF's fighters into the air, where they could be destroyed. It was, in the words of one German officer, the 'only target that Fighter Command would give everything to defend.' That, at least, was Göring's theory, although it did also mark an opportunity for vengeance following Bomber Command's raid on Berlin on 25 August. And London was a vitally important target. It was Europe's largest city, and was the capital city of a nation whose capital was of unparalleled importance. It was the centre of Britain's economy, a major industrial and port city, the seat of government and the home of the King. Small wonder that it was a tempting target.

But just as Göring had rethought his battle plans, so too did Dowding adjust his tactical thinking, and restructured his forces. By coincidence, as the new phase of the Battle began, Dowding's reclassification of his squadrons came into effect. Thereafter, the frontline squadrons in No.11 Group were categorised as Class A squadrons, as were those units in Nos 10 and 12 Groups which Park might call on to reinforce his Group. Class B squadrons were fully manned and fully established, and were ready to be called into action, but might be lacking in combat experience or be suffering from a degree of fatigue. Finally, Class C squadrons were those which had suffered severe losses, and were being rested and re-equipped. Experienced survivors from these units were taken (as soon as they were ready) to act as replacements for pilots killed or wounded in the higher category units. This cut the link between an individual pilot and his original unit, but ensured that newly formed squadrons

would have a core of combat-experienced veterans. Meanwhile, Keith Park instructed his controllers and pilots to henceforth obey altitude orders from Group, without making any personal interpretations of the heights given. He did this to ensure that climbing fighters did not emerge below their targets, but it caused delays and sometimes meant that the RAF fighters fought the escorts instead of the bombers, which often flew slightly lower.

As if to deliberately confuse Fighter Commander, the Luftwaffe began 7 September as it had begun many of the past days, with a handful of reconnaissance sorties, but thereafter, the radar screens remained clear and the plotting tables empty. The long delay seemed ominous. The Air Ministry had already issued an 'Invasion Alert No.1' (meaning attack imminent) without having previously issued Alert Nos 2 and 3 (attack probable within two and three days, respectively).

History records that the first raid counter was placed on the plotting table at Bentley Priory at 1554, and that within minutes counters representing many hundreds of aircraft were on the table. Göring had launched virtually the full strength of KG 1, KG 2, KG 3, KG 26 and KG 76, together with the Bf 110s of ZG 2 and the Bf 109Es of JG 2, JG 3, JG 51, JG 52, JG 54, I./JG 77 and I./ and II./LG 2. This colossal armada numbered 965 aircraft, stepped up from 4268m to 7010m (14,000ft to 23,000ft) advancing along a 32.2km (20-mile) front. Dowding and Park correctly guessed that only London could be the target of such a vast force, and at 1617 11 fighter squadrons were ordered into the air, with 21 units airborne by 1630. All available fighters raced towards the capital, with no thought of standing guard over their airfields. The RAF fighters were massively out-numbered by the German escorts, but tore into the enemy with great ferocity. The German bombers

ABOVE: HEINKEL HE 111 BOMBERS EN ROUTE TO ENGLAND. THIS PHOTOGRAPH SHOWS THE DORSAL AND VENTRAL GUN POSITIONS WELL; THEY WERE ARMED WITH 7.9MM (0.310IN) MG 15 MACHINE GUNS.

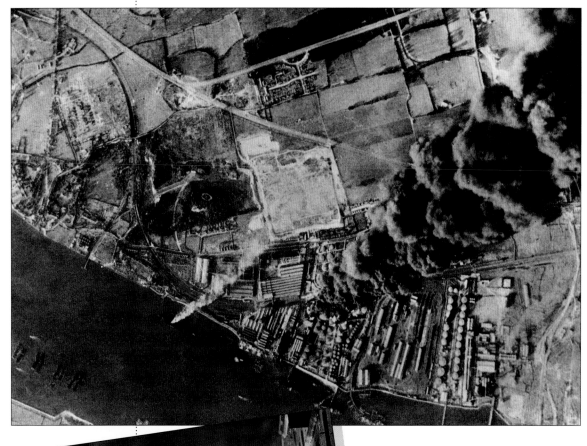

aimed for the docks, but their bombs fell over a wide area, from Kensington in the west but concentrated in the East End, and doing as much damage to the densely packed terraces of working-men's houses as to the docks, gas-works and power stations that were also hit. The enemy bombers turned around and were all en route home by 1745, albeit with huge gaps in the neat formations.

As the skies above London emptied of aircraft, the fight was taken over by the firemen, who fought the spreading fires with a grim determination. They fought to douse the burning buildings, the wooden-block road surfaces on older streets and even the surface of the River Thames itself (where floating liquid sugar ignited), all the while with the warehouses of paint, oil, explosives and ammunition blowing up in terrifying explosions. But it was not just the obviously dangerous materials that exploded – flour and pepper were equally dangerous, and the conflagration threatened to become self-sustaining as the fire sucked in oxygen from the surrounding streets. Burning debris was tossed into the air like straw, setting new fires wherever it landed. The London Fire Brigade classified a fire requiring 30 pumps as a 'Major' fire, yet in the early evening of 7 September, the Fire Brigade were tackling nine fires which were officially rated as 'Conflagrations', in that they required more than 100 pumps each. The largest was in the Surrey Docks, where the fire was too large to classify, and where it was arbitrarily rated as a 300-appliance fire.

At about 2010, the next wave of 318 German bombers began to pour down tons of incendiaries. 306 civilians died in the bombing, and 1337 more were seriously injured in the City, with 142 more killed in the suburbs. An enormous pall of smoke hung over the capital, and the fires burned on.

The first day cost Fighter Command dear, with the loss of 15 Spitfires (and four pilots) and 17 Hurricanes (with seven pilots). But the Luftwaffe lost 38 aircraft, including 14 Bf 109s. The balance of attrition was not very different from that suffered during the past weeks, although this changed as the campaign wore on, and the onslaught on London soon became much more costly to the attacker than to the defenders. And the blitz against London lasted long after the Battle ended, bleeding the Luftwaffe white in the process. The attacks continued on 76 consecutive nights, with only a single exception. This was 2 November, when the weather was too poor to allow the German bombers to operate. Perhaps most crucially, the Fighter Command airfields, and the Chain Home stations were given precious respite by the switch in targeting. Even the pilots themselves were rested when not actually in the air over London. Squadrons spent whole days without coming to readiness, and there was even time for newly arrived pilots to be taken on training and familiarisation sorties – luxuries which would have been unthinkable only days before. And, as in the phrase popularly used at the time, 'London *could* take it'. Dowding was relieved by the switch in targeting, commenting that 'The nearness of London to German airfields will lose them the war.' Churchill put it in typically over-blown fashion. 'London is like some huge prehistoric animal, capable of enduring terrific injury, mangled and bleeding from many wounds yet preserving its life and movement.'

Keith Park flew over the burning city in his personal Hurricane the next day, and later remarked that 'It was burning all down the River. It was a horrid sight. But I looked down and said "Thank God for that!" because I knew that the Nazis had now switched their attack from the Fighter Stations, thinking they were knocked out. They weren't, but they were pretty groggy.' On landing, Park set about formulating the best response to the raids, repairing his control system so as to maintain an effective defence

OPPOSITE TOP: SMOKE BILLOWS FROM OIL STORAGE TANKS AT PURFLEET IN THE WAKE OF THE LUFTWAFFE'S FIRST MAJOR ATTACK ON LONDON ON 7 SEPTEMBER 1940.

OPPOSITE BOTTOM: A 30FT PILLAR OF FLAME LIGHTS UP A LONDON STREET AS A GAS MAIN BLAZES AFTER A NIGHT RAID. THE ASPHALT ROAD AND HOUSES ON THE RIGHT OF THE PHOTOGRAPH ARE ALSO ABLAZE.

BELOW: PILOT AND FRONT GUNNER PICTURED IN THE NOSE OF A HEINKEL HE 111. THE LARGE GLAZED NOSE AREA AFFORDED EXCELLENT VISIBILITY FOR SPOTTING TARGETS OR ENEMY FIGHTER AIRCRAFT.

ABOVE: CLEARING AWAY
RUBBLE IN THE SEARCH FOR
SURVIVORS AFTER AN AIR
RAID. GREAT DISRUPTION
WAS CAUSED BY DELAYED-
ACTION BOMBS, WHICH
WERE A CONSTANT DANGER
TO RESCUE CREWS.

RIGHT: BUSINESS AS USUAL:
PEOPLE QUEUE AT A FRUIT
AND VEGETABLE SELLER'S
STALL IN THE EAST END.
WHILE THE WEALTHY FLED
LONDON, ORDINARY PEOPLE
DID THEIR BEST TO CARRY
ON WITH THEIR LIVES.

at least against the daylight bombing. The new circumstances allowed the withdrawal of the shattered No.111 Squadron, and No.43 Squadron (who had lost their new CO on 7 September), while No.92 Squadron moved from Pembrey in Wales to Biggin Hill. No.92 had roamed over the No.10 Group area for weeks, looking for action and fretting at its enforced idleness. The unit had achieved some successes, and its pilots had become highly-motivated, energetic and skilled. In its first fortnight at Biggin Hill, the squadron was destined to down 16 enemy aircraft, though for the loss of five pilots and 19 Spitfires! Meanwhile, General Pile of Anti-Aircraft Command ordered every spare gun to London, doubling the number of batteries within 48 hours.

The German bombing was certainly effective, at least by the standards of the day, and while it was never as devastating as Bomber Command's later onslaught against cities like Dresden or Hamburg, it was probably the most effective and accurate bombing seen up to that date. Many factories, docks and warehouses were destroyed or badly damaged in the bombing, although the effect on industrial production was negligible. Some of the bombs which fell away from their intended targets had an even greater effect on morale. Most of London's landmark buildings were hit – the Houses of Parliament, St Paul's Cathedral, Victoria Station and even Buckingham Palace, while others (like the Carlton hotel) were entirely demolished by bombs. Leicester Square was in ruins, and the Luftwaffe managed to scar most of the capital's most famous and important streets and thoroughfares.

But the bombing was not the catastrophe that many had predicted in the 1920s as bombing techniques and aircraft developed after World War I. In 1925 it had been predicted that 3000

Londoners would die in the first two days of a bombing onslaught, and that there would be mass panic, even that the Government would be overthrown. In the longer term, the prophets of doom predicted the destruction of 500,000 homes in three weeks, (and the damage of five million more) and the death of between 50,000 and 100,000 people. In fact, the death toll was

DORNIER DO 17

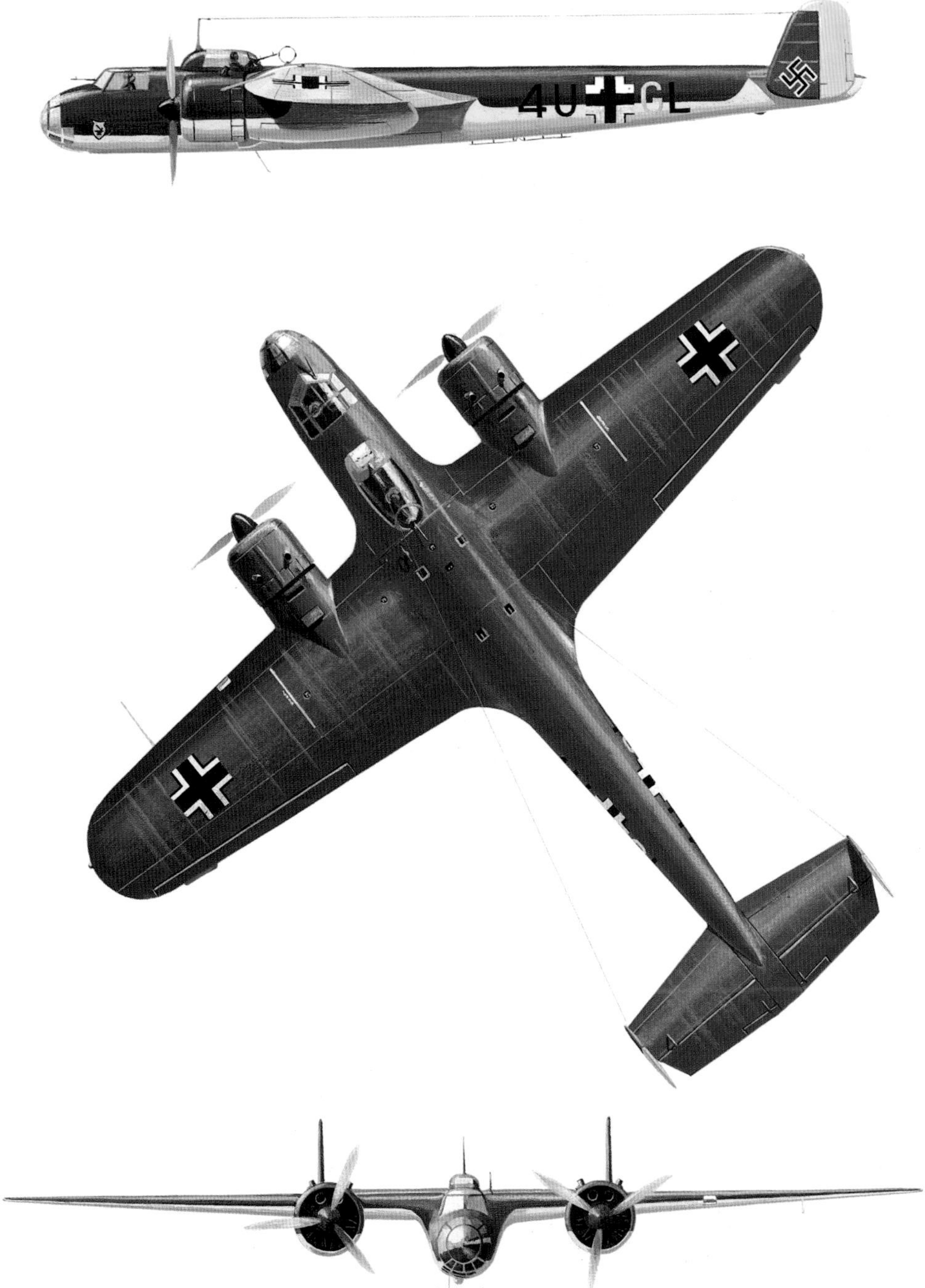

Back at Bentley Priory, General Pile showed a commendable understanding of the value of his anti-aircraft guns by issuing orders to them to fire blind, at their maximum rate of fire, as soon as the enemy were overhead. He didn't expect to shoot down any enemy aircraft, but did expect to lift civilian morale, and perhaps even upset the aim of the enemy bombers. 'I will not dignify the policy by calling it a barrage', he noted, dryly.

mercifully small, and some have even claimed that the change in lifestyle caused by the bombing was actually of more significance than the bombing itself, the use of cold, damp shelters bringing about a 10 per cent rise in the incidences of tuberculosis, for example.

The second day of the bombing of London (8 September) saw minor attacks on Kentish airfields and London suburbs during the day, followed by another prolonged and heavy night attack on London itself. The day witnessed the destruction of 11 enemy aircraft for the loss of five RAF fighters, while the RAF lost 21 fighters on 9 September, for the destruction of about 24 enemy aircraft. The third day saw the Luftwaffe formalising the division of responsibilities between Luftflotte 2 and Luftflotte 3, with Kesselring undertaking daylight raids against military and commercial targets in the western part of the city and the suburbs, and Luftflotte 3 attacking the docks and their environs at night.

As if to underline the danger of over-simplifying the nature of this final phase of the Battle of Britain, 9 September saw a number of attempted daylight attacks against airfields, and some fighter-versus-fighter combat. No.12 Group's famous 'Big Wing' (consisting on this occasion of Nos 19, 242 and 310 Squadrons) went into action, successfully breaking up an attack and claiming 19 Dorniers shot down. Post-war study of German records show that such a claim was somewhat over-ambitious, since not a single Do 17 was lost, and none of the Wing's claims was witnessed by the Observer Corps.

As night fell, London again came under heavy attack, with a school in Silvertown, West Ham being one of the most tragic targets to be hit. In use as a shelter for those bombed-out of their homes, the school was itself hit by bombs, killing 450. The survivors were taken to Epping, where many locals were unwilling to help or give shelter to those who had been bombed out, and many of the East Enders found themselves sleeping out in the open in the forest.

On 10 September, two significant events occurred. On the other side of the Channel, two Wehrmacht divisions hitherto earmarked for Sea Lion quietly packed up and moved east ready for the assault on Russia. Theoretically, at least, final orders for Sea Lion were to have been given only one day later, though the Führer personally intervened and put back the decision day to 14 September. Back at Bentley Priory, General Pile showed a

commendable understanding of the value of his anti-aircraft guns by issuing orders to them to fire blind, at their maximum rate of fire, as soon as the enemy were overhead. He didn't expect to shoot down any enemy aircraft, but did expect to lift civilian morale, and perhaps even upset the aim of the enemy bombers. 'I will not dignify the policy by calling it a barrage', he noted, dryly. Londoners were, indeed, reassured by the noise of the guns, and a letter to the Times newspaper described 10 September as its author's 'first peaceful

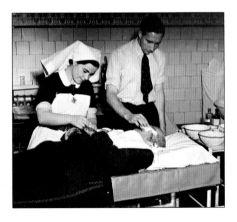

ABOVE: FAMOUS PHOTOGRAPH TAKEN FROM ST PAUL'S AS THE LUFTWAFFE UNLOADS ITS BOMBS INTO THE CITY OF LONDON ON THE NIGHT OF 29/30 DECEMBER 1940.

LEFT: STAFF TENDING AN AIR RAID CASUALTY AT CHARING CROSS HOSPITAL. THE BLITZ TESTED THE BRITISH MEDICAL RESOURCES TO THEIR LIMIT, ALTHOUGH THE WIDESPREAD USE OF AUXILIARY STAFF HELPED GREATLY.

night's sleep!' In the air, the Luftwaffe limited its daylight operations to nuisance raids, due largely to low cloud, and Fighter Command lost no aircraft in combat, though No.72 Squadron managed to shoot down a pair of He 111s passing over Kenley. The onslaught against London continued by night.

On 11 September, a major daylight raid against London was caught by more than 60 RAF fighters after its Bf 109E escort had withdrawn, and seven bombers and five Bf 110s were shot down. Unfortunately, a Free Chase by Bf 109Es caught some RAF fighters as they were climbing to engage, and 12 were shot down. Fighter Command's total combat losses for the day amounted to 30 fighters, while the Luftwaffe lost 22 aircraft to AA fire and fighters, including four Bf 109Es. Seldom mentioned in accounts of the Battle of Britain were the attacks by Bomber and Coastal Command against the enemy invasion barges in the Channel ports. 11 September saw this campaign being expanded, with 100 aircraft dropping more than 80 tonnes of bombs on the docks at Boulogne, Calais, Dunkirk and Le Havre. These attacks continued over the next two nights, and resulted in the destruction of at least 70 landing barges.

Fighter Command enjoyed a rather better day on 12 September, with only a single combat loss, although they only claimed one enemy kill. The scale of Luftwaffe operations during the day was much reduced, with a few reconnaissance sorties and nuisance raids, although by night London again bore the brunt of significant attacks, though even these were lighter than had been suffered on previous nights. Unexploded bombs were made safe at St Pauls Cathedral and outside the Ford showrooms in Regent Street.

Fighter Command losses on 13 September were limited to a single Hurricane (flown by 'Ginger' Lacey and shot down by an He 111 he had just mortally wounded) and an AI-radar equipped Blenheim. A Coastal Command Blenheim was also lost near the Norwegian coast. The Luftwaffe suffered four combat losses, including Lacey's Heinkel and a Ju 88 downed by William Blackadder of No.607 Squadron.

Despite poor weather, the Luftwaffe increased the scope and scale of its daylight operations on 14 September, with raids against London (bombs falling on Kingston and Wimbledon) and (following raids on south-coast Chain Home stations) against Brighton and Eastbourne. Although KG 1's Ju 88s inflicted little damage on the radar stations, the

ABOVE: YET ANOTHER PICTORIAL RECORD OF THE LONDONERS' DETERMINATION TO KEEP THEIR CITY TICKING OVER. THE GOVERNMENT'S MAIN CONCERN WAS THAT CIVILIAN MORALE WOULD CRACK; IT NEVER DID.

ABOVE RIGHT: A CASUALTY OF THE BLITZ IS REMOVED FROM THE RUBBLE. ALTHOUGH LONDON SUFFERED THE WORST CASUALTIES, SOME 8700 PEOPLE WERE KILLED IN ATTACKS ON OTHER TOWNS.

radar was handicapped by the first real use of jamming by the Germans. Fighter Command lost 14 fighters in combat (one, a Hurricane, to an over enthusiastic Spitfire pilot!) and accounted for only seven enemy aircraft. But despite this scoreline, Hitler was finally convinced that the Luftwaffe had failed in its allotted task, and if Sea Lion had ever been a reality, it was certainly cancelled in Hitler's mind on that day, although the Wehrmacht actually issued its first invasion orders. Attacks on London continued, however, especially by night, and the invasion threat remained in place as a weapon of intimidation.

On 14 September, Hans Jeschonnek begged to be allowed to target Britain's civilian population, hoping to encourage 'mass psychosis' and an emigration from the cities. Hitler absolutely forbade any deliberate attacks on residential areas, reserving this as a possible reprisal in case Bomber Command stepped up its own attacks.

BELOW: THIS PHOTO, TAKEN ON **7** SEPTEMBER **1940**, SHOWS A HEINKEL HE III OVER WAPPING. VISIBLE ARE SOME OF LONDON'S DOCKLANDS.

IMPREGNABLE TARGET

Sunday 15 September has come to be regarded as the climax of the entire Battle of Britain, and as the day on which Göring's bombers were finally, decisively beaten. Somehow they continued their attacks for months more, and RAF fighter pilots continued to die in droves, but the official line was that this was the hour of victory, and the day is now remembered annually as 'Battle of Britain Day'. In a campaign without an obvious beginning (witness the various start dates assigned by different historians) and with no clean end, it is difficult to pick one day to represent the entire period, but 15 September did have a better claim than most.

'War knows no Sundays', said one young Battle of Britain pilot who much later joined the Church, and 15 September dawned bright and clear, with only patchy mist which would burn off quickly, Fighter Command anticipated heavy attacks. Standing patrols were maintained from first light, and at each sector airfield one squadron was at readiness from 0700.

Apart from occasional forays by reconnaissance aircraft, nothing happened until shortly before 1100, when Chain Home began reporting a large enemy build-up. Following several missed rendezvous in the past, the 100 or so Do 17s of KG 3 flew from their Belgian bases to the Pas de Calais, where they picked up an escort of Bf 109Es. The raid came under attack as soon as it crossed the coast at Dungeness at 1135, with progressively larger groups of fighters falling on it as it struggled towards London. Twenty minutes later, with London in sight, four Hurricane squadrons attacked from head-on while Bader's Big Wing carved in on the flank, smashing through the escort. The bomber formation began to break up as almost 160 RAF fighters pressed home their attacks, and the majority began a broad curving dive for home, jettisoning or dropping their bombs at random as they fled. As a result, bombs were reported as falling in Battersea, Camberwell, Chelsea, Clapham, Crystal Palace, Kensington, Lambeth, Lewisham, Wandsworth and Westminster. Even Buckingham Palace received two unexploded bombs! Downed aircraft and aircrew fell all over London. Sergeant Raymond Holmes of No.501 Squadron collided with a Do 17 which fell on Victoria Station's forecourt, and three of whose crew baled out to land on or near the Oval cricket ground. One was left dangling from a telegraph wire, his feet only inches from the ground, outside the Oval tube station. Angry Londoners beat him so badly that he died of his injuries. Holmes himself abandoned his Hurricane over Chelsea, landing (according to some accounts) in a large dustbin!

Undaunted, Kesselring soon despatched a second wave of 150 bombers, from KG 2, KG 53 and KG 76, with Galland's JG 26 and Trautloft's JG 54 providing escorts. Fighter Command put up every fighter and pilot it could muster, managing to despatch two full flights from most squadrons, despite the morning's inevitable losses. These pilots included Northolt's 43-year-old Station Commander, who had been commissioned in the RFC in 1915. The massive German formation met 170 RAF fighters over Kent, and struggled on to London, where five squadrons of Duxford's famous 'Big

Wing' joined the fight. The bombers soon dumped their bombs and fled, while the German fighter pilots faced the agonising decision of staying to help (and certainly running out of fuel on the way home) or live to fight another day.

The reception accorded to the two raids on 15 September must have been a grave shock to many of the Luftwaffe participants, many of whom believed the propaganda that the RAF was 'down to its last 50 fighters'. On each occasion the sky must have appeared black with enemy fighters, as around 300 Spitfires and Hurricanes smashed into their huge armada. It became clear that the British were not beaten yet.

There were a number of smaller attacks in the west during the afternoon, but these had little effect, and

ABOVE: A SERGEANT OF No.11 GROUP, ROYAL AIR FORCE, WEARING A STEEL HELMET.

LEFT: 'GINGER' LACEY, AN RAF ACE, POSES IN FRONT OF HIS HURRICANE FIGHTER. THE PICTURE GIVES A GOOD IDEA OF THE SIZE OF THE AIRCRAFT'S 3.3M (10FT 9IN) DIAMETER ROTOL PROPELLER.

were seen off by No.10 and No.11 Groups. At the height of the second major attack, Churchill had visited HQ No.11 Group and had innocently asked Park about reserves. 'There are none', replied the New Zealander, to the obvious consternation of the Prime Minister, who watched the unfolding drama with increased nervousness. Fighter Command lost 27 of its fighters to enemy action on 15 September, but destroyed 55 enemy aircraft, including 19 Bf 109Es. Such losses were unsustainable for the Luftwaffe, which would have lost an entire Luftflotte in less than three weeks had it continued to suffer this level of losses. Many more German bombers made it home only to crash-land on their aerodromes, full of dead or wounded aircrew. In the confusion of this huge battle, both sides over-claimed hugely, with contemporary RAF claims reaching 183 enemy aircraft.

Park, perhaps predictably, was not happy with these results, feeling that 300 fighters could and should have achieved more. Although he had been experimenting with using pairs of squadrons, he now dismissed such formations as too unwieldy to control, and too time-consuming to form up before the engagement. He now issued instructions that in future the Biggin Hill and Hornchurch Spitfire squadrons would concentrate on the BF 109E top cover, while Hurricanes from Tangmere and Northolt would concentrate on the bombers. The Hurricanes could operate in formations of up to three squadrons (if time permitted) and the Spitfire squadrons in pairs.

Göring brushed aside his losses with the assurance that Fighter Command would be crushed within days, failing to realise the growing strength of Dowding's force. He ordered a return to attacks on Fighter Command airfields and fighter factories, unaware that in the

ABOVE: GERMAN AIRCREW GETTING READY FOR A NIGHT SORTIE. THE GERMANS WERE NOT OUTSTANDING NAVIGATORS AT NIGHT, WHICH WAS WHY LONDON, EASILY IDENTIFIABLE ON THE THAMES, WAS A TEMPTING TARGET.

RIGHT: THE PILOT OF A MESSERSCHMITT 109 UNDER POLICE ESCORT AFTER BEING SHOT DOWN OVER SOUTHEAST ENGLAND. HIS SHOES HAVE BEEN REMOVED TO HINDER ANY ESCAPE ATTEMPT.

LEFT: HURRICANES OF NO 1 SQUADRON IN BLAST-PROOF REVETMENTS AT RAF WITTERING, OCTOBER 1940. WITTERING WAS IN THE 12 GROUP AREA, EXTENDING TO THE NORTH OF THE THAMES; NO 11 GROUP WAS TO THE SOUTH.

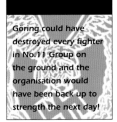

breathing space since 6 September the Command had built up a reserve of 160 new Spitfires and Hurricanes in the Maintenance Units, with another 400 ready for delivery within one week. Pilots were still in short supply, of course, although many of those compulsorily rested after the Battle of France were finally returning to their squadrons. Göring could have destroyed every fighter in No.11 Group on the ground and the organisation would have been back up to strength the next day!

After the carnage of 15 September, there was relatively little daylight activity on 16 September, and Fighter Command lost a Hurricane to Werner Mölders (though this suffered only Category 2 damage, and was repaired) and a Spitfire which ran itself out of fuel while pursuing a Ju 88. The Luftwaffe suffered about five combat losses, including one to a No.600 Squadron Blenheim night fighter.

On 17 September, Kesselring's first move was to launch a single raid consisting of multiple waves of Free Chasing Bf 109Es. Fighter Command generally declined combat, though one formation from II./ and III./JG 53 were set upon by No.501 Squadron (two of whose aircraft were downed without cost to the enemy) and then by No.41 Squadron (who badly damaged two Bf 109Es, but lost one Spitfire) and finally by the Duxford wing, who hacked down three Bf 109Es without loss. Each side lost three aircraft, but only one RAF pilot was killed, while all three German fighter pilots were killed or captured. Fighter Command lost seven aircraft in combat overall that day, one less than the Luftwaffe. After its poor combat record earlier in the Battle, the Boulton Paul Defiant restored some of its credibility by downing a pair of Ju 88s (and damaging another) shortly before midnight.

While Göring continued to believe that the RAF was on its last legs, the German navy were more realistic, and the War Diary of the Naval Staff noted that 'The RAF is

ABOVE: GERMAN GROUND CREW PICTURED WITH A MESSERSCHMITT BF 109E-4 OF III/JG51 IN FRANCE DURING THE BATTLE OF BRITAIN. THE AIRCRAFT HAS BEEN STRIPPED OF ITS ENGINE COWLING.

Göring could have destroyed every fighter in No.11 Group on the ground and the organisation would have been back up to strength the next day!

by no means defeated' at the head of its arguments against launching an invasion. On 17 September, Hitler formally began to consider postponing S-Day to 27 September, though the reality was that the operation had been cancelled, and orders were issued to dismantle the invasion air-transport facilities.

While the Luftwaffe continued to pound London, Bristol, Liverpool and Southampton overnight, Bomber Command had enjoyed a successful night attacking the invasion fleet, destroying an estimated 500 barges and causing huge damage at Antwerp, where an estimated 500 tonnes of ammunition went up.

On the morning of 18 September, Kesselring again launched fighter sweeps over Kent, causing 15 squadrons to scramble, of which six engaged. Five Spitfires were shot down, with the loss of three Bf 109Es and a reconnaissance Dornier Do 215. A subsequent raid by a handful of Ju 88s and more than 100 Bf 109Es was ignored, goading Kesselring into sending over an unescorted raid by the Ju 88s of III./JG 77. Park reacted against these aircraft (correctly identified by the Observer Corps) despatching 14 squadrons of fighters.

Nine of the Ju 88s were shot down, four by the Duxford Wing, who claimed 30! The day ended with the loss of 11 Fighter Command aircraft and 17 enemy aircraft.

Daylight operations were much reduced by poor weather on 19 September, and combat losses were limited to a pair of Ju 88s downed respectively by Nos 249 and 302 Squadrons, another Ju 88 felled by an undetermined RAF unit, and a Do 17 shot down by Count Manfred Czernin of No.17 Squadron.

The wisdom of avoiding the Bf 109Es, when they were not tied to close escort duties, was amply demonstrated on 20 September. The Luftwaffe's sole attack was carried out by two waves of Bf 109Es, each at almost Geschwader strength. Weight of numbers allowed the German fighter pilots to shoot down seven Spitfires (four of whose pilots were killed), for the loss of only two of their own aircraft. What made it worse was that these Spitfires included two from the elite No.92 Squadron, with two more from No.72 (hardly beginners in the air combat game) and three from No.222 Squadron. But even the German bombers were far from being easy targets. The same day, No.41 Squadron's George Bennions (with eight Battle of Britain victories under his belt) was shot down by a Ju 88, though he managed to land his damaged Spitfire at Lympne. The

Germans suffered only three combat losses, though another Bf 109E was so badly damaged that it crashed at Cap Gris Nez on its return.

The German tactic of sending raids consisting entirely of Bf 109Es was beginning to cause Fighter Command some problems, since they could seldom be identified as such until they were too late to intercept. If they were ignored, and then turned out to be bombers, the raiders could dash through to their targets, yet if Dowding waited to scramble until the enemy formation had been positively identified from the ground, some formations would not be intercepted at all, some would be engaged too late, and others would find vulnerable Spitfires or Hurricanes straining to climb up to them. Thus on 21 September, Dowding authorised the formation of a new dedicated unit, No.421 Flight, which flew small formations of Hurricanes (and later Spitfires) on reconnaissance missions over the Channel, reporting the build-up of enemy bomber formations, and confirming the composition of inbound raids. Formed at Gravesend from a nucleus provided by No.66 Squadron in October 1940, No.421 Flight moved to West Malling on 31 October, and to Biggin Hill on 6 November (re-equipping with Spitfires) and then finally to Hawkinge on 15 November. After the Battle, the Flight was expanded to become No.91 Squadron.

It was generally quiet on 21 September, with enemy air activity limited to reconnaissance sorties and nuisance raids. Fighter Command suffered no combat losses, but downed two

ABOVE: ANOTHER LEGENDARY VIEW OF LONDON. A HUGE PALL OF SMOKE HANGS OVER THE CITY OF LONDON AFTER THE BIG LUFTWAFFE ATTACK OF 7 SEPTEMBER 1940. FOR THE LONDONERS, WORSE WAS TO COME.

RIGHT: A FAKED
PHOTOGRAPH OF A SPITFIRE
UNDER ATTACK BY THE
FRONT GUNNER OF A
HEINKEL 111.

BELOW: DOMINION TROOPS
LEARNING THE ART OF
SHOOTING AT LOW-FLYING
AIRCRAFT WITH A BREN
GUN. OF CZECHOSLOVAK
ORIGIN, THE BREN WAS
A VERY EFFECTIVE LIGHT
MACHINE GUN, AND
SERVED THE BRITISH WELL
THROUGHOUT WWII.

enemy aircraft, while AA fire accounted for two more. Another three enemy aircraft crashed on their return after combat with RAF fighters and were totally destroyed, bringing the total to seven. Poor weather ensured that Sunday 22 September was even quieter, and a reconnaissance Ju 88A was the only enemy aircraft engaged by Fighter Command, though German flak accounted for a Bf 110.

Very late that night, Downing Street received a telegram from Roosevelt warning that 'reliable sources indicate that an invasion will begin at 0300 on 23 September'. But with a major storm raging over the Channel, Churchill's staff left the Prime Minister to sleep. One junior adviser was horrified, insisting that the great man should be woken up and told, but a more senior man dismissed the idea with the immortal lines: 'If the Germans really want to commit suicide, the PM will have plenty of time to go and watch them do it after breakfast!'

Fighter Command lost 10 aircraft on 23 September, while the Luftwaffe suffered more than 13 combat losses, including 10 Bf 109Es. On 24 September, the Luftwaffe despatched a Bf 110 raid against the Spitfire factory at Woolston, and a number of daylight attacks against London. Fighter Command lost seven fighters in combat, one Polish pilot being jumped by Bf 109Es after chasing a Do 17 all the way to the French coast. The Luftwaffe suffered only seven combat losses that day, none of them single-engined fighters.

The Sea Lion landing assault had been scheduled for 21 September, and Phase I was originally to have been completed by 27 September. The British finally received fairly incontrovertible evidence that the operation had been cancelled on 25 September, with reconnaissance photographs showing a 40 per cent reduction in the number of barges at Calais, Boulogne and Dunkirk. And as if this were not enough, the fighter and Zerstörer units which had moved to the Pas de Calais to support the landings moved back westwards on 25 September. Even before these units had settled in, raids against the West Country began. A major attack was mounted against the Bristol Aeroplane Company at Filton, with Erprobungsgruppe 210 marking the target and with 58 He 111s of KG 55 dropping almost 100 tonnes of bombs and causing massive damage. The Filton raid was supported by diversionary raids on Falmouth, Plymouth, Southampton and Swanage. The attack on Filton destroyed eight new Beauforts and Blenheims, and many more were damaged, and Blenheim production was halted, but the immediate effect on Fighter Command was negligible. Throughout the day, Fighter Command lost five aircraft, but shot down 11 of the enemy, including four Bf 109Es.

On 26 September, the Luftwaffe finally hit Supermarine's Woolston plant, dropping some 70 tonnes of bombs in a single run. This killed 37 workers and brought Spitfire production briefly to a halt. It would soon be restored, and anyway there were 100 Spitfires awaiting issue in the manufacturing plants and 60 more in dispersed repair sites. More significantly, the raid led to the dispersal of component production to various converted bus garages and other large buildings, scattered over southern England, and thereafter Spitfire production became effectively immune against air attack. That day Fighter Command lost seven fighters (and two pilots, including one who died because no-one rescued him from the sea in time), while the Luftwaffe lost five aircraft in combat, and two more in a collision.

Friday 27 September began with the usual reconnaissance aircraft picking their way carefully past Fighter Command's airfields, their crews hoping against hope that they might be ignored. On that day most of them were, as both Park and Brand wanted to conserve their fighters for the bombers they were sure would follow. Only one of the aircraft, a Ju 88A of 3(F)/123 was shot down. Next to arrive were six groups of Bf 110s, with Bf 109E escorts, which made no attacks, but which flew around Kent and Sussex for as long as their fuel permitted, soaking up attack after

attack by Park's fighters. The German intention had been to sneak through a heavy raid against London when the Fighter Command aircraft were refuelling and re-arming, but the 55 Ju 88s involved were late at their assembly area, and arrived over Kent to meet the full weight of Fighter Command's defences. Some 12 of the attacking bombers were shot down, though Bf 109Es and Bf 110s finally swept in to cover the retreat of the survivors. Further west, Sperrle tried to repeat the raid on Filton, since his intelligence sources had informed him that damage had been light. This time, however, No.10 Group were ready and waiting, and the raid became a costly and fruitless slaughter of some of the Luftwaffe's most experienced aircrew.

The Luftwaffe suffered the loss of at least 49 aircraft in combat, including 18 Bf 110s and 17 Bf 109Es but not including two Bf 109Es which limped home to crash-land on French territory, but which were effectively total losses. 11 Bf 109 pilots failed to return, as well as 36 Bf 110 aircrew, together with 56 bomber personnel. This was far and away the worst day for the Luftwaffe since the 15 September, and since 18 August before that. The RAF suffered the loss of 30 fighters in combat, with 17 pilots killed. Churchill appreciated the extent of the day's success, and the next day sent a message to Dowding. 'Pray congratulate Fighter Command on the results of yesterday. The scale

HIT-AND-RUN RAIDERS

From 8 October 1940, the RAF began intercepting Bf 109s which had been hastily adapted as fighter-bombers by carrying a single SC250 250kg (550lb) bomb on the centreline. Often the Bf 109Es slipped through unopposed, either at very low level (giving the defences little warning time in which to react) or very high (leaving defending fighters insufficient time to climb up to them). Even carrying a 250kg (550lb) bomb the Bf 109E could fly at 9144m (30,000ft), well above the ceiling of the Hurricane, though within reach of the Spitfire. Yet the Jabos actually achieved little. During their initial, rather predictable, Staffel-strength attacks on London, the German perception was that they suffered unacceptably heavy losses, and some of their pilots felt that the role offended their professional pride and didn't even attempt to deliver weapons accurately on a particular target. Over London, for instance, German Jabo pilots dropped their weapons when the section leader did, and specific pinpoint targets were often not briefed. Theo Osterkamp, the German fighter commander was furious, and complained bitterly to Jeschonnek, who absolved himself from blame by claiming that the orders had come directly from the Führer.

Osterkamp's response was bitter and sarcastic, and cost him further promotion. 'Until proven otherwise,' he said 'I take our Führer to be a man who would not order such an idiocy, if he knew what effect it was having. I suggest the following. By God's Grace I still have about 384 fighters left at the moment, that makes 96 sections. Out of these I will send a section off twice a day at different times, with bombs under their bellies. They will reach their targets, because such small formations can slip through anywhere. Above their targets, they will dive down to 400 metres, bail out with their parachutes and let the aircraft with its bomb crash into the docks. The pilots will go into captivity. Result No.1: the bombs will land in the docks, which you all consider "decisive for the war". Result No.2: You will at least know exactly when the fighter weapon will have been completely destroyed – namely in 48 days. On the 49th day I will go the same way with my adjutant. Then you will all have peace. But one thing at least will have been accomplished: my boys will not have sacrificed their lives for a daydream.'

Osterkamp's concerns about vulnerability and losses were addressed by sending fighter Bf 109Es to escort the fighter-bombers, the fighters flying in at 9754m (32,000ft). The fighter-bombers were also increasingly tasked with pinpoint attacks on more important targets, and this helped improve morale.

The increasing emphasis placed on fighter-bomber operations did not go unnoticed by the British. Sandy Johnstone of No.602 Squadron summed up the RAF attitude to the new form of warfare quite well. 'I may be wrong, but things seem to be easing off a bit these days... we only spot 109s cruising around at heights well above 30,000ft. These occasionally make furtive darts at us before soaring up again to their superior position... Could it be that the Germans have had enough?'

and intensity of the fighting and the heavy losses of the enemy make 27th September rank with 15th September and 15th August as the third great and victorious day of Fighter Command during course of the Battle of Britain.'

The Luftwaffe took a measure of revenge on 28 September, downing 14 RAF fighters for the loss of only five of its own aircraft. It achieved this by mounting very high-speed bombing raids by small formations of Ju 88s and Bf 110s which flew in at top speed, escorted by huge numbers of BF 109Es which were at last able to fly at their economical cruising speed. When the RAF fighters were scrambled, they found themselves facing a single Gruppe of bombers and three entire Jagdgeschwadern of fighters, totalling about 250 Bf 109Es.

There was relatively little action on Sunday 29 September, though KG 55 lost an He 111 as they flew up through the Irish Sea to attack Merseyside, and two more were forced to turn back with damage, after being attacked by Hurricanes, three of which were shot down. The day's combat losses totalled five Hurricanes and eight Luftwaffe aircraft.

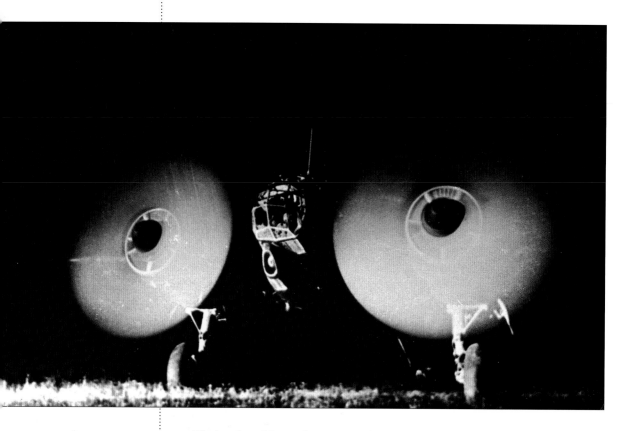

The last day of September saw the final massed daylight raids of the Battle of Britain. Two waves of 200 bombers approached London soon after 0900, but these were turned back over Kent by some 12 RAF fighter squadrons. Later that morning, a sweep by Bf 109Es was similarly turned back after a brief engagement. In the afternoon, a formation of about 100 bombers and 200 fighters attempted to force their way through to London, and suffered heavy losses, while a group of about 40 He 111s, escorted by Bf 110s were mauled by No.10 Group's fighters when they attempted to attack the Westland Aircraft factory at Yeovil. Fighter Command lost 18 aircraft (and two pilots) that day, while the

Luftwaffe suffered 39 losses, including no less than 28 Bf 109Es, with 26 of their pilots. This was one of the few occasions on which Fighter Command inflicted a serious defeat on the enemy's single-seat fighters.

The Luftwaffe had lost large numbers of aircrew during September, including many of its leaders. The toll of dead, missing and PoWs included four Geschwaderkommodoren, 13 Gruppenkommandeuren, and a staggering 31 StaffelKapitanen. The fighting had changed in character, so that the German fighters were now unable to obtain local air superiority (as they had done so many times in the past) except by sending over several Geschwadern at once. Even then, when Fighter Command responded in strength, Luftwaffe fighter losses soon became unbearable.

In view of the mounting bomber losses, it had been decided that most bomber missions would henceforth be carried out at night, and that fighter-bombers would carry out nuisance raids by day. With this in mind, every Jagdgeschwader was ordered to convert one third of its aircraft and pilots to the fighter-bomber (Jagdbomber or Jabo) role. Some did so by assigning one entire Gruppe to the role, others by assigning one Staffel within each Gruppe.

Lehrgeschwader 1 began flying Free Chases with bomb-carrying BF 109E-7s before the new Jabo-roled Jagdgeschwadern, and flew some sorties on 1 October. That day Fighter Command lost seven aircraft (including one Blenheim), while the Luftwaffe suffered only three combat losses.

Waves of fighter-bombers attacked targets in London and the southeast during the morning of 2 October, while heavy raids were made on cities and airfields that night. The RAF lost only a single Spitfire, but the Luftwaffe lost 10 aircraft, including four Bf 109Es. Poor weather effectively grounded Fighter Command on Thursday 3 October, and limited the scope and extent of Luftwaffe operations. One Ju 88 made a daring attack on the de Havilland works at Hatfield, skipping four 250kg (550lb) bombs off the grass into the factory buildings. The Luftwaffe's combat losses for the day totalled five aircraft, and Fighter Command was left untouched.

Poor weather on Friday 4 again restricted operations, though the Ju 88s of LG 1 bombed Hythe and Folkestone

BELOW: A BOMB DISPOSAL TEAM RECOVERING AN UNEXPLODED BOMB, KNOWN AS A **UXB.** SUCH TEAMS WORKED UNDER HUGE STRESS DURING THE BLITZ AND SHOWED GREAT GALLANTRY; THEY ALSO SUFFERED CONSIDERABLE CASUALTIES.

killing 50 civilians. Night attacks concentrated on London's armament factories at Enfield and Woolwich, though accuracy suffered greatly at night, and all the bombs dropped fell on residential areas. Fighter Command lost a single Spitfire during the day's operations, while the Luftwaffe

LEFT: RAF FIGHTER PILOTS MAKE A VERBAL REPORT ON THEIR SORTIE TO THE SQUADRON INTELLIGENCE OFFICER. SUCH REPORTS WERE VITAL IN MAKING ACCURATE ASSESSMENTS OF ENEMY LOSSES.

suffered seven combat losses, plus a Do 17 shot down by its own fighters and a number of aircraft destroyed in accidents.

Despite continuing poor weather on Saturday 5 October, Kesselring launched a five-phase attack, while Sperrle launched three diversionary attacks on West Country targets. Fighter Command ignored the first wave of Bf 109E Jabos and their escorts, but intercepted the Bf 110s of Erprobungsgruppe 210 as they attacked West Malling, disrupting their attack. II./ZG 76 attacked Detling unmolested, but with poor accuracy. Between 1100 and 1200 the Luftwaffe launched six small fighter sweeps, losing five Bf 109Es in these operations. The final major daylight attack was by two Gruppen of Ju 88As against Southampton. Combat losses totalled three Hurricanes, one Ju 88, two Bf 110s and five Bf 109Es.

Near-continuous rain on Sunday 6 October did not prevent fighter bombers from demolishing three barrack blocks at Biggin Hill, while eight bombs fell on Middle Wallop and 12 on Northolt, where one hit a taxiing No.303 Squadron Hurricane. Four parachute mines fell on Uxbridge, and one which failed to detonate threatened No.11 Group HQ itself until it was defused. Luftwaffe combat losses totalled five aircraft.

Improving weather conditions allowed a higher intensity of operations on Monday 7 October. An almost constant procession of Bf 109E sweeps over Kent were met in strength. One intruder was rammed by Pilot Officer MacKenzie of No.501 Squadron when he ran out of ammunition. The major day attack was mounted by 25 Ju 88s and 50 Bf 110s against the Westland factory at Yeovil, but was met by five No.10 Group squadrons and suffered heavy losses. The massacre was ended with the arrival of a force of Bf 109Es which covered the withdrawal of the surviving bombers. The day's combat losses amounted to 15 Fighter Command aircraft and 20 Luftwaffe aircraft, including 10 Bf 109Es.

Tuesday 8 October saw a steady stream of attacks against London by day and night, and although Fighter Command suffered only two combat losses, one of these was of Josef

ABOVE: LONDON'S BURNING: A VIEW OF THE BURNING CAPITAL FROM A GERMAN BOMBER. AS TIME WENT BY, REPRISAL ATTACKS FOR RAF RAIDS ON GERMAN TOWNS BECAME A REGULAR FEATURE OF THE AIR WAR.

ABOVE RIGHT AND RIGHT: LOCAL AUTHORITIES DID THEIR BEST TO GIVE HOUSEHOLDERS INSTRUCTION IN THE USE OF RUDIMENTARY FIREFIGHTING EQUIPMENT SUCH AS THE STIRRUP PUMP, AND IN HOW TO DEAL WITH THE THREAT OF INCENDIARY BOMBS.

LEFT: POLISH PILOTS POSE IN FRONT OF A SPITFIRE. A LARGE NUMBER OF KILL MARKINGS CAN BE SEEN ON THE SIDE OF THE AIRCRAFT.

BELOW: HM KING GEORGE VI AND QUEEN ELIZABETH ON A VISIT TO A TOWN IN THE NORTH OF ENGLAND. SOME NORTHERN TOWNS, IN PARTICULAR HULL, TOOK SEVERE PUNISHMENT DURING THE BLITZ ON BRITAIN.

Frantisek, top scorer of the Battle according to its official definition. By the time Frantisek died, Fighter Command included two fully-operational Czech squadrons, and two Polish, with 240 Czech, Polish, Belgian and French pilots on the frontline. Luftwaffe combat losses for the day totalled seven aircraft.

Despite poor, squally weather, the pattern of attacks and losses continued on 9 October, with Fighter Command losing five aircraft and the Luftwaffe eight, including five Bf 109Es. Night attacks on London resulted in the death of 50 geriatric patients in a hospital which received a direct hit, while the University of London announced that the University College Library had lost 100,000 rare books in one of the previous night's attacks.

On 10 October, large numbers of fighter bombers attacked London, souteast airfields and Weymouth by day, while night bombers attacked London, Manchester, Merseyside and Fighter Command airfields. Fighter Command lost five aircraft in action that day, while the Luftwaffe lost a single Bf 109E in combat, and six more in accidents. The 11 October was similar, with fighter-bomber attacks on the aerodromes at Biggin Hill, Kenley and Southend, and on Canterbury, Deal, Folkestone and Weymouth, and night raids on London, Manchester, Merseyside, Teeside and Tyneside.

RIGHT: A BATTLE-SCARRED
LONDON BUS STANDS AMID
THE RUBBLE OF A STREET.
RUBBLE-CHOKED STREETS
CAUSED SEVERE PROBLEMS
FOR THE FIRE AND RESCUE
SERVICES, CREATING DELAYS
IN REACHING THE SCENE OF
AN INCIDENT.

BELOW: THE END OF A
MESSERSCHMITT 110,
TAKEN FROM AN RAF
FIGHTER'S GUN-CAMERA
FILM.

The RAF lost 10 aircraft in combat, while the Luftwaffe suffered three combat losses. The latter did not include one Do 17 which was set on fire, and from which two crew-members baled out before the aircraft returned safely to Brest.

On 12 October, Keitel finally announced that Hitler had decided that preparations for Sea Lion would henceforth be continued only to 'maintain pressure on England'. On that same day, the Luftwaffe lost seven aircraft in combat, while Fighter Command lost eleven. On 13 October poor weather again limited the scope and extent of operations. RAF combat losses totalled four aircraft, though these included a Blenheim shot down by the over-enthusiastic Czech pilots of No.312 Squadron, and a Hurricane shot down by Chatham's anti-aircraft guns. The Luftwaffe suffered two combat losses.

Although London and other major cities had been under nightly attack since the beginning of September, some historians choose to date the start of the Blitz as being the 14 October. Certainly the day marked the renewal of really heavy and concentrated attacks, and 591 civilians died when some 200 Ju 88s and He 111s dropped over 1000 bombs on London, causing 900 fires and heavy damage. Fighter Command flew 50 night-fighter sorties, but not one night fighter made contact with the enemy. The day's combat losses were very light, with each side losing a single aircraft. The RAF Hurricane that was lost was shot down by friendly AA, or may have crashed into a British barrage balloon.

The attack on London continued by day and night on 15 October, with BF 109E fighter-bombers wrecking the approach to Waterloo

Station, temporarily closing several railway lines and also hitting a number of South Bank factories. Accurate prediction of Bf 109E heights allowed the Biggin Hill and Hornchurch Spitfire Wings to dive out of the sun on several enemy formations, destroying five Bf 109Es in one engagement. Night raids included an attack by 20 Do 17s of KüFlGr 606 against Birmingham. One of these aircraft bombed RAF Ternhill, demolishing a hangar and wrecking 20 training aircraft and a No.29 Squadron Blenheim inside. Other Luftwaffe bombers destroyed more dock facilities and damaged Paddington, Liverpool Street, Waterloo and Victoria railway stations, as well as Beckton gasworks and Battersea Power Station. 512 civilians were killed, and 11,000 were made homeless, and only two bombers were shot down. These brought the Luftwaffe's combat losses to 12 aircraft, while Fighter Command lost 16 aircraft.

Poor weather prevented the Luftwaffe from launching more than single-aircraft and flight-strength nuisance raids during the daylight hours of 16 October, though London was attacked by night. Fighter Command lost a single Hurricane in combat, while the Luftwaffe lost four aircraft. The next day was rainy, with sunny intervals, and the Luftwaffe launched attacks against a number of targets, including HQ Fighter Command and a number of south-coast towns. The RAF lost seven fighters in combat, while the Luftwaffe suffered the loss of four Bf 109Es. Despite widespread fog, Friday 18 October followed a similar pattern of attacks, though Fighter Command completed the day without any combat losses, and shot down two enemy aircraft. But while the Luftwaffe failed to claim any RAF fighters, the weather did not fail, and four Hurricanes were destroyed (with the loss of all four pilots) when they became lost and began to run out of fuel. The formation leader ordered the flight to land at Sandown Park racecourse, but all crashed.

Herman Göring chose this Friday to issue a typically boastful and bombastic message which he hoped would boost the morale of his pilots. 'In the past few days and nights you have caused the British World Enemy disastrous losses by your constant destructive blows. Your indefatigable attacks at the heart of the British Empire (the City of London) have reduced the British Plutocracy to fear and terror. Those losses which you

LEFT: FOR MANY LONDONERS, THE UNDERGROUND WAS A HAVEN OF REFUGE DURING THE BLITZ, PROVIDING THOUSANDS WITH A SECURE – IF NOT EXACTLY UNDISTURBED – NIGHT'S SLEEP.

BELOW: KEEPING THE NIGHT OFFENSIVE GOING; GERMAN ARMOURERS BOMBING-UP A STUKA IN PREPARATION FOR A NIGHT-TIME SORTIE AGAINST ENGLAND SOMETIME IN LATE 1940.

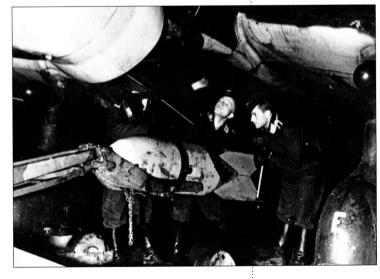

have inflicted on the much-vaunted RAF with your determined fighter combat are irreplaceable.' (The Luftwaffe had actually destroyed about 50 RAF fighters during the previous week's fighting, and had lost 36 aircraft to enemy action, and many more in accidents). Unfortunately, most of the Jagdwaffe veterans merely laughed at this latest illustration of posturing by 'Der Dicke' (the Fat Man).

Some have described Saturday 19 October as the quietest day of the entire Battle of Britain, and although two Staffeln of Bf 109Es ventured over Kent, there were no combat losses on either side. Sunday 20 October was rather more active, with 300 Jabo sorties launched in two distinct waves. These resulted in the loss of four RAF fighters in combat, and seven Bf 109Es and one Bf 110. Targets hit that night included St Dunstan's hospital for the blind. One of the night attackers (a Do 17) suffered engine problems, and was abandoned near Salisbury by its crew. It flew on for over 160km (100 miles) and landed itself so gently on the mud flats in Essex that only salt-water damage prevented the aircraft from being recovered to fly again.

By 21 October the weather was becoming steadily more wintry, and the day saw an unpleasant combination of fog, rain, and thick, low cloud. There were a handful of raids on London and Merseyside during the day, but the weather was better in the west, where there were various nuisance raids. One Ju 88, having failed to find Gloster's Brockworth works, attacked Old Sarum, where it was seen by Spitfires from Middle Wallop, who chased it and shot it down. The aircraft became one of two Luftwaffe combat losses that day.

Cloudy weather persisted for the rest of October, sometimes with rain, sometimes with fog or mist. London and other cities were attacked nightly, with airfield attacks as well on the night of 27 October. The daylight raids were usually by single aircraft or small formations, and seldom caused much damage, except to civilians.

Operations were very restricted on Tuesday 22 October, with three fairly fruitless convoy attacks in the Thames Estuary and Channel. Despite the lack of operational work to do, KG 27 had a very bad day, losing three He 111s in fatal accidents, one of which

ABOVE: THE REGIA AERONAUTICA (ITALIAN AIR FORCE) SENT A MIXED FIGHTER AND BOMBER FORCE TO BELGIUM AT THE TAIL-END OF THE BATTLE OF BRITAIN. IT SUFFFERED HEAVILY, AND WAS WITHDRAWN. PHOTOGRAPH SHOWS A FIAT BR20 BOMBER BEING WAVED OUT FOR TAKE-OFF.

RIGHT: A HEINKEL HE 111 CAMOUFLAGED FOR THE NIGHT BLITZ AGAINST ENGLAND.

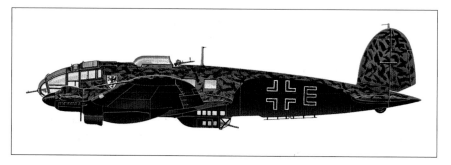

also resulted in the death of 13 ground personnel. Combat losses were limited to two Spitfires, two Hurricanes (one falling to 'friendly' AA fire) and three Bf 109Es. Slightly clearer conditions permitted an expansion of operations on Wednesday 23 October, and there were attacks on the airfields at Biggin Hill and Tangmere, and on Cromer, Harwich and Southampton. These resulted in the loss of one Hurricane and a Ju 88 in combat. The night raids included a long-range attack on Glasgow by KG 26.

Despite sporadic hit-and-run raids, there was only a single combat loss on 24 October, this being a Bf 109E which crashed off Cap Gris Nez after being damaged by RAF fighters. Things went much the same way on 25 October, though there were more engagements, and combat losses totalled nine from Fighter Command and 14 from the Luftwaffe, including 11 Bf 109Es. That night saw an He 111 of KG 26 bombing Montrose airfield at dusk, and the first major operation by the Italian force based in Belgium. Some 16 Fiat BR.20Ms took off to attack Harwich, though one was lost on take off and two more ran out of fuel on their return journeys, and crashed.

Saturday 26 October saw frequent fighter-bomber raids against London and the south east of England, and there was a half-hearted attack on a Channel convoy. During these various attacks, Fighter Command lost four Hurricanes and a Spitfire, while Luftwaffe combat losses totalled four aircraft. The day also saw the crippling of the 42,000-tonne liner SS *Empress of Britain* by an Fw 200 of KG 40. The ship was set ablaze, and was subsequently torpedoed by a U-boat and sank.

ABOVE: THIS BF 109E-4 WAS THE PERSONAL AIRCRAFT OF MAJOR HELMUT WICK, WHO GAINED **56** VICTORIES BEFORE BEING SHOT DOWN AND DROWNED IN THE CHANNEL IN NOVEMBER **1940**.

ITALIAN INVOLVEMENT IN THE BATTLE OF BRITAIN

Bomber Command's raids on Italy (and a desire to share in the glory of defeating England) spurred Mussolini into offering the use of Italian aircraft and aircrew in the Battle of Britain. A fully-autonomous, self-supporting group, the Corpo Aereo Italiano was formed on 10 September 1940, moving to its Belgian bases in late September with eight squadrons of Fiat BR.20M bombers, a single squadron of Cant Z1007.bis reconnaissance aircraft and six fighter squadrons.

The Regia Aeronautica was inexperienced, poorly equipped, and untrained in German tactical and strategic doctrine, and the arrival of the Italians in Belgium as part of Luftflotte II presented Kesselring with an immediate problem – what to do with his new-found allies. Several aircraft were lost during the long flight to Belgium, and this gave Kesselring the excuse to insist that the Italians initially confine themselves to training. They finally began flying operations on 25 October, with a 16-aircraft night attack on Harwich. Fifteen BR.20Ms, escorted by about 70 CR.42s, then

made an abortive daylight raid on Ramsgate four days later, on 29 October, amazingly suffering no losses despite heavy anti-aircraft fire. The Italians mounted another daylight raid on Ramsgate on 11 November (after the official end of the Battle) which was intercepted by Hurricanes. The Italians lost five of the 10 BR.20Ms involved in the mission, as well as seven of their escorting fighters. The Italian fighter pilots fought with great courage, but their ancient biplanes were out-classed.

Two more night attacks were mounted on 17 November (against Harwich, with six BR.20Ms) and 20 November (against Harwich and Ipswich, by 12 BR.20Ms). The BR.20Ms were withdrawn from the Blitz in January and returned to Italy, and the CR.42s were withdrawn from Belgium in February 1941. This left only three squadrons of Fiat G.50 fighters. Used mainly as night-fighters, the G.50s were finally withdrawn in April 1941.

Amazingly, Sunday 27 October saw Fighter Command fly its highest total number of sorties of the entire Battle (1007), strongly responding to a series of fighter and fighter-bomber sweeps, some of which involved as many as 50 enemy aircraft. These targeted convoys, London, Southampton and Martlesham Heath airfield. Combat losses totalled nine RAF fighters and 11 Luftwaffe aircraft. Unusually, Luftwaffe night operations included attacks on Coltishall, Driffield, Feltwell, Hawkinge, Honington, Kirton in Lindsey and Leconfield.

Among the daylight attacks on 28 October were eight groups of Bf 109Es sent out over Kent and the Thames Estuary, which suffered four combat losses, resulting in a Luftwaffe total of five losses (all Bf 109Es) that day. The RAF lost no aircraft in action.

The next two days saw the last gasp of the Battle of Britain, the final occasions on which the Luftwaffe

LEFT: THE REMAINS OF A BF 109E-4 OF 8/JG27, SHOT DOWN BY SPITFIRES AT FISHER FARM WEST WICKHAM, ON 27 OCTOBER 1940. THE PILOT, LT BUSCH, BALED OUT WITH SLIGHT INJURIES AND WAS CAPTURED.

BELOW: THE LUCKY SURVIVOR IN THIS PHOTOGRAPH WAS A MR NEWMAN, PULLED ALIVE FROM A BUILDING IN THE LONDON AREA AFTER BEING BURIED FOR 14 HOURS. EMERGENCY SERVICES WERE STRETCHED TO THE LIMIT DURING THE BLITZ.

made a major effort to attack targets heavily by daylight, albeit primarily using single-engined fighter-bombers and the high-speed Ju 88s.

After the usual scattering of reconnaissance missions, Kesselring unleashed his first wave of Bf 109Es, with two Staffeln of fighters escorting a single Staffel of Jabos. These crossed the coast near Deal at 1110, and while the fighters tangled with a small force of Spitfires, the Jabos dashed through to drop their bombs on London, hitting railway lines near Charing Cross station. Four of the German fighters were lost in the mêlée, but the RAF Spitfires returned to base without loss. The Duxford 'Big Wing' was scrambled but failed to contribute, taking 17 minutes to get airborne and another 20 to form up and leave the area. Park had five Spitfire and four Hurricane squadrons in position ready for the next raid, which consisted of the Bf 109E fighter-bombers of I./ and II./LG 2 escorted by about 100 Bf 109Es from I./ and II./JG 51. This time, the defenders shot down at least nine Bf 109Es.

Further raids that day included a brilliant attack by 12 Ju 88s of LG 1 (escorted by two Gruppen from JG 2) against Portsmouth, and an attack by 15 Fiat BR.20Ms and 73 escorting CR.42s against Ramsgate. 3./Erprobungsgruppe 210 attacked North Weald with its Bf 110s and Bf 109Es, catching Nos 249 and 257 Squadrons as they scrambled, damaging one aircraft, destroying another, and damaging another badly enough that all its pilot could do was

climb high enough to bale out. The fighter-bombers also caused significant damage to the airfield infrastructure, and lost only two aircraft in doing so. The Duxford Wing were in action again in the afternoon, but the very heavy radio traffic between the five squadrons prevented the controllers from being able to use them effectively. Leigh-Mallory then recalled the Wing early, worried about recovering the huge formation in the deteriorating weather conditions. Total combat losses for the day reached seven for the RAF, and 17 for the Luftwaffe.

Whereas 29 October had been one of Jabo attacks, 30 October was marked by the despatch of several formations of bombers. Good warning from Chain Home and a well-planned deployment of Fighter Command squadrons prevented most of the attackers from breaking through the screen of fighters, however. A formation of 80 bombers and fighter bombers appeared over the Thames Estuary at noon, and two more formations (totalling about 100 aircraft) crossed the coast at Dymchurch about quarter of an hour later. Later in the afternoon, a single attack was made by about 130 enemy aircraft. The day closed

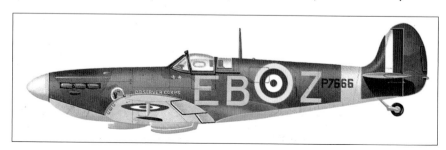

with Fighter Command having lost six Spitfires and a Hurricane, and with Luftwaffe combat losses totalling five aircraft. Night operations were light, due to exceptionally poor weather, and London's 'All Clear' sounded early enough for many Londoners to enjoy their best night's sleep for weeks.

The Battle of Britain did not end decisively on a particular date, though it had petered out by the end of October. Thereafter, the Luftwaffe's campaign was one of continuing night attacks against British cities, while Fighter Command was able to go onto the offensive. By the end of October, the monthly ratio of Fighter Command kills to losses had grown to 2:1, and was steadily improving. Over the whole course of the Battle, Fighter Command lost between 900 and 925 aircraft in combat (sources vary) and the Luftwaffe lost between 1590 and 1740. Fighter Command lost just over 400 pilots and aircrew killed, while the Luftwaffe suffered much heavier personnel losses, losing five aircrew for every Fighter Command pilot killed. At the time, Fighter Command claimed 2698 enemy aircraft, while the Luftwaffe claimed 3058 kills. Appropriately enough, the last day of October was exceptionally quiet, and there were no combat losses on either side.

RAF AIR ORDER OF BATTLE (FIGHTER COMMAND UNITS) 15 SEPTEMBER 1940

NO.10 GROUP

Middle Wallop Sector

No.238 Squadron	RAF Middle Wallop	Hurricane
No.23 Squadron	RAF Middle Wallop	Blenheim
No.604 Squadron	RAF Middle Wallop	Blenheim/
	Beaufighter	
No.56 Squadron	RAF Boscombe Down	Hurricane
No.152 Squadron	RAF Warmwell	Spitfire
No.609 Squadron	RAF Warmwell	Spitfire

Filton Sector

No.79 Squadron	RAF Pembrey	Hurricane

Exeter Sector

No.601 Squadron	Exeter	Hurricane
No.87 Squadron	Exeter	Hurricane

St. Eval Sector

No.234 Squadron	RAF St. Eval	Spitfire
No.236 Squadron	RAF St. Eval	Blenheim
No.247 Squadron	Roborough	Gladiator

NO.11 GROUP

North Weald Sector

No.23 Squadron	RAF North Weald	Blenheim/
	Beaufighter	
No.249 Squadron	RAF North Weald	Hurricane
No.46 Squadron	RAF Stapleford	Hurricane

Hornchurch Sector

No.41 Squadron	RAF Hornchurch	Spitfire
No.222 Squadron	RAF Hornchurch	Spitfire
No.600 Squadron	RAF Hornchurch	Blenheim/
	Beaufighter	
No.603 Squadron	RAF Hornchurch	Spitfire

Biggin Hill Sector

No.72 Squadron	RAF Biggin Hill	Spitfire
No.92 Squadron	RAF Biggin Hill	Spitfire
No.141 Squadron	RAF Biggin Hill	Defiant
No.66 Squadron	RAF Gravesend	Spitfire

Kenley Sector

No.253 Squadron	RAF Kenley	Hurricane
No.501 Squadron	RAF Kenley	Hurricane
No.605 Squadron	Croydon	Hurricane

Northolt Sector

No.229 Squadron	RAF Northolt	Hurricane
No.264 Squadron	RAF Northolt	Defiant
No.303 Squadron	RAF Northolt	Hurricane
No.504 Squadron	RAF Northolt	Hurricane
No.1 (RCAF) Squadron	RAF Northolt	Hurricane

Tangmere Sector

No.213 Squadron	RAF Tangmere	Hurricane
No.607 Squadron	RAF Tangmere	Hurricane
No.23 Squadron	RAF Ford	Blenheim
No.602 Squadron	RAF Westhampnett	Spitfire

Debden Sector

No.17 Squadron	RAF Debden	Hurricane
No.73 Squadron	RAF Castle Camps	Hurricane

No.25 Squadron	RAF Martlesham Heath	Blenheim
No.257 Squadron	RAF Martlesham Heath	Hurricane

NO.12 GROUP

Church Fenton Sector

No.85 Squadron	RAF Church Fenton	Hurricane
No.306 Squadron	RAF Church Fenton	Hurricane
No.64 Squadron	RAF Leconfield	Spitfire

Kirton in Lindsey Sector

No.264 Squadron	RAF Kirton in Lindsey	Defiant
No.307 Squadron	RAF Kirton in Lindsey	Defiant
No.616 Squadron	RAF Kirton in Lindsey	Spitfire

Digby Sector

No.29 Squadron	RAF Digby	Blenheim/
	Beaufighter	
No.151 Squadron	RAF Digby	Hurricane

Wittering Sector

No.1 Squadron	RAF Wittering	Hurricane
No.266 Squadron	RAF Wittering	Spitfire

Duxford Sector

No.242 Squadron	RAF Duxford	Hurricane
No.302 Squadron	RAF Duxford	Hurricane
No.310 Squadron	RAF Duxford	Hurricane
No.312 Squadron	RAF Duxford	Hurricane
No.19 Squadron	RAF Fowlmere	Spitfire
No.611 Squadron	RAF Fowlmere	Spitfire

Coltishall Sector

No.74 Squadron	RAF Coltishall	Spitfire

NO.13 GROUP

Aldergrove Sector

No.245 Squadron	RAF Aldergrove	Hurricane

Wick Sector

No.232 Squadron	RAF Wick	Hurricane

Dyce Sector

No.145 Squadron	RAF Dyce and Montrose	Hurricane

Turnhouse Sector

No.3 Squadron	RAF Turnhouse	Hurricane
No.65 Squadron	RAF Turnhouse	Spitfire
No.141 Squadron	RAF Turnhouse	Defiant
No.111 Squadron	RAF Drem	Hurricane
No.263 Squadron	RAF Drem	Hurricane/
		Whirlwind
No.615 Squadron	RAF Prestwick	Hurricane

Usworth Sector

No.43 Squadron	RAF Usworth	Hurricane
No.32 Squadron	RAF Acklington	Hurricane
No.219 Squadron	RAF Acklington	Blenheim
No.610 Squadron	RAF Acklington	Spitfire

Catterick Sector

No.54 Squadron	RAF Catterick	Spitfire
No.219 Squadron	RAF Catterick	Blenheim/
		Beaufighter

LUFTWAFFE AIR ORDER OF BATTLE (BATTLE OF BRITAIN UNITS) 15 SEPTEMBER 1940

LUFTFLOTTE 2

1(F)/22 Do 17, Bf 110	
2(F)/122	Ju88A
4(F)/122	He111H, Ju88A, Bf 110

I Fliegerkorps

Stab KG 1	He 111H
I./KG 1 He 111H	
II./KG 1 He 111H	
III./KG 1Ju 88A	
Stab KG 30	Ju 88A
I./KG 30	Ju 88C
III./KG 30	Ju 88C
Stab KG 76	Do 17Z
I./KG 76	Do 17Z
II./KG 76	Ju 88A
III./KG 76	Do 17Z
Stab KG 77	Ju 88A
I./KG 77	Ju 88A
II./KG 77	Ju 88A
III./KG 77	Ju 88A
5(F)/122	He111H, Ju88A

II Fliegerkorps

Stab KG 2 Do 17Z	
I./KG 2 Do 17Z	
II/.KG 2 Do 17Z	
III./KG 2Do 17Z	
Stab KG 3	Do 17Z
I./KG 3 Do 17Z	
II./KG 3 Do 17Z	
III./KG 3Do 17Z	
Stab KG 53	He 111H
I./KG 53	He 111H
II./KG 53	He 111H
III./KG 53	He 111H
Stab StG 1	Ju 87B
II./StG 1Ju 87B	
Stab StG 2	Ju 87B
II./StG 2Ju 87B	
IV(St)/LG 1	Ju 87B
II(Schlacht)/LG 2	Bf 109E
Erprobungsgr 210	Bf 109E, 110C,D
1(F)/122	Ju 88A
7(F)/LG 2	Bf 110

VIII Fliegerkorps

I./StG 1 Ju 87R	
III./StG 1	Ju 87B
I./StG 2 Ju 87B	
Stab/StG 77	Ju 87B
I./StG 77	Ju 87B
II./StG 77	Ju 87B
III./StG 77	Ju 87B
2(F)/11 Do17	
2(F)/123	Do17P

9 Fliegerdivision

Stab KG 4	He 111P
I./KG 4 He 111H	
II./KG 4 He 111P	
III./KG 4Ju 88A	
Stab KG 40	Ju 88A
K.Fl.Gr.106	Do 18, He 115
3(F)/122	He111H, Ju88A
Jafu 1	
I./JG 77 Bf 109E	
V(Z)/LG 1	Bf 110

Jafu 2

Stab JG 3	Bf 109E
I./JG 3 Bf 109E	
II./JG 3 Bf 109E	
III./JG 3 Bf 109E	
Stab JG 26	Bf 109E
I./JG 26	Bf 109E
II./JG 26	Bf 109E
III./JG 26	Bf 109E
Stab JG 51	Bf 109E
I./JG 51	Bf 109E
II./JG 51	Bf 109E
III./JG 51	Bf 109E
Stab JG 52	Bf 109E
I./JG 52	Bf 109E
II./JG 52	Bf 109E
III./JG 52	Bf 109E
Stab JG 54	Bf 109E
I./JG 54 Bf 109E	
II./JG 54	Bf 109E
III./JG 54	Bf 109E
Stab/ZG 26	Bf 110C
I./ZG 26	Bf 110C/D
II./ZG 26	Bf 110C
III./ZG 26	Bf 110C

LUFTFLOTTE 3

1(F)/123	Do 17, Ju 88A
2(F)/123	Do 17, Ju88A
3(F)/123	Do 17, Ju88A

IV Fliegerkorps

3(F)/121	He 111, Ju88A
Stab LG 1	Ju 88A
I(K)/LG 1	Ju 88A
II(K)/LG 1	Ju 88A
III(K)/LG 1	Ju 88A
Stab KG 27	He 111P
I./KG 27	He 111P
II./KG 27	He 111P, H
III./KG 27	He 111P
Kampfgrüppe 100	He 111H
Kampfgrüppe 606	Do 17
Kampfgrüppe 806	Ju 88A

Stab/StG 3	Ju 87B
I./StG 3 Ju 87B	
I./KG 40	Fw 200C
Stab JG 53	Bf 109E
I./JG 53	Bf 109E
II./JG 53	Bf 109E
III./JG 53	Bf 109E
Stab ZG 76	Bf 110
I./ZG 76	Bf 110
II./ZG 76	Bf 110
III./ZG 76	Bf 110
3(F)/31 Do17P, Bf 110	

V Fliegerkorps

Stab KG 51	Ju 88A
I./KG 51	Ju 88A
II./KG 51	Ju 88A
III./KG 51	Ju 88A
Stab KG 54	Ju 88A
I./KG 54	Ju 88A
II./KG 54	Ju 88A
Stab KG 55	He 111P
I./KG 55	He 111H, P
II./KG 55	He 111H, P
III./KG 55	He 111P
Stab JG 2	Bf 109E
I./JG 2 Bf 109E	
II./JG 2 Bf 109E	
III./JG 2 Bf 109E	
Stab JG 27	Bf 109E
I./JG27	Bf 109E
II./JG 27	Bf 109E
III./JG 27	Bf 109E
Stab ZG 26	Bf 110
I./ZG 26	Bf 110
II./ZG 26	Bf 110
III./ZG 26	Bf 110
4(F)/14 Do17M,P, Bf 110	
4(F)/121	Do17P, Ju 88A

LUFTFLOTTE 5

X Fliegerkorps

II./JG 77	Bf 109E
Stab/KüFlGr 506	He 115
1./KüFlGr 506	He 115
2./KüFlGr 506	He 115
3./KüFlGr 506	He 115
1(F)/120	He 111H, Ju 88
1(F)/121	Do 17, Ju 88A
2(F)/22 Do 17P/M	
3(F)/122	Do 17P/M

CHAPTER 7

Who Won the Battle of Britain?

LEFT: A TIRED RAF PILOT CLIMBING DOWN FROM HIS SPITFIRE AFTER A SORTIE. VISIBLE BEHIND HIM IS THE SANDBAGGED WALL OF THE REVETMENT WHICH PROTECTS THE AIRCRAFT FROM ANY FLYING DEBRIS OR SHRAPNEL SHOULD THE AIRFIELD BE ATTACKED.

ABOVE: 'TWICE IN THE FIRES
OF SACRIFICE CONSUMED
HAS LONDON LAIN: TWICE
HAS LONDON BURNED –
AND TWICE SHALL LONDON
RISE AGAIN!' WHAT BETTER
COMPLEMENT TO THIS
PICTURE OF ST PAUL'S THAN
THOSE WORDS OF THE POET
FRANCIS BRETT YOUNG?

RIGHT: MESSERSCHMITT
TRAVELLING LOW AND FAST.
THIS AIRCRAFT IS A
BF 109F, WHICH DID NOT
ENTER FULL OPERATIONAL
SERVICE UNTIL EARLY 1941;
NOTE THE ABSENCE OF
TAILPLANE STRUTS AND THE
ROUNDED WINGTIPS.

Everyone 'knows' that the Battle of Britain marked a historic victory for the RAF, and a humiliating defeat for the Luftwaffe. This is, however, a dangerously simplistic conclusion. Long after the end of the Battle, German aircraft were able to operate over Britain, attacking targets with virtual impunity. The Luftwaffe had been unable to achieve the air supremacy required for an invasion, and admittedly failed to crush its enemy. But at the same time the RAF had similarly failed to destroy the Luftwaffe, and was unable to win complete control of its own airspace.

In the end, Fighter Command achieved its stated (and relatively modest) aim by surviving intact long enough to keep Britain in the war and to deny Hitler any chance of invading, while the Luftwaffe failed to achieve its more ambitious aims. In that sense, at least, the RAF 'won' the Battle. An official Luftwaffe report on the Battle concluded gloomily that the 'enemy's power of resistance was stronger than the means of attack', and even dismissed claims that the effect of the Blitz on civilian morale had been worthwhile. It noted Allied reports claiming that the Battle of Britain had changed the course of the war, and acknowledged Allied assessments of why the Luftwaffe failed – 'Insufficient defensive power and bombload of German bombers' and 'fragmentation of effort' with 'insufficient follow-up to attacks on specific targets'.

A study of the overall numbers of aircraft downed and aircrew lost on each side would also support the verdict of a British victory, though the German single-engined fighters (despite operating at the end of their range) more than held their own, and could arguably have been said to have won their part of the battle.

Some serious historians have concluded that the Battle of Britain marked the beginning of the end for Germany, confidently stating that the Luftwaffe never again mounted a

serious challenge to Allied superiority in the air. This at least is extremely questionable, even if we accept that the Battle of Britain marked a victory for the RAF. No-one can seriously claim that the RAF's disastrous probing raids of 1941 and 1942 (and especially the wasteful fiasco that was Dieppe) were anything but a long-running and costly defeat for the RAF.

Some German historians have argued that there was no Battle of Britain (at least as defined by the British), and that the air campaign against Britain continued throughout the Blitz of 1941 until the invasion of Russia. By including the RAF's own bomber losses throughout this longer period, and by adding in the heavy losses over France in May 1940 and in early 1941, some have even claimed a massive victory. In late 1940, the official German propaganda was that Britain was beaten, needing only a coup de grace – patently an exaggeration, if not actually untrue. When von Ribbentrop made this claim to Molotov, his Russian counterpart, the Soviet Foreign Minister retorted that 'one should not speak of victory when British bombs are still falling on Berlin!'

Whatever the various historical angles, there was a very definite and distinctive battle for air superiority over southern England in the summer of 1940, and this was very different in extent and character from the sporadic raiding and night bombing which followed

ABOVE: A WOUNDED GERMAN PRISONER OF WAR BEING REPATRIATED. THE LOSS OF HIS RIGHT ARM DOES NOT APPEAR TO BE ACCOMPANIED BY ANY LOSS OF ARROGANCE.

it. And while the RAF did not manage to destroy the Luftwaffe, it did prevent the Germans from gaining air supremacy over Britain, and did impose such high costs that daylight bombing by massed formations had to be abandoned. If the threat of invasion was ever more than a heavily crafted illusion, then the RAF prevented that from happening too, and kept Britain in the war. At the very least it represented a modest and partial victory for Britain. It gave a glimpse of what was possible, opening a chink in the myth of Nazi invulnerability, and almost certainly saved Britain from the same fate as France.

But it was not without cost, with 515 fighter pilots killed, and many more seriously wounded, while the loss of aircraft was also staggering. Hitler's bombers caused massive damage to British cities, and had an appreciable effect on short-term production figures. Many civilians lost their lives, while the concentration on home defence may have sowed the seeds of later British defeat in the Balkans and Far East. The Royal Navy's withdrawal of destroyers from convoy escort duties to await an invasion also cost the Merchant Navy huge casualties from U-boats and the Luftwaffe. However, the Battle of Britain can be seen to have turned the tide of the war. There were, admittedly, further defeats to come for the British, but the Battle of Britain kept the United Kingdom, its dominions and empire in the war. This in turn forced Hitler to fight a war on two fronts, and it was the subsequent overstretch on resources that was to eventually bring total defeat for the Third Reich.

BOULTON PAUL DEFIANT

Specifications: Crew: 2 Maximum Speed: 504km/h (313mph) Range: 748km (465 miles) Armament: 4 7.7mm (0.303in) machine guns **Britain**

Folklore would have us believe that the Boulton Paul Defiant represented a flawed concept, and that it was a fighter which owed its only successes to being mistaken for something else, lulling enemy fighter pilots into making attacks from the wrong direction (for them). It is generally believed to have suffered such cripplingly high losses that its withdrawal from the fighting was rapid, and that it made little contribution, except to kill fine airmen who would have been better employed flying something else. This (as with so much Battle of Britain folklore) falls far short of the whole truth.

In fact, when the Defiant was designed there was little prospect of enemy bombers being escorted all the way to the target by single-engined single-seat fighters, given that the latter had much shorter ranges, and the concept of a dedicated 'Bomber Destroyer' seemed eminently sensible. France no longer represented a credible threat, and it was inconceivable that bombers flying from Germany (or even from Holland) could bring fighter escort with them.

It soon became apparent that a single-seat fighter with eight wing-mounted machine guns would have only a limited firing time during a typical attack, and that its pilot would have to concentrate on manoeuvring, on keeping in formation with his leader and/or wingmen as well as aiming his machine at the enemy. It was clear that a two-seat fighter equipped with four similar machine guns in a power operated turret might enjoy a longer firing opportunity, while a dedicated air gunner might well achieve greater accuracy. The concept had been demonstrated (to a rather more modest extent) by the Hawker Demon, and the first Specification for a monoplane Demon replacement was issued in 1933. This was revised and reissued in 1935 (as F.9/35) and six companies responded. Boulton Paul's P.82 was regarded as the most promising runner up to Hawker's Hotspur, which was based on the Henley light bomber (basically a two-seat Hurricane). Two prototypes were therefore ordered of each type.

Boulton Paul designed a neat and graceful single-engined monoplane, with a licence-built French SAMM turret behind the cockpit, containing four of the new 0.303-in Colt-Browning machine guns, with 600 rounds per gun. Forward firing armament was not fitted. Provision was made, however, for the carriage of up to eight 20lb fragmentation bombs for use in the Army Co-operation role. The aircraft itself was exceptionally clean with fine, almost delicate lines, though because double-curvature was avoided wherever possible, promised to be simple and cheap to manufacture.

Hawker were barely able to cope with Hurricane production, and accordingly the Defiant became the only contender to meet the requirement, though it was probably also the best. The prototype made its maiden flight on 11 August 1937, achieving 320 mph in service trials at Martlesham Heath in December. Even before the maiden flight, Boulton Paul had received a contract for the first 87 P.82, to be officially known as Defiants.

No.264 Squadron formed at RAF Sutton Bridge on 30 October 1939, intended as the first Defiant squadron. Initially equipped with Battles and Magisters, it received Defiants that December. The unit was declared operational on 20 March, and began flying convoy patrols. The Squadron flew many patrols during the invasion of France and the Low Countries, and proved most successful when deployed in mixed formations, supported by single-engined single-seat fighters. The aircraft rapidly proved its effectiveness as a bomber destroyer, but was less successful against fighter targets, except when mistaken for Spitfires or Hurricanes and attacked from above and behind. Otherwise, the Defiant proved very vulnerable to Bf 109s, and fourteen aircraft were lost by the end of the Dunkirk operation. But in turn, No.264 had claimed 65 enemy aircraft - 37 of them on one day. While the actual total of kills was very much lower, there is little doubt that the Defiant gave as good as it got.

The story was much the same during the Battle of Britain, in which two Defiant Squadrons were involved. No.141 Squadron served at West Malling from 3 June until withdrawn to Prestwick on 21 July after suffering five losses when taking off for a patrol. No.264 was posted to Hornchurch on 22 August and withdrew on 28 August, after the loss of eleven aircraft, five pilots and nine air gunners in only eight days. They had accounted for 15 enemy aircraft confirmed and one more unconfirmed, however, including three Bf 109s.

Though it dealt out more punishment than it received, the Defiant was recognised as being pitifully vulnerable, and the type was never committed to daylight operations within range of enemy fighters again, though it did go on to play a vital role as a night-fighter, target tug, and air sea rescue support aircraft.

BATTLE OF BRITAIN DEFIANT SQUADRONS

SQUADRON	CODES	BASES
No.141	'TW-'	West Malling
No.264	'PS-'	Hornchurch

BRISTOL BLENHEIM

Specifications: Crew: 3 Max Speed: 459km/h (285mph) Range: 1810km (1155 miles) Armament: 6 7.7mm (0.303in) machine guns   **Britain**

Delays to the Defiant led to the idea of using surplus short-nosed Blenheim Is (replaced in the bomber role by long-nosed Mk IVs) as interim fighters, allowing the withdrawal of the last biplane Hawker Demons. The decision was taken that the Fighter Blenheim would have a four-gun battery in the former bomb-bay, but No.11 Group and No.12 Group argued about whether the gun turret (and gunner) should be retained. Dowding and No.11 Group favoured a single-seat version, though they were overruled by the Air Staff.

Blenheim losses during the German invasion of France and the Low Countries underlined the type's vulnerability (especially to single-engined fighters), and increasingly, the Fighter Command Blenheims were tasked with night-fighter duties. No.600 Squadron began flying with AI radar in June/July 1940, and the aircraft began to achieve limited successes against the German night raids.

The Blenheims eventually had their turrets removed from October 1940, by which time replacement Beaufighters were beginning to arrive. Although insanely slow, the Blenheim was quite agile, and could even out-turn a Bf 109 at certain heights. The Blenheim fighter also served with Coastal Command, three of whose squadrons (Nos 235, 236 and 248) were regarded by the RAF as 'Qualifying' for the list of participants in the Battle. In total, the Blenheims claimed 30 kills during the Battle of Britain period.

BATTLE OF BRITAIN BLENHEIM SQUADRONS

SQUADRON	CODES	BASES
No.23	'YP-'	Wittering, Ford, Middle Wallop
No.25	'ZK-'	Martlesham Heath, North Weald
No.29	'RO-'	Digby and Wellingore
No.219	'FK-'	Catterick and Redhill
No.235	'LA-'	Detling, Bircham Newton, Thorney Is.
No.236	'FA-'	Thorney Island, St.Eval
No.248	'WR-'	Sumburgh
No.600	'BQ-'	Manston, Hornchurch, Redhill, Catterick
No.604	'NG-'	Manston, Gravesend, Middle Wallop
FIU	'ZQ-'	Tangmere, Shoreham

GLOSTER GLADIATOR

Specifications: Crew: 1 Max Speed: 407km/h (253mph) Range: 689km (428 miles) Armament: 4 7.7mm (0.303in) machine guns   **Britain**

The last of the RAF's biplane fighters, the Gloster Gladiator introduced many refinements by comparison with its forebears, including an enclosed cockpit, four-gun armament, landing flaps, and (later) a three-bladed variable pitch propellor. The Gladiator's replacement by the Hurricane in Fighter Command was virtually complete by 1940. However the type was still felt to have a role to play in North Africa, and Gladiators had been deployed to Norway due to their ability to operate from poorly prepared airstrips in the most primitive and hostile conditions. But it was widely recognised that the Gladiator was obsolete, and should not be committed where it might run up against single-engined monoplane single-seat fighters.

With the Gauntlet, the Gladiator had formed the backbone of Fighter Command during much of the 1930s, and two squadrons (Nos 607 and 615) had even been sent to France with the BEF, though these soon converted to the Hurricane. Nevertheless, some sources credit the BEF Gladiators with scoring as many as 72 kills between 10 and 20 May 1940. By the time the Battle of Britain began, the Gladiator remained in home-based frontline service only with the Shetland Fighter Flight defending Scapa Flow. However an expanded Flight of Gladiators was moved to Roborough, a small grass strip incapable of sustaining operations by more modern fighters, to protect Plymouth's dockyards. The Shetland Gladiators moved south, initially to St.Eval, becoming No.247 Squadron on 1 August and being declared operational at Roborough on 13 August.

The Gladiator was in service in larger numbers with the Fleet Air Arm, but the only RN Gladiator Squadron to participate in the Battle of Britain was No.80 at Hatston, flying patrols in defence of Scapa Flow. The Gladiator engaged the enemy only once during the Battle of Britain, on 28 October, when a No.247 Squadron aircraft attacked a Heinkel 111 over Plymouth.

BATTLE OF BRITAIN GLADIATOR SQUADRONS

SQUADRON	CODES	BASES
No.247	'HP-'	Roborough and St. Eval

HAWKER HURRICANE

Specifications: Crew: 1 Max Speed: 521km/h (324mph) Range: 716km (445 miles) Armament: 8 7.7mm (0.303in) machine guns **Britain**

During the Battle of Britain, the Spitfire tended to hog the headlines and steal the limelight, although the Hurricane equipped twice as many (36) Fighter Command squadrons, and accounted for 477 more enemy aircraft than the Spitfire. The Hurricane units accounted for some 1593 kills, averaging 44.25 enemy aircraft destroyed per squadron. And if, on average, Spitfire squadrons performed better than those flying Hurricanes (more than 60 kills per squadron), it must be remembered that the Hurricane was quicker, cheaper and easier to build and repair, and it would not have been possible to equip the whole of Fighter Command with Spitfires.

Although not the equal of the Spitfire in terms of manoeuvrability and performance, the Hurricane was an extremely effective fighter that could survive far more battle damage than the 'flimsy' Spitfire. Like the Spitfire, the Hurricane turned better than the more modern Messerschmitt Bf 109E, making it a better dogfighter, and reducing the German fighter pilots to making slashing attacks which exploited their superior speed, especially in the dive.

Designed to meet the 1934 specification F.36/34, the Hurricane began life as the 'Fury Monoplane' armed with only two machine guns above the engine. When the prototype was built, designer Sydney Camm substituted a battery of eight wing-mounted machine guns. But apart from this, the retractable undercarriage, the cantilever monoplane wing and Merlin engine, the Hurricane was little more advanced than the Gladiator, which had already introduced landing flaps and a fully-enclosed cockpit.

The Hurricane combined high performance (the prototype had a level speed of 315 mph, and a climb to 15,000 ft in 5.7 minutes) with the ability to operate from biplane-type aerodromes, while posing relatively few difficulties or unfamiliar features for engineers and groundcrew. From a RAF fighter pilot's point of view, the transition to the Hurricane was simple and quick.

In March 1936, Hawker began production of 1000 aircraft. Minor teething troubles delayed delivery of the first production aircraft to No.111 Squadron until November 1937. By the time the Munich crisis broke, the Hurricane also equipped Nos. 3 and 56 Squadrons, though the latter was non-operational.

The early Hurricane Is used fixed-pitch, two-bladed wooden Watts propellors, had fabric-covered wings, and lacked a ventral fin. A few survived to see active service during the early part of the war and the Battle of Britain, but by late 1939, most frontline Hurricanes had three-bladed constant speed propellors, stressed-skin metal wings, and a ventral fin. Hurricanes formed the backbone of the RAF's fighter force in France, and were also used in Norway.

BATTLE OF BRITAIN HURRICANE SQUADRONS

SQUADRON	CODES	BASES
No. 1	'JX-'	Northolt, Tangmere, Manston, N. Weald, Heathrow, Wittering.
No. 3	'QO-'	Wick, Castletown, Turnhouse
No. 17	'YB-'	Debden, Tangmere, Martlesham Heath
No. 32	'GZ-'	Biggin Hill, Acklington.
No. 43	'FT-'	Tangmere, Usworth
No. 46	'PO-'	Digby, Stapleford
No. 56	'US-'	North Weald, Boscombe Down.
No. 73	'TP-'	Church Fenton, Castle Camps
No. 79	'NV-'	Hawkinge, Acklington, Pembrey
No. 85	'VY-'	Debden, Croydon, Church Fenton
No. 87	'LK-'	Church Fenton, Exeter, Hullavington, Bibury, Colerne
No. 111	'JU-'	Croydon, Debden
No. 145	'SO-'	Tangmere, Westhampnett, Drem, Dyce
No. 151	'DZ-'	North Weald, Digby,
No. 213	'AK-'	Exeter, Tangmere
No. 229	'HB-'	Wittering, Northolt.
No. 232	'EF-'	Sumburgh, Castletown
No. 234		St Eval, Middle Wallop
No. 238	'VK-'	Middle Wallop, St.Eval, Chilbolton
No. 242	'LE-'	Coltishall, Duxford
No. 245	'DR-'	Hawkinge
No. 249	'GN-'	Church Fenton, Boscombe Down, North Weald
No. 253	'SW-'	Kenley
No. 257	'DT-'	Hendon, Debden, Martlesham Heath, N. Weald
No. 263	'HE-'	Scotland
No. 302	'WX-'	Leconfield, Duxford, Northolt
No. 303	'RF-'	Northolt
No. 310	'NN-'	Duxford
No. 312	'DU-'	Duxford, Speke
No. 501	'SD-'	Croydon, Middle Wallop, Gravesend, Kenley
No. 504	'TM-'	Wick, Castletown, Catterick, Hendon
No. 601	'UF-'	Tangmere, Debden, Exeter
No. 605	'UP-'	Hawkinge, Croydon
No. 607	'AF-'	Usworth, Tangmere, Turnhouse
No. 615	'KW-'	Kenley, Prestwick, Northolt
No.1 (RCAF)	'YO-'	Middle Wallop, Croydon, Northolt
No.421 Flt	no	Gravesend, West Malling
No.422 Flt	no	Shoreham

BRISTOL BEAUFIGHTER

Specifications: *Crew:* 2 *Max Speed:* 488km/h (303mph) *Range:* 5118km (3180 miles) *Armament:* 4 20mm, 6 7.7mm (0.303in) MGs   **Britain**

The Beaufighter was designed as a Private Venture cannon-armed fighter version of the Beaufort, with a new fuselage married to the same basic wing and engines. Intended as an interim replacement for the Whirlwind, the Beaufighter promised to pack a heavy punch

BATTLE OF BRITAIN BEAUFIGHTER SQUADRONS		
SQUADRON	CODES	BASES
No.23	'YP-'	Middle Wallop
No.25	'ZK-'	North Weald
No.29	'RO-'	Wellingore
No.219	'FK-'	Redhill
No.600	'BQ-'	Redhill, Catterick
No.604	'NG-'	Middle Wallop
FIU	'ZQ-'	Tangmere, Shoreham

while offering a top speed of 361 mph, though in the event this was not achieved. First flown on 20 July 1939, the Beaufighter proved inferior in performance to the cannon-armed version of the Hurricane, but its long range and twin-engined, two-crew configuration held out the promise of greater multi-role versatility. The first two aircraft were built in June 1940, with five more in July, 23 in August and 15 in September. Unusually, the new aircraft were scattered among existing Blenheim units in small numbers, allowing squadrons to evaluate the new type and develop tactics and techniques for using it. The first examples went to the FIU on 12 August and to Nos. 29, 604 and 25 squadrons on 2 and 3 September. Nos. 23 and 600 each received a Beaufighter on 8 September. Some 28 aircraft had been delivered by 31 October, most being concentrated within Nos. 25 and 219 Squadrons. The Beaufighter began flying sporadic operational sorties from 18 September, initially by day.

FAIREY FULMAR

Specifications: *Crew:* 2 *Max Speed:* 398km/h (247mph) *Range:* 1255km (780 miles) *Armament:* 8 7.7mm (0.303in) machine guns   **Britain**

Between September 1940 and August 1942, the Fairey Fulmar shot down 112 enemy aircraft, accounting for an astonishing 30% of the FAA's tally during the period. Developed from Fairey's unsuccessful P.4/34 high speed light bomber (competing against the Hawker Henley) the Fulmar was developed as an interim fighter pending the availability (and anticipating the possible failure) of the Blackburn Roc and Skua. Designed to patrol for up to six hours, and to be capable of 265 mph, the Fulmar was armed with a battery of eight 0.303-in machine guns - like the Spitfire and Hurricane, but with a mind-boggling 750 rounds per gun (double that of the two RAF aircraft), and later 1,000 rounds per gun. But despite the fact that the aircraft was a two-seater no rearward facing armament was provided. It was also planned to be capable of rapid conversion to floatplane configuration (taking four men not more than two hours!), though this requirement was later dropped. The first Fulmar made its maiden flight on 4 January 1940, and proved slow in level flight, with a very limited ceiling, but enormously fast

in even a shallow dive, thanks to its heavy weight. Easy to deck-land, the Fulmar was a very much better aircraft than specification figures might suggest, and some 600 were eventually built. No.806 Squadron was the first Frontline Fulmar unit, equipping at Eastleigh from June 1940. The Squadron then embarked on HMS Illustrious for an abbreviated work-up before heading to the Mediterranean. The second Fulmar unit was No.808 Squadron, which formed at Worthy Down in July and then took up station at Hatston in the Orkneys in September. Although the unit saw no action, it was officially part of Fighter Command's Battle of Britain order of battle, one of only two Royal Navy units so included.

BATTLE OF BRITAIN FULMAR SQUADRONS		
SQUADRON	CODES	BASES
No.808	No codes	Casteltown

WESTLAND LYSANDER

Specifications: *Crew:* 2 *Max Speed:* 396km/h (229mph) *Range:* 966km (600 miles) *Armament:* 3 7.7mm (0.303in) machine guns   **Britain**

The number of Westland Lysanders on charge in October 1940 (almost 700) was felt by some to be an embarrassing waste of valuable aero engines, and the type was dismissed as being 'only really suitable for use on the North-West Frontier'. Army Co-operation Command's Lysanders had flown 600 sorties during the Battle of France, losing 34 of their number and prompting a host of modifications aimed at reducing the type's vulnerability. Some were fitted with rearward-firing machine guns, and some with 20-mm cannon on their stub wings. Before the Battle, the aircraft were used intensively for anti-invasion patrols, and some envisaged the type taking on a close support role (perhaps spraying gas) had an invasion materialised. Later in the Battle, Lysanders were used to try

and find downed aircrew in the Channel, but it was after the Battle, when the type was used for agent-dropping and retrieval, that the Lysander found its niche.

Only one Lysander was ever involved in the shooting during the Battle of Britain, as far as can be ascertained. The RAF's Lysander units were never part of the Fighter Command order of battle, and so did not officially participate. For the record, the Lysander-equipped units were No.II Squadron, No.4 Squadron, No.13 Squadron, No.16 Squadron, No.26 Squadron, No.110 Squadron, No.225 Squadron, No.231 Squadron, No.239 Squadron, No.241 Squadron, No.416 Squadron, No.613 Squadron, No.614 Squadron, and No.419 Flight.

SUPERMARINE SPITFIRE

Specifications: Crew: 1 Max Speed: 580km/h (362mph) Range: 637km (395 miles) Armament: 8 7.7mm (0.303in) machine guns   **Britain**

For many years regarded as the aircraft that won the Battle of Britain, the Spitfire was indisputably the best fighter aircraft available to the RAF in 1940, and, despite its lightweight armament and an engine which could cut out under negative g, was probably superior to the Bf 109 as well. Small wonder that most German fighter pilots claimed to have shot down (or been shot down by) Spitfires, and not the less glamorous Hurricane, even though this was used in far greater numbers.

Some 18 Spitfire Squadrons, accounted for 1,116.5 kill claims, only 477 fewer enemy aircraft than were claimed by twice as many Hurricane squadrons. This averaged out at 62 per Squadron (compared to 44 per squadron for the Hurricane), making the average Spitfire squadron 50% more effective than the average Hurricane unit (shooting down18 more enemy aircraft per squadron on average). There are also some grounds for suspecting that Spitfire claims, while undeniably inflated, were closer to reality than those by some Hurricane units! Taking this to its logical conclusion, one might conclude that if only the 36 Hurricane units had actually had Spitfires, Fighter Command's score might have been 648 or more higher! But this could never have been an option, since production of the simpler, quicker-to-build Hurricane allowed Fighter Command to be a much larger organisation than an all-Spitfire Command could have been, and allowed it to protect a greater proportion of Britain's airspace. But while acknowledging the contribution of the Hawker fighter, it is perhaps fair that the Spitfire is remembered as the aircraft that won the Battle.

Legend has it that the Spitfire was directly decended from the sleek floatplanes which won Britain the prestigious Schneider Trophy in 1931. These dedicated racers had been evolved by Supermarine's RJ Mitchell, who also created the Spitfire, and were similarly all-metal, stressed-skin monoplanes powered by inline engines. But there the similarity ended. The original Supermarine Type 224 (unofficially dubbed Spitfire) was a landplane fighter derivative of the dainty floatplanes, but featured a cranked wing, fixed 'trousered' undercarriage and a steam-cooled Goshawk engine. But the ungainly Type 224 was so plainly unsatisfactory that Mitchell began drawing more refined Goshawk-engined fighters, and these bore a greater similarity to the eventual Spitfire.

The availability of the Rolls Royce PV-12 engine (later the Merlin) resulted in the Type 300, which Mitchell drew up to meet Air Ministry Specification F.5/34. This featured an elliptical wing (like that of the Heinkel He 70 used by Rolls Royce as a Merlin test-bed) and eight wing-mounted machine guns. The Type 300

went far beyond the requirements of Specification F.5/34, and a new specification was written around it. A single prototype was ordered for evaluation and this flew for the first time on 5 March 1936, only four months after the rival Hurricane. The prototype impressed those who evaluated it at Martlesham Heath, and the type was ordered into production as the Spitfire in June 1936.

While the Spitfire and Hurricane were near-contemporaries, and although they shared a common powerplant and armament, they represented entirely different generations of fighter. While the Hurricane was the last of the old style, the stressed skin Spitfire was very much the first of the new. Unfortunately for the RAF, this meant that the Spitfire was more expensive and more difficult to build, even without the fact that the Hurricane was built in its entirety by the massive and well-established Hawker operation, while the tiny Supermarine company could originally build only the

BATTLE OF BRITAIN SPITFIRE SQUADRONS

SQUADRON	CODES	BASES
No. 19 Sqn	'QV-'	Duxford, Fowlmere, Eastchurch
No. 41 Sqn	'EB-'	Hornchurch, Catterick
No. 54 Sqn	'KL-'	Rochford, Hornchurch, Catterick
No. 64 Sqn	'SH-'	Kenley, Leconfield, Biggin Hill, Coltishall
No. 65 Sqn	'YT-'	Hornchurch, Turnhouse
No. 66 Sqn	'LZ-'	Coltishall, Kenley, Gravesend, West Malling
No. 72 Sqn	'RN-'	Acklington, Biggin Hill, Leconfied, Coltishall,
No. 74 Sqn	'ZP-'	Hornchurch, Wittering, Kirton on Lindsey, Coltishall
No. 92 Sqn	'QJ-'	Pembrey, Biggin Hill,
No. 152 Sqn	'UM-'	Acklington, Warmwell
No. 222 Sqn	'ZD-'	Kirton in Lindsey, Hornchurch
No. 266 Sqn	'UO-'	Wittering, Collyweston, Eastchurch, Hornchurch
No. 602 Sqn	'LO-'	Drem, Westhampnett
No. 603 Sqn	'XT-'	Turnhouse, Hornchurch
No. 609 Sqn	'PR-'	Northolt, Middle Wallop, Warmwell
No. 610 Sqn	'DW-'	Biggin Hill, Acklington
No. 611 Sqn	'FY-'	Digby, Ternhill, North Coates
No. 616 Sqn	'YQ-'	Leconfield, Kenley, Coltishall, Kirton in Lindsey
No.421 Flt	'DL-'	Biggin Hill

aircraft's fuselage, sub-contracting wings to General Aircraft and Pobjoy, wing ribs to Westland, leading edges to The Pressed Steel Co., ailerons and elevators to Aero Engines Ltd, tails to Folland, wing tips to General Electric and fuselage frames to J.Samuel White & Co. Ltd.

The limited production capacity of Supermarine's Woolston factory led, in 1938, to the placing of an order with the Nuffield Organisation. This called for the construction of 1000 Spitfires at a new Shadow Factory at Castle Bromwich. By 3 September 1939 some 2,143 Spitfires were on order, and nine Squadrons had been equipped with the aircraft, with two more undergoing conversion. Squadrons would continue to re-equip with the Spitfire right through the Battle of Britain itself.

The first Spitfires in service had simple two-bladed, fixed-pitch Watts wooden propellors, but from the 78th aircraft were fitted with a three-bladed variable pitch (two-position, coarse and fine) de Havilland propellor. From the 175th aircraft new Spitfires had 1030 shp Merlin III engines with provision for either Rotol or de Havilland three-bladed variable pitch propellors. Between late June and early August de Havilland engineers visited fighter stations to supervise the conversion of airscrews fitted to existing aircraft to constant speed (fully variable) standards, while new-build aircraft were fitted with constant speed propellors on the production line. Constant speed propellors allowed propellor pitch to be varied to suit airspeed, and dramatically improved the Spitfire's climb performance and ceiling.

In service, Spitfires received a range of other modifications, including a castoring tailwheel, ejector exhausts and a domed cockpit canopy giving improved all-round visibility (adopted before the war), as well as armoured windscreens and head-armour behind the pilot. Some 30 Spitfire Mk IBs were delivered to No.19 Squadron for operational trials during the Battle. These had two 20-mm Hispano cannon (with 60-round ammunition drums) in place of the four inboard 0.303-in machine guns, but these were prone to stoppages and jamming, and the type was never widely adopted.

The Spitfire II designation was applied to the aircraft built at the Castle Bromwich 'Shadow Factory', which began being delivered in July 1940. These naturally had all the usual features of late production Mk Is, incorporated on the production line, and were powered by the new 1175 shp Merlin XII, which ran on 100 octane fuel, was fitted with a Coffman starter and drove a Jablo Rotol constant speed airscrew. The Spitfire II remained something of a rarity during the Battle, equipping only a few units, but it rapidly re-equipped Fighter Command squadrons afterwards.

The Spitfire went on to perform wide variety of roles in World War II, from photo-reconnaissance to fighter-bomber, and served in virtually every theatre of operations. Although surpassed by other, more modern designs as a pure fighter, it remained an important type, and was more than capable of holding its own against potential opponents. After the war many countries' air forces had at least one of the Spitfire marks in service, and it remained in front-line service with various air forces for many years (the last RAF Spitfires flew as late as 1954). However it will forever be synonymous with the Battle of Britain, its 'finest hour'.

BELOW: A SPITFIRE OF NO.66 SQUADRON BASED AT GRAVESEND IN SEPTEMBER 1940, WITH A 501 SQUADRON HURRICANE, ALSO BASED THERE, VISIBLE IN THE BACKGROUND.

DORNIER DO 17

Specifications: Crew: 4 Max Speed: 410km/h (255mph) Range: 1500km (932 miles) Armament 4-8: 7.92mm (0.31in) machine guns **Germany**

The \Dornier Do 17 was the least numerous of the Luftwaffe bombers deployed against Britain during the Battle, but has been claimed by some to have been the most effective. Most German military aircraft of the period were designed from the start as warplanes, but were first revealed in a civil guise - masquerading as airliners or 'high speed mailplanes'. For example, Dornier itself had built Do 11Cs in Switzerland as 'freight transports'. The Do 17, by contrast, was really designed as a high speed mailplane, with tiny cramped cabins fore and aft of the wing accomodating six passengers with very difficult access. This was realised too late, and the three prototypes were soon placed in storage, where they remained until discovered by a curious RLM test pilot, who flight-tested one and was so impressed by its performance that he suggested the type's conversion for use as a high-speed bomber.

Dornier were by then working on the long-range Do 19, a four-engined heavy bomber, and were not greatly interested in the idea. Nor, until the death of General Walther Wever, was the Luftwaffe. But Wever's successor as Chief of Staff, Albert Kesselring was a tactical man, through and through, and preferred large fleets of relatively cheap, lightweight bombers optimised for what was, in essence, a close support role. The Do 17 soon won his approval, while the Do 19 (probably the aircraft the Luftwaffe really needed for the Battle of Britain) was unceremoniously scrapped.

Three further Do 17 prototypes were built with twin endplate fins in place of the original aircraft's single fin, and the forward fuselage was deepened and fitted with extensive glazing to accomodate a full bomber crew. The aircraft retained much of the appearance of the original, and this led to the type's 'Flying Pencil' nickname.

BATTLE OF BRITAIN DO 17 UNITS

SQUADRON	TYPE	CODES	BASES	SQUADRON	TYPE	CODES	BASES
Stab KG 2	Do 17Z-2	U5+*A	Saint Leger	4(F)/11	Do 17		
I/KG 2	Do 17Z-2,-3	U5+*B, H, K, L	Cambrai	4(F)/14	Do 17P		Raum Cherbourg
II/KG 2	Do 17Z-2,-3	U5+*C, M, N, P	Saint Leger	1(F)/22	Do 17P		Lille
III/KG 2	Do 17Z-2	U5+*D, R, S, T	Cambrai	2(F)/22	Do 17P/M		Stavanger
Stab KG 3	Do 17Z-2	5K+*A	Le Culot	3(F)/22	Do 17P/M		Stavanger
I/KG 3	Do 17Z-2	5K+*B, H, K, L	Le Culot	3(F)/31	Do 17P		St Brieux
II/KG 3	Do 17Z-2,-3	5K+*C, M, N, P	Antwerp/Deurne	1(F)/120	Do 17P		Stavanger
III/KG 3	Do 17Z-2	5K+*D, R, S, T	Saint-Trond	4(F)/121	Do 17P		Villacoublay
Stab KG 28	Do 17M	+*A		5(F)/122	Do 17P		Haute Fontaine
Stab KG 76	Do 17Z	F1+*A	Cormeilles en Vexin	1(F)/123	Do 17P		
I/KG 76	Do 17Z-1	F1+*B, H, K, L	Beauvais/Tille	2(F)/123	Do 17P		
II/KG 76	Do 17Z	F1+*C, M, N, P	Creil	3(F)/123	Do 17P	4U+*L	Buc
(converted to Ju 88A)				1(F)/124	Do 215		
III/KG 76	Do 17Z-2,-3	F1+*D, R, S, T	Cormeilles en Vexin	1(F)/Aufkl.Gr.OkL	Do 215		Berlin
Kampfgrüppe 606	Do 17		Brest/Cherbourg	2(F)/Aufkl.Gr.OkL	Do 215		
Stab StG 1	Do 17M		Saint Pol	3(F)/Aufkl.Gr.OkL	Do 215		Stavanger
Stab StG 2	Do 17M		Tramecourt	Westa 1 ObdL	Do 17Z		Oldenburg
Stab StG 3	Do 17M, Z		Bretigny	Westa 26 ObdL	Do 17Z		Brussels-Grimberghen
3(F)/10	Do 17			Westa 51	Do 17U		Buc bei Versailles
2(F)/11	Do 17P		Raum Bernay	Aufkl.Staffel zbV	Do 17M		
3(F)/11	Do 17						

The original Do 17E-1 bomber was easily capable of 240 mph (a stripped aircraft had demonstrated 283 mph) and great emphasis was placed on this 'high speed' capability. In fact, this was not even as fast as Britain's modest Bristol Blenheim. To its credit, the Dornier could at least carry a meaningful internal bombload (by the standards of the day), and its crew of three were clustered close together, where they could work together and communicate easily. The Do 17 entered service in 1937, undergoing trials in Spain with the Condor Legion. The Do 17F-1 was a reconnaissance aircraft equipped with two floor-mounted Rb50/18 or Rb50/30 cameras.

The Do 17E and Do 17F gave way to the broadly similar Do 17M and Do 17P, which were bomber and reconnaissance variants respectively, differing from the earlier versions in being powered by 900 hp Bramo Fafnir 323A or BMW 132N radial engines in place of the inline DB600s originally fitted. These raised the maximum speed to fractionally above 300 mph. The DB600-powered versions remained in limited use at the beginning of the war, but by the Battle of France all had vanished from frontline service. On 10 May, 188 serviceable Do 17Ms and Do 17Ps were available, together with 338 examples of the further improved Do 17Z.

Production Do 17Zs featured more powerful (1,000 hp) Bramo 232P radial engines with two-stage superchargers, but more obviously had an entirely redesigned forward fuselage, much deeper, more extensively glazed, and with a huge underslung ventral gondola. This had first appeared on the Do 17S (built in pre-production form only) and made the aircraft look much more like a Ju 88. It raised the crew complement to five, though the bombload remained a paltry 2200lb. Defensive armament was increased to six 7.9-mm

machine guns, one fixed and one free-mounted firing forward, one firing aft in each of the dorsal and ventral positions, and two in the side windows. But these weapons were mounted singly, and had relatively limited arcs of fire. By comparison with the multi-gun powered turrets fitted to aircraft like the Wellington and Blenheim they represented little more than a last-ditch defence, although Do 17 gunners did down surprising numbers of RAF fighters which pressed their attacks too closely, or failed to break away aggressively enough. The Do 17U was basically a hybrid combining the new nose with the engines of the Do 17M. The 15 aircraft built were used as dedicated pathfinders by Kampfgrüppe 100, and carried a second radio operator.

Aircraft losses suffered during the invasion of the Low Countries and France were not fully restored, while some units were already converting to the newer, faster and more effective Ju 88. Do 17 numbers dropped throughout the Battle of Britain. On 1 September 1940, the frontline bomber Kampfgrüppen had 158 Do 17Ms and 212 Do 17Zs on charge. These won a reputation for low level pin-point bombing attacks, but also flew their share of medium level area attacks. The Do 17 was highly manoeuvrable, and its crews could dive at speeds which bordered on the unbelievable. If sufficient height were available, and the defending fighters low on fuel, Dorniers could sometimes escape by pushing their noses down and diving for home 'flat out' - much like the Ju 88.

A final version of the 'Flying Pencil' in use during the Battle of Britain was the Do 215B, 18 of which were designed and built for export (to Sweden) but were then embargoed and re-directed to the Luftwaffe, which used them for reconnaissance duties.

DORNIER DO 18

Specifications: Crew: 4 Max Speed: 267km/h (166mph) Range: 3500km (2175 miles) Armament: 1 20mm cannon, 1 13mm MG   **Germany**

The Do 18 was developed as a successor to the Do 15 Wal (Whale) flying boat, and used a similar configuration, with a high, pylon-mounted braced parasol wing, tandem pusher and tractor engines above the centre section, with sponsons on each side of a two-step hull. The original military Do 18D was on the verge of obsolescence by 1939, but the type was retained due to delays with the planned successor, the Blöhm und Voss Bv 138.

The Do 18G was hastily produced as an interim solution, and introduced improved aerodynamics and more powerful engines. It replaced the Do 18D from mid-1940. The related Do 18H was a dedicated trainer, and the Do 18N a conversion specifically intended for the Seenotdienst.

BATTLE OF BRITAIN DO 18 UNITS	
SQUADRON	**BASES**
2./KüFlGr 106	Rantum
1./KüFlGr 406	Stavanger
2./KüFlGr 406	Stavanger
3./KüFlGr 406	Hörnum
1./KüFlGr 606	Brest
2./KüFlGr 606	Brest
3./KüFlGr 606	Brest
2./KüFlGr 906	Hörnum
3./KüFlGr 906	

DORNIER DO 24

Specifications: Crew: 4 Max Speed: 340km/h (211mph) Range: 2900km (1802 miles) Armament: 1 20mm, 2 7.92mm MGs   **Germany**

The Do 24 was originally designed for export use - specifically for Dutch use in the Netherlands East Indies. The type was in many respects an enlarged and modernised derivative of the Do 18, but with three conventional tractor engines above the wing, and with twin 'endplate' fins instead of a single central fin.

With the invasion of the Low Countries in 1940, the licence manufacturing plant for the Do 24 fell into German hands, along with three (Wright Cyclone-engined) completed aircraft. Two German-built, Jumo-powered prototypes had already been pressed

into service, and were used in support of the invasions of Denmark and Norway. The three new (ex-Dutch) Do 24s were evaluated for Seenotdienst use, and after the Battle the type entered service in large numbers.

BATTLE OF BRITAIN DO 24 UNITS	
KGzbV 108	See Do 24V1, 2

HEINKEL HE 111

Specifications: Crew: 5 Max Speed: 405km/h (252mph) Range: 1930km (1199 miles) Armament: 7 7.92mm (0.31in) machine guns   **Germany**

The Heinkel 111 is probably the best known of the German bombers in the Battle of Britain, though it was out-numbered and out-performed by the newer Ju 88, and was probably less effective than the Do 17. The He 111 was typical of the Luftwaffe's bombers - fast by 1930s standards, but showing its age and best suited to tactical operations under conditions of air superiority. The aircraft was poorly suited for the role it was called upon to carry out in the Battle of Britain - carrying too small a bombload and proving much too vulnerable to fighters. A great aircraft in its day, the He 111 should have been replaced by faster, heavier, four-engined bombers by mid-1940, but such aircraft had failed to materialise, and the He 111 was forced to 'soldier on' for the remainder of the war.

The Heinkel 111 was ostensibly designed as a high-speed passenger transport and mailplane, but future conversion to the bomber role was the real design driver. Thus the first prototype (which flew in early 1935) had three provisional gun positions and provision for a 2200lb bombload, though the second and fourth prototypes, which were shown off in public, were configured as ten-seat airliners, with a 'smoking compartment' in the former bomb bay! But even these aircraft were not what they seemed. The second prototype, for example, was ostentatiously decked out in Lufthansa colours and used for what the airline called 'route proving'. It later transpired that the He 111V-2 was actually a well-equipped photo reconnaissance aircraft, much used for target photography in preparation for the Blitzkrieg, until it crashed. Early versions of the aircraft (the He 111B, D, E and F) fought in Spain, but had been withdrawn from the frontline by the Battle of Britain. Even as early as September 1939, 749 of the 808 He 111s on charge were

HEINKEL 111 UNITS IN THE BATTLE OF BRITAIN

SQUADRON	TYPE	CODES	BASES	SQUADRON	TYPE	CODES	BASES
Stab KG 1	He 111H	V4+*A	Rosieres en Santerre	III/KG 53	He 111H-2,3,4	A1+*D, R, S, T	Lille-Nord
				Stab KG 55	He 111P-2	G1+*A	Villacoublay
I/KG 1	He 111H	V4+*B, H, K, L	Montdidier	I/KG 55	He 111H, P	G1+*B, H, K, L	Dreux
II/KG 1	He 111H-1, 2?	V4+*C, M, N, P	Montdidier	II/KG 55	He 111H-3, P	G1+*C, M, N, P	Chartres
III/KG 1	He 111H-2	V4+*D, R, S, T	Rosieres en Santerre	III/KG 55	He 111P-2	G1+*D, R, S, T	Villacoublay
				Kampfgrüppe 100	He 111H-1,2,3	6N+	Vannes-Meucon
I/KG 3	He 111H-2	5K+*B, H, K, L	Le Culot	Kampfgrüppe 126	He 111H		Marx
Stab KG 4	He 111P	5J+*A	Soesterberg	1(F)/120	He 111H		Stavanger
I/KG 4	He 111H-4	5J+*B, H, K, L	Soesterberg	1(F)/121	He 111H		Stavanger/Aalborg
II/KG 4	He 111P-2	5J+*C, M, N, P	Eindhoven	3(F)/121			North-West France
III/KG 4	He 111P	5J+*D, R, S, T	Schipol	2(F)/122			Brussels/Melsbroek
				3(F)/122	He 111H-2		Eindhoven
Stab KG 26	He 111P	1H+*A	Gilze-Rijen	4(F)/122			Brussels
I/KG 26	He 111H-3,4	1H+*B, H, K, L	Moerbeke, Courtrai	5(F)/122	He 111H		Haute-Fontain
II/KG 26	He 111H-1,3,4,5	1H+*C, M, N, P					
III/KG 26	He 111H-3,4	1H+*D, R, S, T	Gilze-Rijen	Westa Kette X Flk	He 111H		Stavanger
				1(F)/Aufkl.Gr.OkL	He 111H/P		Berlin
Stab KG 27	He 111P	1G+*A	Tours	2(F)/Aufkl.Gr.OkL	He 111P		
I/KG 27	He 111P	1G+*B, H, K, L	Tours	3(F)/Aufkl.Gr.OkL	He 111P		Stavanger
II/KG 27	He 111P, H-3	1G+*C, M, N, P	Tours	Westa 1 ObdL	He 111H		Oldenburg
III/KG 27	He 111P	1G+*D, R, S, T	Tours	Westa 2 ObdL	He 111H		Brest/Lanveoc-Poulmic
Stab KG 53	He 111H-2	A1+*A	Lille-Nord	Westa 26 ObdL	He 111H		Brussels-Grimberghen
I/KG 53	He 111H-2	A1+*B, H, K, L	Lille-Nord				
II/KG 53	He 111H-2,3	A1+*C, M, N, P	Lille-Nord	Westa 51	He 111H		Buc bei Versailles

He 111Ps and He 111Hs. These were the first He 111 versions to feature the redesigned fully glazed nose section, in addition to a streamlined ventral gondola, a 4410lb bombload and a straight-tapered wing planform. The bombs were accomodated in four vertical cells, four on each side of a central gangway, each capable of carrying a single 250kg bomb. In the new variants the pilot sat offset to port, with the forward-firing nose cannon to starboard, where it could be fired by the navigator. The heavily-glazed nose offered superb all-round visibility (apart from the heavy framing) but was some six feet ahead of the pilot's eyes and was prone to reflections at night, and in some lights. For landing in such conditions, the pilot could slide back a roof panel, elevate his seat and sit higher, with his head projecting above the normal nose glazing, protected from the slipstream by a small retractable windscreen. The He 111P and He 111H were extremely similar, and differed only in their powerplants. The He 111P was powered by a pair of DB601 engines, but because of demand for these for the Bf 109 and Bf 110, the He 111H was designed using a pair of Jumo 211A-1s.

The He 111P-4 and He 111H-2 had improved defensive armament, with an additional forward-firing machine gun, MG 15 machine guns in the 'beam positions' and (on some aircraft) a remotely operated 'scare gun' in the tailcone. The new variants also introduced a fifth crew member (a gunner), increased armour, and a reduced bombload. The port bomb cell was occupied by extra fuel and oil tanks, but twin carriers could be added below the new tanks.

The He 111P-6 and H-3 introduced more powerful engines, the P-6 with 1175hp DB601Ns, the H-3 with 1200hp Jumo 211D-1s. But by the Battle of Britain the He 111 was recognised as being well past its prime, and was being replaced by the Ju 88. Only four Kampfgeschwader remained fully-equipped with He 111s by Adlertag, and these suffered alarmingly high loss rates, though they were prized for carrying a heavier bombload than any other Luftwaffe bomber. Once expected to avoid heavy casualties by dint of its high speed, the He 111 was, by 1940 a lumbering leviathan, markedly inferior to the Ju 88, and less successful than the Do 17. The aircraft was remarkably robust, however, and easy to keep serviceable. It was an accurate bombing platform, and its vast wing gave it superb load-carrying capability. The He 111 could roam far from its bases, and its resilience meant that many aircraft limped home, even after being riddled with 0.303in hits. This was a mixed blessing however, since the Heinkels normally made it home only to crash land on or near their airfields. They were seldom easily repaired, and morale on the bomber bases was not well served by aircraft which returned home with dead or dying aircrew aboard.

HEINKEL HE 59

Specifications: Crew: 4 Max Speed: 220km/h (137mph) Range: 1530km (950 miles) Armament: 3 7.92mm machine guns   **Germany**

Designed as a reconnaissance bomber, the He 59 first flew in September 1931, and had been withdrawn from operational use by the time war broke out. The aircraft were then used for training and (in He 59C-2 form) for search and rescue duties. During the Norwegian and Dutch campaigns, some He 59s were used for transport missions, and for landing assault squads on a canal to allow them to capture a bridge. But by the Battle of Britain, the He 59 was a search and rescue aircraft, pure and simple. Variants in use were the He 59C-2 and the He 59D-1 (which combined the roles of the SAR He 59C-2 and the He 59C-1 trainer).

While British pilots were shocked when reports emerged of German aircraft shooting at pilots as they descended by parachute, the Germans were equally scandalised by RAF attacks on their unarmed search and rescue aircraft (usually He 59s). At the start of the Battle these were unarmed, civil-registered, white-painted and bore huge red crosses – not the most inconspicuous paint scheme. Britain's propagandists insisted that the aircraft were also used for mine-laying and landing agents, and refused to allow them free passage. After a few He 59s were lost to RAF fighters the aircraft were hastily camouflaged, and defensive guns were introduced.

German records show that 21 of these aircraft were lost to enemy action between July and the end of October, with others failing to return after collisions, sea landing accidents, and, in one case, landing in a minefield.

Due to incomplete records that were lost or damaged during the war, it is not possible to determine the units involved.

HEINKEL HE 115

Specifications: Crew: 3 Max Speed: 295km/h (183mph) Range: 2600km (1616 miles) Armament: 2 7.92mm machine guns   **Germany**

The He 115 was originally designed as a patrol, torpedo and bomber aircraft, though it was always too slow, and too lightly armed to perform all of these roles credibly. The first aircraft made its maiden flight in August 1937, and the type soon set a number of 'speed with load' records. Various sub-variants were produced, and the type saw useful service in the invasion of Norway. The type was used for anti-convoy attacks, mine-laying, and maritime reconnaissance, playing a peripheral role in the Battle of Britain.

BATTLE OF BRITAIN HE 115 UNITS

SQUADRON	CODES	BASES	SQUADRON	CODES	BASES
1./KüFlGr 106			3./KüFlGr 506		
1./KüFlGr 406	K6+*H		7./KüFlGr 606		
Stab/KüFlGr 506			1./KüFlGr 706		
1./KüFlGr 506			7./KüFlGr 906	8L+*H	
2./KüFlGr 506					

MESSERSCHMITT BF 110

Specifications: Crew: 2/3 Max Speed: 560km/h (248mph) Range: 1095km (680 miles) Armament:2 20mm, 5 7.9mm (0.31 in) MGs   **Germany**

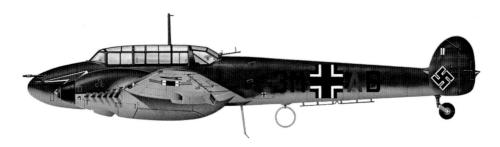

The concept of a dedicated 'bomber destroyer' was seductive - in the inter-war years few could imagine bombers operating with a single-seat fighter escort, so an aircraft which combined speed and a heavy weight of fire promised a great deal. But in Germany the 'bomber destroyer' concept was taken one step further to produce a 'Zerstörer' (Destroyer) whose task would be not only to destroy enemy bombers in friendly airspace, but to clear a path for bombers through enemy airspace. This would inevitably bring the Zerstörer face to face with enemy single-seat fighters, which would be smaller, lighter and carrying less fuel.

This did not necessarily invalidate the concept, as was shown by the Lockheed P-38 Lightning, which proved able to escort friendly bombers over enormous distances, and then to fight enemy fighters on favourable terms. Britain's Westland Whirlwind could probably have performed equally well had it been given a better powerplant, which effectively limited the type to low level attacks. But these successful long range fighters were all single-seaters, and every

effort had been made to keep their weight, and size low, and to ensure that agility did not suffer unduly.

The Messerschmitt Bf 110 had a modern stressed-skin structure, with Handley Page automatic leading edge slats and hydraulically-actuated slotted flaps. Its engines (in the Bf 110C used in the Battle) were DB601s, and these drove three-bladed constant speed propellors. The Bf 110 was undeniably modern, and as a high speed light bomber or recce aircraft, the aircraft could have been formidable. The biggest mistake made by its designers was the two-seat configuration, since this necessitated carrying not only the 'dead weight' of a navigator/radio operator, but also his seat, oxygen, armour, an intercom system, and the extra fuel needed to carry the weight. It also made sense to provide a (heavy) long range radio, extra navigation equipment (more than the usual single map!) and even a rearward facing machine gun and ammunition. As a single-seat long range fighter, the Bf 110 could have been made considerably smaller and lighter, even with two engines.

As it was the Bf 110 had a heavier empty weight than a British Blenheim bomber, and though it was elegantly streamlined, it was never as fast as it needed to be, and was too sluggish to manoeuvre with single-seat fighters. As a fighter the aircraft was a non-starter.

Unfortunately, during the Battle of Britain the Bf 110 fell victim to the Luftwaffe's propaganda machine. It created a record of 'invincibility' in Poland, the Low Countries and the Battle of France. Senior Luftwaffe officers had helped create the Zerstörer (including Göring himself) and they were more than happy to hear their expectations confirmed. Göring even let his own nephew fly Bf 110s, losing his relative on 11 July when he fell victim to No.87 Squadron's Hurricanes over Portland.

In fact, the Bf 110 had performed poorly in Poland, with many aircraft falling to the obsolescent P.11 fighters. In Scandinavia the story was much the same, with some losses to Gladiator biplanes! The aircraft was devastatingly effective against unescorted British bombers, but the Battle of France proved a less happy experience. Bf 110s did manage to down French Morane single-seaters, and some Hurricanes, but in fighter-versus-fighter combat, it was clear that the big Messerschmitt was out-classed.

When it came to the Battle of Britain, the Zerstörergrüppen began with 237 serviceable aircraft, and lost an astonishing 223 during the course of the Battle. Losses were, in fact, so heavy that the Bf 110 Geschwaders could not be maintained at full strength, and it was this that forced their withdrawal from the Battle, and re-assignment to night fighter, coastal patrol and convoy escort duties.

BATTLE OF BRITAIN BF 110 UNITS

SQUADRON	TYPE	CODES	
Erprobungsgruppe 210	Bf 110C-6,D-0	S9+	

SQUADRON	TYPE	CODES	BASES
V(Z)/LG 1	Bf 110C,D	L1+*F, X, Y, Z	Caen
Stab/ZG 2		2S+*A	Toussus le Noble
7./LG 2	Bf 110C-5		
Stab ZG 2	Bf 110C	2S+*A	Toussus-le-Noble
I/ZG 2	Bf 110D	2S+*B, H, K, L	Caen-Carpiquet
II/ZG 2	Bf 110C-2,5,D	2S+*C, M, N, P	Guyancourt
Stab/ZG 26	Bf 110C	U8+*A	Lille
I/ZG 26	Bf 110C/D	U8+*B, H, K, L	Yvrench-St Omer
II/ZG 26	Bf 110C	U8+*C, M, N, P	Crécy-St Omer
III/ZG 26	Bf 110C-2,4	U8+*D, R, S, T	Barly-Arques
Stab/ZG 76	Bf 110C	M8+*A	Laval
I/ZG 76		M8+*B, H, K, L	Stavanger-Forus
II/ZG 76		M8+*C, M, N, P	Abbeville-Yvrench
III/ZG 76		M8+*D, R, S, T	Laval
4(F)/14			Normandy
1(F)/22			Lille
3(F)/31	Bf 110C		St Brieux
4(F)/121	Bf 110C-4		
4(F)/122			Brussels

JUNKERS JU 87

Specifications: Crew: 2 Max Speed: 383km/h (238mph) Range: 790km (491 miles) Armament: 3 7.92mm (0.31in) machine guns   **Germany**

The Junkers Ju 87 was an exceptionally pleasant aircraft to fly, combining light, well harmonised controls with good all-round visibility and excellent manoeuvrability. It was ugly and cumbersome looking, and laden with character and charisma. The aircraft had amassed an enviable combat record in Spain and Poland, operating as a type of 'Flying Artillery'. But even in Poland, the Ju 87's flaws were plain to see. For while the Ju 87 was an exceptionally accurate way of placing bombs on target (with twice the accuracy of its closest rivals) the aircraft was also frighteningly vulnerable to any enemy defences, and especially to enemy fighters.

The Luftwaffe gained an early enthusiasm for dive-bombing even before its existence was officially acknowledged. Udet bought a pair of Curtiss BFC-2 Hawk IIs for dive bombing trials in 1933, and personally evaluated the SB2C Helldiver, while dive bombing was already one of the primary roles of the Junkers K-47. The Henschel Hs 123 biplane was ordered as an interim dive bomber, and a requirement for a definitive dive bomber aeroplane was issued in January 1935. This led directly to the design of the Ju 87, whose prototype made its maiden flight in early 1935.

The Ju 87 looked anachronistic even before it flew, with its fixed, 'trousered' undercarriage and angular appearance. The competing Heinkel He 118 was faster, more manoeuvrable and more modern, but the sole prototype was destroyed during competitive trials, leaving the Ju 87 as the overall winner of the competition.

Ju 87s fought with conspicuous success in Spain, but the type was felt to be almost obsolescent as World War II broke out. Even the arrival of the Ju 87B, with its more powerful 1200 hp Jumo 211Da engine and minor aerodynamic refinements was felt to be a step which would delay the type's inevitable retirement very little.

But the almost complete lack of air opposition in Poland and the Low Countries (and the Stuka's corresponding success) led some to re-evaluate the aircraft's capabilities. Some senior officers began to think that perhaps it was still a viable weapon. Proper operational analysis would have shown that when the Ju 87 had come up against enemy air opposition it had generally performed very poorly indeed. The air operations over Dunkirk would have reinforced this point - had people not been too busy celebrating the historic overall victory over France. It was too easy to see only the Ju 87's strengths - its ability to spread fear and panic among enemy soldiers and refugees, its pinpoint accuracy, and its ability to respond rapidly to demands for close air support. But Dunkirk showed that even when heavily escorted, the Ju 87 was hopelessly vulnerable, being too slow, too cumbersome, with inadequate armour and inadequate defensive armament. The aircraft's lack of range had been partially addressed, however – relatively large numbers of improved Ju 87B-2s and longer-range Ju 87Rs were available among the 316 Stukas gathered for the Battle.

The Stuka played its part in the Kanalkampf, attacking Channel shipping and some coastal targets. Most of the Stuka raids in early July were quick 'hit-and-run' raids, often heavily escorted. Once the Ju 87s turned their attentions to Fighter Command's airfields, the RAF had even more time to react, and the Stuka's losses increased steadily. More often than not, formations of Ju 87s would lose up to half their number, or would be forced to turn back without attacking their targets. On 18 August the Luftwaffe lost 17 Stukas, and the type was withdrawn from active operations after a last dive-bombing attack on 30 August. The only units retained were II/StG 1, II/StG 2, and IV (St)/LG 1 for possible night operations, and I/StG 3 for anti-shipping use. But the Stuka's part in the Battle was over, apart from sporadic anti-convoy missions flown in early November.

JU 87 STUKA UNITS OF THE BATTLE OF BRITAIN

SQUADRON	TYPE	CODES	BASES
Stab/StG 1	Ju 87B	A5+*A	Angers
I/StG 1	Ju 87R	A5+*B, H, K, L	Angers
II/StG 1	Ju 87B	A5+*C, M, N, P	Pas de Calais
III/StG 1	Ju 87B-2	A5+*D, R, S, T	Angers
Stab/StG 2	Ju 87B	T6+*A	St Malo
I/StG 2	Ju 87B	T6+*B, H, K, L	St Malo
II/StG 2	Ju 87R-1, B7	T6+*C, M, N, P	Lannion
III/StG 2	Ju 87B-1	T6+*D, R, S, T	
Stab/StG 3	Ju 87B	S7+*A	Caen
I/StG 3	Ju 87B	S7+*B, H, K, L	Caen
I/StG 76	Ju 87B	F1+*B, H, K, L	
II/StG 76	Ju 87B	F1+*C, M, N, P	
Stab/StG 77	Ju 87B	S2+*A	Caen
I/StG 77	Ju 87B	S2+*B, H, K, L	Caen
II/StG 77	Ju 87B	S2+*C, M, N, P	Caen
III/StG 77	Ju 87B	S2+*D, R, S, T	Caen
I(St)/TrGr 186	Ju 87B	+*B, H, K, L	
IV (St)/LG 1	Ju 87B-2	L1+*E, U, V, W	Tramecourt

JUNKERS JU 88

Specifications: Crew: 4 Max Speed: 470km/h (292mph) Range:2730km (1696 miles) Armament: 7 7.92mm (0.31in) machine guns   **Germany**

The Junkers Ju 88 was one of the outstanding aircraft of the Second World War, and despite being designed originally as a dedicated fast day bomber ('Schnellbomber'), later became known for its near-legendary versatility. This was a direct result of the aircraft's superb performance characteristics, which in turn resulted from its revolutionary technical innovations. When the original (anti-Nazi) Professor Junkers was replaced, his successor, Heinrich Koppenberg, hired American engineers to supervise his team, laying the foundations for a genuinely modern bomber. Dive brakes were added below each wing during development, as a result of combat experience with other types in Spain and Poland, which showed that dive attacks dramatically improved accuracy, and the fact that dive-bombing was fashionable in Luftwaffe circles.

The Ju 88 prototype made its maiden flight on 21 December 1936, and soon demonstrated great potential. In March 1939 the

fifth prototype set a 1000km (621 mile) closed circuit record of 517km/h (321,25mph), whilst carrying a 2000kg (4409lb) payload. The initial production version of the aircraft, the Ju 88A-1, was entering service just as the Second World War broke out, and the type flew its first operational missions in late September 1939, but was too late to see service in the Polish campaign.

The Ju 88 had a heavier empty weight than either the Dornier Do 17 or the Heinkel He 111, but it had 1200 hp Jumo 211B-1 engines from the start, and its airframe was exceptionally clean and aerodynamic. The aircraft carried 28 50kg bombs internally and could carry two 500kg bombs or two 250kg bombs below each inner wing. Defensive armament consisted of a fixed forward-firing 7.9mm machine gun operated by the pilot, with two similar weapons firing aft through limited arcs of fire, one in the cockpit roof and one in the ventral gondola. A second gun was soon added

JU 88 UNITS IN THE BATTLE OF BRITAIN

SQUADRON	TYPE	CODES	BASES	SQUADRON	TYPE	CODES	BASES
III/KG 1	Ju 88A-1	V4+*D, R, S, T	Rosieres en Santerre	III/KG 77	Ju 88A-1	+*D, R, S, T	Laon
III/KG 4	Ju 88A-1,5	5J+*D, R, S, T	Schipol	Kampfgrüppe 806	Ju 88A		Nantes, Caen
Stab KG 30	Ju 88A-1	4D+*A	Brussels	Stab LG 1	Ju 88A	L1+*A	Orléans-Bricy
I/KG 30	Ju 88C, A-5	4D+*B, H, K, L	Brussels	I(K)/LG 1	Ju 88A-5	L1+*B, H, K, L	Orléans-Bricy
II/KG 30	Ju 88A-1,5	4D+*C, M, N, P	Gilze-Rijen	II(K)/LG 1	Ju 88A-1	L1+*C, M, N, P	Orléans-Bricy
III/KG 30	Ju 88A-5,C-2	4D+*D, R, S, T		III(K)/LG 1	Ju 88A-5	L1+*D, R, S, T	Chateaudun
Stab KG 40	Ju 88A-1	??+*A	Brest-Guipavas	1(F)/120			Stavanger
Stab KG 51	Ju 88A-1	9K+*A	Orly	1(F)/121			Stavanger/Aalborg
I/KG 51	Ju 88A-1	9K+*B, H, K, L	Melun	3(F)/121			North-West France
II/KG 51	Ju 88A-1	9K+*C, M, N, P	Orly	4(F)/121			Villacoublay
III/KG 51	Ju 88A-1	9K+*D, R, S, T	Étampes	1(F)/123			
				1(F)/122			
Stab KG 54	Ju 88A-1	B3+*A	Evreux	2(F)/123			Brussels/Melsbroek
I/KG 54	Ju 88A-1	B3+*B, H, K, L	Evreux	3(F)/122			Eindhoven
II/KG 54	Ju 88A-1	B3+*C, M, N, P	St André	4(F)/122			Brussels
				5(F)/122			Haute-Fontain
II/KG 76	Ju 88A-1	+*C, M, N, P	Creil	1(F)/123			
				2(F)/123			
Stab KG 77	Ju 88A-1	+*A	Laon	3(F)/123			Buc
I/KG 77	Ju 88A-1	+*B, H, K, L	Laon				
II/KG 77	Ju 88A-1,5	+*C, M, N, P	Asch	1(F)/Aufkl.Gr.OkL	Ju 88A		Berlin

in the cockpit roof, and eventually two more lateral firing guns were added. But even with all of these weapons, the aircraft was not well-equipped to defend itself against Allied fighters, as active operations proved. One man (the already-overworked Flight Engineer) had to operate four of the machine guns, theoretically hopping from one to the other as an enemy fighter flashed past. Needless to say, this was hardly a viable proposition, and the plethora of guns merely added weight and expense. A single gun with a better arc of fire (and preferably in a powered turret) would undoubtedly have been more effective.

For the Battle of France, the Ju 88 equipped one three Gruppe Geschwader, and four Gruppen within other Geschwaders. By Adlertag, the Luftwaffe included 13 Gruppen of Ju 88s, and these were able to play a decisive part in the Battle of Britain, highlights including a mass raid on Portsmouth by 63 Ju 88s on 12 August. The Ju 88 was far and away the best of the Luftwaffe bombers operating during the Battle of Britain, and suffered a correspondingly lower attrition rate than either the He 111 and Do 17. The aircraft was vulnerable to single seat fighters, of course, but there were numerous instances documented where Ju 88s were able to escape from an attack by diving away from their pursuers at very high speed.

The original Ju 88A-1 which formed the backbone of the Kampfgeschwaderen during the Battle of Britain were prone to a number of problems, some relatively minor, others much more serious. These led to the imposition of a number of fairly restrictive limitations on speed and manoeuvring. These limitations were not applied to the later Ju 88A-4, though problems with this version's 1350 hp Jumo 211J engines meant that it did not reach the frontline until after the Battle, and nor did its specialist reconnaissance equivalent, the Ju 88D-1. Fortunately, an interim 'improved Ju 88' was available to the Luftwaffe in time for Adlertag. This was the Ju 88A-5 (with the Ju 88D-2 as the recce equivalent), which featured a longer-span, strengthened wing with inset metal-skinned ailerons, and a much-increased bombload. For the first time, the Luftwaffe had a Ju 88 not choked by artificial limitations, and the Ju 88A-5 performed with great distinction. The final variant to participate in the Battle was the initial reconnaissance Ju 88D-0, a handful of which flew from Norway.

Following the Battle of Britain, the Ju 88 continued from strength to strength, being built in a bewildering array of sub-types,

and being successfully adapted by Junkers to perform virtually every conceivable role that an aircraft could fulfil in World War II. The next, Ju 88C, series were in effect heavy fighters, with solid noses mounting three MG 17 machine guns and a 20mm MG FF cannon. Two additional MG 15 machine guns were mounted for greater defensive armament. The Ju 88-C6 and C7s were nightfighter variants, and proved the type to be highly effective in this specialist role. The Ju 88R series were night-fighters uprated with the BMW 801MA engines, which had become more freely available by this stage of the war.

The Ju 88D series were long-range reconnaissance aircraft based on the Ju88A-4. The Ju 88G series were the definitive night-fighters of the latter stages of the war. Equipped with airborne interception radar and bristling with weapons, the Ju 88Gs were extremely formidable, and took a heavy toll of RAF night bombers over Germany, with the assistance of German radar and other night-fighter control systems. They were followed into service by a few Ju 88H aircraft, versions with a lengthened fuselage, which gave the airframe greater internal fuel capacity. The Ju 88H-1 reconnaissance and Ju 88H-2 fighter aircraft thus had a significantly increased range.

By the latter stages of the war the Russian tank forces were overwhelming those of the Wehrmacht, and as a measure to help stem the Russian tide the Luftwaffe therefore brought into service the Ju 88P tank-busting airframe, developed from the Ju 88A-4. The Ju 88P-1 mounted a 75mm PaK 40 cannon, and the Ju 88P-2 to P-4 versions carried other types of anti-tank armament.

As Allied fighters became more and more capable towards the end of the war, German losses began to rise, and the final production versions of the Ju 88 were an attempt to redress parity. The Ju 88S was a high-performance bomber, whilst the Ju 88T was a similarly-uprated photo-reconnaissance platform.

When production ended shortly before the war's end, almost 15,000 examples of the Ju 88 had been built, emphasising the significant role that the aircraft played for the Luftwaffe throughout the duration of the conflict. The type even saw some limited service with the reformed French air force after the war, as an interim measure before French manufacturers could build the next generation of French bomber aircraft. Had the Luftwaffe had more Ju 88s for the Battle of Britain, it may not have turned the tide towards Germany, but Britain would have suffered far greater damage.

FOCKE WULF FW 200 KONDOR

Specifications: Crew: 6 Max Speed: 360km/h (224mph) Range: 4440km (2795 miles) Armt: 1 20mm cannon, 2 13mm, 2 7.9mm MGs **Germany**

The Fw 200 was designed by Kurt Tank as a long range airliner, and attracted little interest from the Luftwaffe when it first flew on 27 July 1937, although the third prototype was adapted as Adolf Hitler's personal transport. Able to fly the Atlantic 'non-stop', the aircraft had obvious potential as a maritime patrol aircraft, and Japan ordered a maritime patrol derivative. When war loomed, the planned Luftwaffe long-range maritime reconnaissance/strike aircraft (the He 177) was far from ready, and the Japanese Fw 200 was pressed into Luftwaffe service as the Fw 200C.

KG 40 began flying missions against British shipping on 8 April 1940, transferring to Bordeaux in June, from where it participated in the Battle of Britain. The unit flew solo long range sweeps, usually West of Cornwall and on up to Norway, from where the aircraft returned a few days later. The unit's aircraft participated in night

bombing attacks on Liverpool and Birkenhead in late August, but its principal role remained anti-shipping.

By October the Fw 200Cs had accounted for 90,000 tonnes, and on 26 October a KG 40 Fw 200 captained by Oberleutnant Bernhard Jope attacked the liner *Empress of Britain*, south-west of Donegal. A U-Boat finished-off the crippled vessel by torpedo. The Kondor remained in service until the end of the war.

BATTLE OF BRITAIN FW 200 UNITS		
SQUADRON	CODES	BASES
Stab/KG 40		Bordeaux
I/KG 40		Bordeaux

MESSERSCHMITT BF 109

Specifications: Crew: 1 Max Speed: 560km/h (348mph) Range: 660km (410 miles) Armament: 2 20mm, 2 7.92mm (0.31in) MGs   **Germany**

During the Battle of Britain the Luftwaffe used a single type of single-seat fighter - the Messerschmitt Bf 109. These were augmented by heavier, longer-range, twin-engined Bf 110s, but these were to prove inadequate in the face of determined opposition, and the Bf 109 was destined to bear the brunt of the Luftwaffe's air campaign against the RAF. On May 10, when the Luftwaffe had begun its war in the West, it had included 1,016 Bf 109s, and after surprisingly heavy losses over France and the Low Countries, and after surprisingly modest (and slow) production of attrition replacements, was able to muster 809 aircraft (656 of which were serviceable) on 20 July. By August 10, three days before Göring's ambitious Adlertag, the numbers had risen to 934 Bf 109Es, 805 of which were serviceable. But this was far short of the number necessary to seriously challenge Fighter Command, which was able to increase its strength as the Battle continued, thanks to rapid production and repair, while Luftwaffe fighter strength steadily 'bled away'. But despite this, the Bf 109 remained a deadly and much-feared adversary, and rightly so.

The prototype of Messerschmitt's Bf 109 made its maiden flight in September 1935, powered by a British Rolls Royce Kestrel engine. Subsequent prototypes used a Junkers Jumo 210 engine, and deliveries of production Bf 109Bs began in 1937, initially to JG 132 'Richthofen' and 2/Jagdgruppe 88 of the Condor Legion, fighting in Spain. Subsequent versions used variable pitch propellors and more powerful engines, culminating in the Bf 109E, powered by the 1,100-hp DB601A engine.

The Bf 109E-3 and E-4 sub-variants were the principal types in use during the Battle of Britain, and armament was a pair of nose-mounted 7.9-mm MG17 machine guns with a pair of MG 17s (Bf 109E-3) or 20-mm MG FF cannon (Bf 109E-4) in the wings. The E-4 had no provision for a third engine-mounted cannon, and by 1940 this was seldom fitted to the E-3 either. Some earlier Bf 109Es remained in use, including some E-1s, a few of which were modified as fighter-bombers under the designation E-1/B, as were some E-4/Bs and the E-7, which could carry an external fuel drop tank, though these were not routinely used until after the Battle.

BATTLE OF BRITAIN BF 109 UNITS

SQUADRON	TYPE	BASES	SQUADRON	TYPE	BASES
Stab JG 2	Bf 109E	Beaumont le Roger	II/JG 51	Bf 109E	Marquise-Ouest
I/JG 2	Bf 109E	Beaumont le Roger	III/JG 51	Bf 109E	St.Omer-Clairmarais
II/JG 2	Bf 109E	Beaumont le Roger			
III/JG 2	Bf 109E	Le Havre	Stab JG 52	Bf 109E	Coquelles
			I/JG 52	Bf 109E	Coquelles
Stab JG 3	Bf 109E	Wierre au Bois	II/JG 52	Bf 109E	Peuplingues
I/JG 3	Bf 109E	Grandvilliers	III/JG 52	Bf 109E	Zerbst
II/JG 3	Bf 109E	Samer			
III/JG 3	Bf 109E	Desvres u Le Touquet	Stab JG 53	Bf 109E	Cherbourg
			I/JG 53	Bf 109E	Rennes
Stab JG 26	Bf 109E	Audembert	II/JG 53	Bf 109E	Dinan
I/JG 26	Bf 109E	Audembert	III/JG 53	Bf 109E	Brest
II/JG 26	Bf 109E	Marquise-Ost			
III/JG 26	Bf 109E	Caffiers	Stab JG 54	Bf 109E	Campagne-les-Guines
			I/JG 54	Bf 109E	Guines-en-Calaises
Stab JG 27	Bf 109E	Cherbourg-Ouest	II/JG 54	Bf 109E	Hermelingen
I/JG27	Bf 109E	Plumetôt	III/JG 54	Bf 109E	Guines-en-Calaises
II/JG 27	Bf 109E	Crépon			
III/JG 27	Bf 109E	Arcques	Stab JG 77	Bf 109E	
			I/JG 77	Bf 109E	
Stab JG 51	Bf 109E	Wissant	II/JG 77	Bf 109E	Stavanger Trondheim
I/JG 51	Bf 109E	Pihen bei Calais	II(S)/LG 2	Bf 109E-7	Böblingen

Many have suggested that the Bf 109, in its 'Emil' form, was the best fighter aircraft of its generation. Certainly, the 109 enjoyed a margin of superiority over previous-generation aircraft like the Hawker Hurricane, though this superiority was never as marked as has sometimes been claimed. Many Bf 109Es fell to Hurricanes, and even to fixed-gear, open cockpit PZL P.11s. This was hardly the mark of total superiority.

But the Bf 109E was clearly superior to the old-fashioned Hurricane, in most respects, and its relative strengths usually outweighed its few disadvantages. Against the Spitfire, it was a very different story. The extent of the Bf 109's inferiority has been camouflaged by a few very obvious advantages. The Spitfire I began the war with a fixed-pitch, two-blade propeller, and only received a fully-variable, constant-speed propeller as the Battle of Britain began. The Spitfire I also relied on inadequate rifle-calibre machine gun armament, which quite clearly packed a smaller punch than the Bf 109's cannon. The Bf 109's direct fuel injection also allowed the pilot to push into a dive without the engine cutting out.

But these 'advantages' were less important than has sometimes been inferred. The Bf 109Es seldom used the troublesome engine-mounted cannon, so had only two 20-mm cannon, rather than three, and these fired very slowly. The Bf 109Es much-vaunted ability to 'push-over' into a dive was also less significant than has sometimes been claimed. Human pilots do not withstand negative g easily, and if a Bf 109 pilot wanted to enter a steep dive, it was actually quicker to snap inverted and pull hard, pulling positive g while inverted. In any case, the ability to run away quickly is of limited usefulness in shooting down the enemy.

The Spitfire (and even the Hurricane) enjoyed superior handling characteristics and greater manoeuvrability throughout most of the envelope, with lighter control forces at high speed, lower wing loading, and were equipped with rudder trimmers. The British fighters also lacked any equivalent to the Bf 109E's terrible automatic opening leading edge slats and were able to out-turn the Bf 109 at all altitudes. The British pilots also enjoyed better visibility from their cockpits, and bulletproof windscreens were more commonly fitted.

If the Bf 109E enjoyed any greater success in action than the Spitfire, as it seems to have done during the early part of the war, then it would seem safe to attribute this success to the superior training and tactical expertise of its pilots. Once RAF pilots began to obtain combat experience, they were every bit as successful as their German counterparts, and once the Bf 109s were ordered to 'stick close' to the bombers, the tide of the battle turned decisively away from them. Whatever the relative merits of the Bf 109E and the Spitfire I, it is now clear that the Messerschmitt had reached the apogee of its development potential, while much of the Spitfire's potential remained unguessed at. There were subsequent Bf 109 variants, but while faster, and sometimes packing a heavier punch, they were no more agile than the Emil, while RAF fighters underwent all-round improvements.

The next version of the Messerschmitt fighter was too late to influence the course of the Battle of Britain. This was the Bf 109F, which was redesigned to exploit extra engine power. The Friedrich was more streamlined, lightened by the reduction in armament to a single engine-mounted cannon and two nose-mounted machine guns, and had extended-span rounded wingtips. A handful of early Bf 109F-1s were delivered to Stab/JG 51 for evaluation, and these were flown in action. Teething troubles meant that full service entry did not take place until March 1941. Introduction of the Spitfire V variant more than restored that aircraft's superiority.

ABOVE: GUNTHER LÜTZOW, A GERMAN ACE OF THE BATTLE OF BRITAIN WITH JAGDGESCHWADER 3.

ARADO AR 196

Specifications: Crew: 2 Max Speed: 320km/h (199mph) Range: 1070km (665 miles) Armament: 2 7.92mm (0.31in) machine guns   **Germany**

The Arado Ar 196 was originally designed as a floatplane for shipborne use. The first of four prototypes flew in 1937, and the four aircraft were evaluated with two float arrangements. The conventional twin-float arrangement (on V1 and V2) was eventually selected over the single main float with stabilisers configuration.

The Ar 196 was subsequently used by a number of coastal 'land-based' units, principally for reconnaissance, but also for light attack, using fixed wing-mounted machine guns and small bombs. The type was also pressed into use for search and rescue, though its configuration meant that its open-sea landing capability was negligible, and landing to pick up survivors was seldom an option. In practice the role usually fell to the Heinkel He 59.

BATTLE OF BRITAIN AR 196 UNITS

SQUADRON	CODES	BASES
1./Bo.Fl.Gr.196	Ar 196A	Wilhelmshaven

CANT Z1007.BIS

Specifications: Crew: 5 Max Speed: 466km/h (290mph) Range: 1750km (1087 miles) Armament: 2 12.7mm and 2 7.7mm machine guns   **Italy**

A single squadron of reconnaissance aircraft formed part of Mussolini's Corpo Aereo Italiano, deployed to Belgium to participate in the closing stages of the Battle of Britain. This was equipped with the Cant Z.1007bis Alcione (Kingfisher), a three-engined medium bomber with a power operated single-gun dorsal turret and a ventral gun position, with provision for a further

BATTLE OF BRITAIN Z.1007BIS UNITS

SQUADRON	CODES	BASES
172a	RST	Chiévres

machine gun in each beam. The original Cant Z.1007 had first flown in March 1937, but was soon superseded by the much-improved Z.1007bis, with more powerful engines and twin endplate fins to allow the defensive armament a better arc of fire. The Cant Z.1007bis aircraft of the 172a Squadriglia Ricognnizione Strategica Terrestre were attached to the 43° Stormo Bombardamento (operating BR.20Ms) at Chievres. With a maximum speed of 289 mph and a ceiling of 26,900 ft, the ungainly Cant was an impressive performer by Italian standards, but carried only a modest 2200 kg bombload, and so was a natural choice as a reconnaissance aircraft.

FIAT BR20

Specifications: Crew: 5 Max Speed: 430km/h (267mph) Range: 1240km (770.5 miles) Armament: 4 7.7mm (0.303in) machine guns   **Italy**

Mussolini cleverly took Italy into the war days before the Fall of France, winning himself a cheap share in the German victory. Some have attributed Italy's late and rather limited showing in the Battle of Britain to a similar motivation.

In fact the Corpo Aereo Italiano dispatched to Belgium to participate in the Battle was never intended as more than a token, a gesture of solidarity with the Germans. Formed on 10 September, the Corpo moved to its Belgian bases in late September, coming under the command of Luftflotte 2. It was intended as a fully-autonomous, self-supporting group with a core bomber force having its own escort fighters and reconnaissance support. The bomber force around which the Corpo Aereo Italiano was

formed consisted of eight squadrons of Fiat BR.20Ms, totalling almost 80 aircraft. The BR.20M was an improved version of the original BR.20 Cigogna (Italy's first all-metal bomber), with a new, aerodynamically improved and lengthened fuselage, modified wings and revised defensive armament. The basic BR.20 was combat-proven in Spain and had replaced the ageing Savoia Marchetti SM.81 in service, along with the famous SM.79. It had flown for the first time on 10 February 1936. By the time Italy entered the war, replacement by the improved BR.20M was well underway, and both versions took part in operations against French targets in early June. Some of the new BR.20Ms were newly built, while others were produced through conversion of existing BR.20s.

BATTLE OF BRITAIN BR20 UNITS

13° Stormo Bombardamento			43° Stormo Bombardamento		
SQUADRON	CODES	BASES	SQUADRON	CODES	BASES
172a	RST	Chiévres	98° Gruupo		
1a	BR.20M	Melsbroek	240a	BR.20M	Chiévres
3a	BR.20M	Melsbroek	241a	BR.20M	Chiévres
4a	BR.20M	Melsbroek	99° Gruupo		
5a	BR.20M	Melsbroek	242a	BR.20M	Chiévres
			243a	BR.20M	Chiévres

Several BR.20Ms were lost during the long flight to Belgium, falling victim to bad weather, and the ill-preparedness of Italian aircrew for such conditions. The type began flying operations on 25 October, with a 16-aircraft night attack on Harwich. One aircraft crashed on take-off and two aircraft were abandoned when their crews became lost on the return journey. Fifteen BR.20Ms, escorted by about 70 CR.42s, made an abortive daylight raid on Ramsgate on 29 October. Further attacks included a daylight raid on Ramsgate on 11 November (after the official end of the Battle) in which five of the ten attacking BR.20Ms were shot down, along with several of their 40 CR.42 escorts. Despite instrument flying training by the Luftwaffe, the BR.20Ms were withdrawn from the air offensive in January and returned to Italy, having lost about one quarter of their original strength.

FIAT CR.42 FALCO

Specifications: Crew: 1 Max Speed: 430km/h (267mph) Range: 775km (482 miles) Armament: 2 12.7mm (0.5in) machine guns   **Italy**

Although of biplane configuration the CR.42 was a remarkably fast and agile fighter, and one derived from the CR.32 which had gained an enviable combat record in Spain. First flown in 1939, the CR.42 was used in action in the brief fighting against France in early June 1940, proving remarkably effective against monoplane Bloch and Dewoitine fighters of the Armée de l'Air.

The aircraft was a natural choice for the Corpo Aereo Italiano, although the RAF's Hurricanes and Spitfires would prove to be a very different proposition than any of the Falco's previous opponents. The Corpo's BR.20M bombers were generally escorted by large numbers of CR.42s when they made daylight raids, and the CR.42s suffered heavy casualties. The Italian pilots fought with courage and skill, but were simply out-classed, and were withdrawn

BATTLE OF BRITAIN CR.42 UNITS

56° Stormo Caccia
18° Gruupo CT (attached from 3° Stormo)

SQUADRON	CODES	BASES
83a	CR.42	Meldegem
85a	CR.42	Meldegem
95a	CR.42	Meldegem

from Belgium in February 1941. The type went on to fight in North Africa, where it gained some successes, and proved superior to the British Gladiator in many respects.

FIAT G.50

Specifications: Crew: 1 Max Speed: 472km/h (293mph) Range: 670km (416 miles) Armament: 2 12.7mm (0.5in) machine guns   **Italy**

Rather more modern than the biplane CR.42, the G.50 was still essentially an obsolete design, with an open cockpit and poor performance. Had the G.50s been committed to escorting daylight attacks, they would probably have suffered heavier losses than the marginally slower but rather more agile CR.42s. As it was, the G.50s were used primarily at night, and for air defence purposes along the coast of Brittany. They were finally withdrawn back to Italy in April 1941.

RAF SQUADRONS AND ACES OF THE BATTLE OF BRITAIN

The twelve-aircraft (18 pilot) squadron has always been the basic organisational component of the Royal Air Force, and during the Battle of Britain it was also the standard tactical fighting unit. Squadrons were based together in Wings, but except in the case of No.12 Group, these Wings rarely flew together as cohesive units. RAF fighter squadrons were themselves further divided into two Flights (usually 'A' and 'B') each Flight consisting of two three-aircraft sections. The Battle of Britain saw a rapid evolution in tactics, and a switch from the three aircraft 'vic' to a two-aircraft 'pair' as the smallest fighting unit, a switch which sometimes dispensed with the six-aircraft section too.

The victory tallies of individual pilots are here given for the period from 1 July to 31 October 1940, and combine wartime claims with information researched by Shores and Williams for their definitive book *Aces High*. The most reliable figures for squadron tallies cover a slightly longer period, from July to November. The various locations of the squadrons during the Battle of Britain, unless otherwise stated, here indicate British air bases or regions.

Note: the abbreviation 'KIFA' stands for 'Killed in Flying Accident'

No. 1 (FIGHTER) SQUADRON
Nantes (France), Tangmere, Northolt, Wittering

P/O G.E. Goodman	4 kills, + 3 shared	KIA 1941

No. 3 SQUADRON
France, Kenley, Wick

No. 17 SQUADRON
France, Tangmere, Debden, Martlesham Heath

NO. 19 SQUADRON

No.19 was the RAF's first Spitfire unit, and thus it fielded highly experienced Spitfire pilots for the Battle of Britain, even though it had been split in two to form No.66 Squadron, while other pilots were detached to pass their knowledge on to new RAF units. Between June and September, No.19 had some cannon-armed Mk IBs, but unreliable cannon installation resulted in frequent jams and stoppages. New Spitfire Mk IIAs were received in September. Although based within No.12 Group at Duxford and Fowlmere for most of the Battle, No.19 Squadron was never as prone to over-claiming as were some No.12 Group squadrons, even though a detachment to Eastchurch gave the unit more scoring opportunities than many. Thus its score of 68½ between June and November probably represented something close to the truth, and the unit should probably be ranked higher than 18th place. No.19 was led by Squadron Leader Pinkham between May and September, and then by B.J. Lane, DFC (Distinguished Flying Cross), who gained four kills during the Battle, adding to four scored in June. The unit's Spitfires wore the code letters 'QV-'.

F/O Count Manfred Czernin	7 kills, + 4 shared	
Sgt G. Griffiths	5 kills, + 1 shared	
F/L A.W.A. 'Alfie' Bayne	5 kills, + 6 shared	

No. 19 SQUADRON
Duxford, Fowlmere, Eastchurch (detachment)

F/Sgt George 'Grumpy' Unwin	9 kills	
F/O L.A. Haines	6 kills, + 2 shared,	KIA 1941
Sub Lt A.G. Blake	6 kills, + 1 shared	
F/L W. Clouston	4 kills, + 2 shared	

No. 23 SQUADRON
Wittering, Collyweston, Ford

No. 25 SQUADRON
Martlesham Heath, North Weald

No. 29 SQUADRON
Wellingore, Digby

No. 32 SQUADRON
Biggin Hill, Gravesend, Manston, Wittering

F/L Mike 'Red Knight' Crossley	13 kills, + 2 shared	
Sgt R.T. Llewellyn	10 kills, + 1 shared	
P/O Karol Pniak	5 kills, + 1 shared	
F/L P.M. Brothers	8 kills + 2 kills with No.257 Sqn	
P/O A.R.H. Barton	5 kills, + 3 shared	KIFA 1943
P/O B.A. Wlasowilski	5 kills	
P/O R.F. Smythe	4 or 5 kills	
P/O A.F. 'Shag' Eckford	4 kills	
P/O P.M. Gardner	4 kills	
Sgt W.B. Higgins	4 kills	

No. 41 (FIGHTER) SQUADRON
Catterick, Hornchurch

P/O Eric Lock	21 kills	
P/O George Bennions	11 kills	
F/O J.T.Webster	9 kills, + 1 shared	KIA 5/9/40
P/O J.N. McKenzie	6 kills	
F/L J.G. Boyle	5 kills, + 2 shared	KIA 28/9/40
F/O Edgar Ryder	5 kills, + 1 shared	
F/O A.D.J. Lovell	5 kills, + 1 shared	KIFA 1945

No. 43 (CHINA-BRITISH) SQUADRON
Tangmere, Usworth

Sgt Herbert Hallowes	11 kills, + 1 shared	
F/O H.C. Upton	10 kills, + 1 shared	
F/L T.F. Dalton-Morgan	7 kills, + 2 shared	
P/O C.A. 'Wombat' Woods-Scawen	7 kills	KIA 2/9/40
P/O Frank 'Chota' Carey	5 kills	KIA 1944
S/L J.V.C. Badger	8 kills, + 2 shared	
	Died of wounds, June 1941	

No. 46 (UGANDA) SQUADRON
HMS Glorious, Stapleford

F/L A.C. Rabagliati	6 kills	KIA 1943

NO. 41 (FIGHTER) SQUADRON

An early 'expansion-period' unit, No.41 (F) Squadron briefly operated Hawker Furies before receiving its Spitfires which would wear the codes 'EB-'. Moving from Catterick to Hornchurch on 26 July 1940, it rapidly won a fearsome reputation, eclipsing many older units. It moved back to Catterick on 8 August, and back to Hornchurch again on 3 September, remaining there for the rest of the battle. No.41 Squadron gained an impressive record, its tally of 92²/₅ ranking it sixth in the league table, and a number of high-scoring pilots served with the squadron during the Battle. The unit was led by Squadron Leader H.R.L. Hood until September, and then by Squadron Leader Findlay and then by Squadron Leader Gaunce. George Bennions joined No.41 (F) as a Sergeant Pilot on Hawker Furies, and was commissioned in April 1940. He scored all of his victories in the Battle, and was wounded twice, losing an eye the second time and then being limited to day flying only.

NO. 54 SQUADRON

Rochford, Hornchurch, Catterick

P/O Colin Gray (NZ)	15 kills, + 1 shared	
F/O Al Deere	6 kills	
P/O D.G. Gribble	5 kills, + 1 shared	
F/O D.A.P. MacMullen	4 kills, + 2 shared	
	+ 5 kills + 2 shared with No. 222 Sqn	

NO. 56 (PUNJAB) SQUADRON

France, Digby, North Weald, Boscombe Down

Sgt F.W.Higginson	9 kills	
F/O P.S. Percy Weaver	7 kills, + 2 shared	KIA 31/8/40
P/O E.J. 'Jumbo' Gracie	5 kills, + 2 shared	KIA 1944

NO. 64 SQUADRON

Church Fenton, Kenley, Leconfield, Biggin Hill, Coltishall

S/L A.R.D. MacDonnell	8 kills, + 1 shared	
Sub Lt F. Dawson Paul	7 kills, + 1 shared	KIA July 1940
F/L J. 'Orange' O'Meara	8 kills, + 2 shared	

NO. 65 (EAST INDIA) SQUADRON

Hornchurch, Northolt, Turnhouse

Sgt W.H. Franklin	8 kills	
	KIA December 1940	

NO. 66 SQUADRON

Coltishall, Kenley, Gravesend, West Malling

P/O Bobby Oxspring	8 kills, + 1 shared	
P/O C.A.W. 'Bogle' Bodie	7 kills, + 3 shared	KIFA 1942

NO. 72 (BASUTOLAND) SQUADRON

Gravesend, Acklington, Biggin Hill, Leconfield, Coltishall

F/L J.W.Villa	8 kills, + 3 shared	
	+ 2 kills, + 1 shared with No. 92 Sqn	
Sgt W.T.E. Rolls	7 kills	
P/O T.A.F. 'Jimmie' Elsdon	6 kills	

NO. 73 SQUADRON

France, Church Fenton, Castle Camps

P/O J.E. Storrar	5 kills, + 3 shared	

NO. 74 (TRINIDAD) SQUADRON

Hornchurch, Rochford, Wittering, Kirton on Lindsey, Coltishall

F/O H.M. Stephen	9? kills, + 1 shared	
P/O J.C. Freeborn	7 kills, + 1 shared	
F/O J.C. Mungo-Park	7 kills	KIFA 1941
F/O A.G. Malan	6 kills, + 1 shared	
P/O P.C.F. Stevenson	5 kills, + 1 shared	KIA 1943
F/O W.H. Nelson	5 kills	KIA 1/11/40
F/L Henryk 'Sneezy' Szczesny	3 kills	

NO. 79 (MADRAS PRESIDENCY) SQUADRON

France, Biggin Hill, Digby, Hawkinge

P/O W.H. Millington	8 kills, + 1 kill, + 2 shared with No. 249 Sqn	
		KIA 30/10/40

NO. 85 SQUADRON

France, Debden, Croydon, Church Fenton

Sgt G. 'Sammy' Allard	9 kills, + 3 shared	
S/L Peter Townsend	6 kills	
F/O P.P. Woods-Scawen	5 kills, + 2 shared	KIA 1/9/40
P/O W.H. 'Ace' Hodgson	5 kills, + 2 shared	KIFA 1943
Sgt H.N. Howes	4 kills, + 1 shared	
P/O A.G. Lewis (S.African)	1 kill + 8 kills, + 1 shared with No.249 Sqn	

NO. 74 (TRINIDAD) SQUADRON

No.74 Squadron spent the early part of the war shuttling between Hornchurch and its satellite base at Rochford, gaining some Spitfire IIAs in June 1940, and beginning the Battle of Britain at Hornchurch. The squadron moved to Wittering for one week from 14 August, then to Kirton on Lindsey, and, on 9 September, to Coltishall. It returned to No.11 Group on 15 October, taking station at Biggin Hill. No.74's most famous pilot was Adolf Malan, a South African former merchant seaman who became a Flight Commander on No.74 in 1938. Malan officially scored only six confirmed kills during the Battle (adding to eight confirmed kills before it), but was credited with four more enemy aircraft damaged, plus one unconfirmed and two probables. After the Battle his score eventually reached 32 kills – making him the RAF's top-scorer until overtaken by Johnnie Johnson. It was also his practise to 'give' kills to young wingmen to encourage them and increase their confidence, making it likely that his real score was significantly higher. Malan took command of No.74 from F.L. White in August 1940. No.74 Squadron pilots were extremely punctilious in their claims, and most pilots had a higher proportion of probable and damaged claims than on other units. The squadron's tally between June and November of 86 kills should be viewed in this light, as does its relatively modest ranking at No.8 in the list of Battle of Britain fighter units. Its aircraft wore 'ZP-' codes.

NO. 85 SQUADRON

Allocated to the BEF's Air Component, No.85 Squadron returned to the UK from France with only four surviving aircraft on 23 May 1940. After re-equipping at Debden, the squadron moved to Croydon on 19 August, but following heavy losses, it effectively retired to Church Fenton in early September, but began training in the night-fighter role. Its aircraft wore 'VY-' codes, and usually the white hexagon marking which had been used during the Great War. The unit scored 59 confirmed kills during the period June–November, and was led throughout the Battle by the charismatic Peter Townsend. Two of No.85's most prominent pilots were 'Sammy' Allard and Albert Lewis. Allard had been a Sergeant Pilot with No.85 Squadron when war broke out, and he scored two confirmed (and several unconfirmed) kills in France before becoming a prolific scorer in the Battle of Britain (although only one kill was with No.85 Squadron). South African Albert Lewis was one of the Battle's greatest fighter pilots, a fact he demonstrated in May by becoming the first RAF pilot to score five kills in one day. After losing eight pilots in five days, No.85 Squadron was withdrawn from the fray in early September. Allard, with 19 kills, was rested, though his rival, Lewis (with seven kills in France and two in the Battle of Britain), moved on to No.249 Squadron and on 27 September, downed three Bf 109s, two Bf 110s and a Ju 88 in the course of four sorties.

NO. 87 (UNITED PROVINCES) SQUADRON
France, Debden, Church Fenton, Exeter, Colerne

P/O W.D. David	5 kills, + 1 shared	
	+ 1 kill with No.213 Sqn	
P/O D.T. Jay	5 kills, + 1 shared	KIA 24/10/40
P/O J.R. Cock	5 kills	
F/O I.R. 'Widge' Gleed	5 kills	KIA 1943

NO. 92 (EAST INDIA) SQUADRON
Northolt, Pembrey, Biggin Hill

P/O A.R. Wright	6 kills, + 2 shared	
F/O C.B.F. Kingcome	5 kills, + 4 shared	
F/L R.S. Tuck	4 kills, + 3 shared	
	+ 5 kills with No.257 Sqn	
F/L J.W. Villa	2 kills, + 1 shared	
	+ 8 kills, + 3 shared with No. 92 Sqn	

NO. 111 SQUADRON
Northolt, Scotland, Digby, Croydon, Debden

Sgt Thomas Wallace	6 kills, + 2 shared	
F/O S.D.P. Connors	5 kills, + 1 shared	KIA 18/8/40
Sgt W.L. Dymond	5 kills	
F/L J.M. Thompson	4 or 5 kills	

NO. 141 SQUADRON
West Malling, Biggin Hill (detachment), Prestwick

F/O H.N. Tamblyn	1 kill	
	+ 4 kills, + 1 shared with No.242 Sqn	
	KIA 1941	

NO. 145 SQUADRON
Tangmere, Westhampnett, Drem and Dyce

F/L A.H. Boyd	6 kills, + 4 shared
F/O R.G. Dutton	7 kills, + 3 shared
F/O Witold Urbanowicz (Polish)	2 kills
	+ 13 kills with No.303 Sqn

NO. 151 SQUADRON
North Weald, Manston (detachment), Rochford (detachment)

F/O R.M. Milke	5 kills, + 1 shared

P/O I.S. 'Black' Smith	5 kills, + 1 shared	

NO. 152 (HYDERABAD) SQUADRON
Acklington, Warmwell

F/L D.P.A. Boitel Gill	8 kills	KIFA 1941
P/O Hon. Walter Beaumont	6 kills, + 2 shared	KIA 23/9/40
P/O E.S. 'Boy' Marrs	5 kills, + 2 shared	KIA 1941

NO. 213 SQUADRON
France, Manston, Biggin Hill, Tangmere

F/O J.E.J. Sing	7 kills, + 2 shared	
P/O H.D. Atkinson	6 kills	
P/O J.E.P. Laricheliere	6 kills	
P/O J.A.L. Philipport	6 kills	KIA 25/8/40

NO. 92 (EAST INDIA) SQUADRON

With 317½ kills scored during the War, No.92 was probably the RAF's most successful wartime fighter squadron, an achievement whose foundations lay in the unit's performance in the dark days of 1940. With an astonishing 94⅖ kills, the unit was ranked fourth among Battle of Britain fighter units, despite its late arrival in the No.11 Group area. Formed from a nucleus provided by No.601 Squadron, No.92 Squadron swapped unwieldy Blenheims for Spitfires in March 1940, moving to Northolt in May from where it participated in the slaughter over Dunkirk. Withdrawn to Pembrey on 9 June, No.92 Squadron re-joined the fight on 8 September 1940 at Biggin Hill, where it remained for the rest of the Battle. Squadron Leader P.J. Sanders led the unit until September, when A.M. MacLachlan took over. The squadron had relatively few pilots who scored five kills during the Battle itself, but several pilots opened their scores with No.92 before continuing their successes after the Battle or with other units. Sergeant Don Kingaby, who gained the distinction of being the only recipient of two bars to a DFM (Distinguished Flying Medal), began his scoring (including 3 kills) during the Battle of Britain with No.266 Squadron, but gained his honours and most of his kills with No.92, eventually gaining a reputation as a '109 specialist' and downing prodigious numbers of Messerschmitts. No.92 Squadron was allocated the code letters 'QJ-'.

Sgt E.G. Snowdon	5 kills	
F/O J.M. Strickland	5 kills, +1 shared	KIFA 1941
P/O W.D. David	1 kill	
	+ 5 kills, + 1 shared with No.87 Sqn	

No. 219 Squadron
Catterick, Redhill

No. 222 Squadron
Digby, Hornchurch, Kirton on Lindsey

Sgt E. Scott	5 kills	
F/O D.A.P. MacMullen	5 kills, +2 shared	
	+ 4 kills, +2 shared with No.54 Sqn	
P/O T.A. Tim Vigors	4 kills, +2 shared	

No. 229 Squadron
Wittering

No. 232 Squadron
Sumburgh, Castletown

No. 234 Squadron
Church Fenton, St Eval, Middle Wallop

P/O P.C. Hughes (Australian)	13 kills, + 4 shared
P/O R.F.T. Doe	11 kills, + 2 shared
	+ 3 later kills with No.238 Sqn
Sgt A.S. Harker	7 kills, + 2 shared
Sgt M.C.B. Boddington	5 kills, + 1 shared

No. 235 Squadron
Detling, Thorney Island, Bircham Newton

No. 236 Squadron
Thorney Island, St Eval

No. 238 Squadron
Tangmere, Middle Wallop, St Eval, Chilbolton

P/O J.R. Urwin-Mann	8 kills, + 2 shared	
F/O D.P. Hughes	5 kills,	KIA 11/9/40
P/O C.T. Davis	4 kills, + 6 shared	KIFA 1941
P/O R.F.T. Doe	3 kills	
	+ 11 kills, +2 shared with No.234 Sqn	
F/L M.L. Robinson	2 kills	
	+ 2 kills, + 1 shared with No.601 Sqn,	
	+ 2 kills with No.609 Sqn	

No. 242 (Canadian) Squadron

S/L Douglas Bader	11 kills	
P/O W.L. MacKnight	6 kills, + 2 shared	
Sub Lt R.J. Cork	5 kills	
F/O H.N. Tamblyn	4 kills + 1 shared	
	+ 1 with No.141 Sqn	KIA 1941

No. 245 (Northern Rhodesia) Squadron
Scotland, Northern Ireland, Hawkhinge (detachment)

No. 247 (China British) Squadron
St Eval, Roborough

NO. 242 (CANADIAN) SQUADRON

No-one could deny the aggressive spirit of the Duxford Wing squadrons, and particularly of Douglas Bader's 'own' No.242 Squadron. Unfortunately, however, even the most sketchy research casts the veracity of the Wing's claims into doubt, and the tallies of squadrons and individual pilots are, at best, somewhat inflated. No.242's claimed 'bag' of 68½ kills (placing it above No.s 19, 17, 72 and 54 Squadrons, at 16th equal on the list) should be seen in this light. Bader himself remains a controversial figure. Invalided out of the RAF in 1933 after losing both legs in an accident, he re-joined when war broke out, flying briefly with No.19, then as a Flight Commander with No.222. Charismatic and cocky, Bader's style alone helped him rebuild a demoralised No.242 Squadron into a unit with superb morale. But Bader was also argumentative and boastful, and is still blamed by many for the downfall of Dowding and Park. Kill claims apart, Bader told a good story, claiming, for example, that he collided with a Bf 109 after shooting down another, when in fact he was shot down by one of JG 26's youngest and most inexperienced pilots! He was then the Tangmere Wing leader, and his total score had at this point reached 20 confirmed kills, plus four shared and six probables. No.242 Squadron's Hurri-canes wore 'LE-' codes, and most also wore an unofficial squadron marking, with a jack-booted Hitler being booted by a British-looking foot!

No. 248 Squadron
Sumburgh

No. 249 (Gold Coast) Squadron
Church Fenton, Leconfield, Boscombe Down, North Weald

P/O T.F. Neil	8 kills, + 4 shared	
P/O A.G. Lewis (S.African)	8 kills, + 1 shared	
	+ 1 kill with No.85 Sqn	
F/O R.G. Barclay	5 kills	
Sgt J.M.B. Beard	5 kills	
P/O J.R.B. Meaker	7 kills, +2 shared	KIA 27/9/40
P/O W.H. Millington	1 kill, + 2 shared	
	+ 8 kills with No.79 Sqn	
		KIA 30/10/40
P/O K.T. Lofts	1 kill, + 2 shared adding to	
	3 kills, + 2 shared with No.615	

No. 253 (Hyderabad) Squadron
France, North England, Kenley

S/L G.R.Edge	11 kills

No. 257 (Burma) Squadron
Hendon, Debden, Martlesham Heath, North Weald

F/L R.S.Tuck	5 kills
	+ 4 kills, + 3 shared with No.92 Sqn
F/L P.M. Brothers	2 kills
	had scored 8 kills with No.32 Sqn

No. 263 Squadron
Scotland

NO. 310 (CZECH) SQUADRON

No.310 Squadron was actually the first RAF squadron to form manned mainly by foreign nationals, doing so at Duxford on 10 July, three days before the creation of the first Polish units. The squadron's first action, on 26 August, saw the destruction of a Bf 110, though three Hurricanes were lost (fortunately not their pilots). Under the command of Squadron Leader G.D.M. Blackwood, No.310 joined the Duxford 'Big Wing' on operations in September. Although No.310 Squadron was one of the Duxford units, it may have been less prone to over-claiming than some No.12 Group units. Its Czech pilots were (like the Poles) more interested in shooting down Germans than in talking about it, and it was fortunate in having noteably good RAF Flight Commanders. Some pilots had gained many successes with the Armée de l'Air, like P/O A. Vasatko who had gained four kills (and eleven shared) with the French. Between June and November, the unit accounted for 40 enemy aircraft (37 of them by the end of October), giving it a No.32 ranking. The squadron disbanded in 1946.

NO. 264 (MADRAS PRESIDENCY) SQUADRON
Duxford, Horsham St Faith, Martlesham Heath

F/O E.G. Barwell	(1) + 5 during May*

NO. 266 (RHODESIA) SQUADRON
Wittering, Collyweston, Eastchurch, Hornchurch

NO. 302 (POZNAN) SQUADRON
Leconfield, Duxford, Northolt

F/L S.J. Chalupa	1 kill (+ others in Poland and France)
F/O W.S. Krol	1 kill (+ others in Poland and France)

NO. 303 (KOSCIUSZKO) SQUADRON
Northolt

Sgt Josef Frantisek (Czech)	17 kills	KIA 8/10/40
F/L Witold Urbanowicz (Polish)	13 kills + 2 kills with No.145 Sqn	
F/O Z.K. Henneberg	8 kills, +1 shared	
PO J.E.L. Zumbach	8 kills	
Sgt E. Szapoznikow	8 kills	
P/O M. Feric	7 kills	KIFA 1942
F/L Athol Forbes	7 kills	
Sgt S. Karubin	6 kills	
F/O L.W. Paszkiewicz	6 kills	KIA 27/9/40
S/L R.G. Kellett	5 kills	
P/O W. Lokuciewski	4 kills, + 1 shared (+ others in Poland and France)	
F/L J.A. Kent	4 kills	
F/O M. Pisarek	4 kills (+ others in Poland)	

NO. 310 (CZECH) SQUADRON
Duxford

P/O E.T. Fechtner	6 kills, + 4 shared	KIFA 29/10/40
F/O Gordon Sinclair	10 kills	

NO. 312 (CZECH) SQUADRON
Duxford

NO. 501 (COUNTY OF GLOUCESTER) SQUADRON
Croydon, Middle Wallop, Gravesend, Kenley

Sgt J.H. 'Ginger' Lacey	18 kills
P/O J.A.A. Gibson	8 kills
Sgt Anton Glowacki	8 kills
P/O S. Skalski	7 kills (+ 6 in Poland)
Sgt K.W. MacKenzie	6 kills, + 3 shared
Sgt P.C.P Farnes	6 kills

S/L H.A.V. Hogan	5 kills, + 3 shared
F/L E. Holden	4 kills, + 1 shared

NO. 504 (COUNTY OF NOTTINGHAM) SQUADRON
France, Debden, Wick, Hendon, Castletown, Catterick, Filton

NO. 600 (CITY OF LONDON) SQUADRON
Manston, Hornchurch, Dedhill, Catterick

NO. 601 (COUNTY OF LONDON) SQUADRON
Tangmere, Debden, Exeter

P/O J.K.U.B. McGrath	15? kills	
F/O Carl Davis (US)	9 kills, + 1 shared	KIA 6/9/40
P/O Thomas Grier	8 kills, + 5 shared	KIA 1941
P/O H.C. Mayers	7 kills	
F/O W.P. Clyde	6 kills, + 2 shared	
F/O W.H. Rhodes-Moorhouse	5 kills, + 4 shared	KIA 6/9/40
Sgt L.N. Guy	3 kills, + 2 shared	KIA 18/8/40
F/L M.L. Robinson	2 kills, + 1 shared + 4 with Sqns 238 & 609 later	

NO. 602 (CITY OF GLASGOW) SQUADRON
Drem, Westhampnett

Sgt A. MacDowell	11 kills, + 2 shared	
F/L R.F.Boyd	9 kills, + 6 shared	
Sgt B.E.P. Whall	6 kills, + 3 shared	KIA 7/10/40
F/L A.V.R. Johnstone	6 kills, + 2 shared	
Sgt Cyril Babbage	6 kills	
F/O P.C. Webb	6 kills	

NO. 603 (CITY OF EDINBURGH) SQUADRON
Turnhouse, Hornchurch

F/O B.J.G. Carbury (NZ)	15 kills, + 1 shared	
P/O R. 'Ras' Berry	8 kills, + 3 shared	
F/O B.G. 'Stapme' Stapleton	5 kills, + 2 shared	
F/L H.K. MacDonald	5 kills	KIA 28/9/40
P/O Richard Hillary	5 kills	KIFA 1943

NO. 604 (COUNTY OF MIDDLESEX) SQUADRON
Northolt, Manston, Gravesend, Middle Wallop

NO. 605 (COUNTY OF WARWICK) SQUADRON
Scotland, Hawkhinge, Croydon

F/L Archie McKellar	17 kills, + 1 shared
P/O Bunny Currant	9 kills, + 5 shared

NO. 501 (COUNTY OF GLOUCESTER) SQUADRON

Despite having fought throughout the Battle of France with the AASF, No.501 Squadron remained in, or immediately adjacent to, No.11 Group for the duration of the Battle, not being sent north (or west) for rest or to reform. As a result, the squadron set a Hurricane squadron record of 35 days on which it engaged the enemy (the next best, only 24 days, was achieved by No.238 Sqn). It also remained under a single Commanding Officer, Squadron Leader H.A.V. Hogan. This unique combination of stable leadership and hard-won experience made No.501 a particularly capable unit, with 93 kills scored between June and November (plus thirty scored in France), making the unit the second most successful Hurricane unit and the fifth-highest scoring squadron overall (behind Sqns 303, 602, 603 and 92). While Sgt J.H. 'Ginger' Lacey took the headlines, the unit produced 11 Hurricane aces. These statistics were not without cost, however, and No.501 Squadron lost 43 of its 'SD-' coded Hurricanes during the Battle – unfortunately another record. No.501 Squadron moved from Croydon to Middle Wallop on 4 July, and to Gravesend on 25 July. It finally moved to Kenley on 10 September.

Sgt H.N. Howes	4 kills +4 with No.85 Sqn	
	KIA December 1940	

NO. 607 (COUNTY OF DURHAM) SQUADRON
France, Usworth, Tangmere, Turnhouse

P/O P.A. Burnell-Phillips	5 kills, + 1 shared	KIFA 1941
F/L J.M. Bazin	2 kills (+ 1 damaged, 1 probable, + 2 in France)	
	DFC citation says 10 kills	

NO. 609 (WEST RIDING) SQUADRON
Scotland, Northolt, Middle Wallop, Warmwell

F/L J.C. Dundas	11 kills, + 3 shared	
F/L J.H.G. McArthur	8 kills	
F/L J. Curchin	7 kills, + 3 shared	
Sgt A.N. Feary	5 kills, + 1 shared	KIA 7/10/40
F/O D.M. Crook	5 kills, + 3 shared	
F/O F.J. Howell	5 kills, + 3 shared	
P/O M.E. Staples	5 kills, +1 shared	KIA 9/11/40
F/L M.L. Robinson	2 kills + 4 kills + 1 shared earlier with Sqns 601 & 238	

NO. 610 (COUNTY OF CHESTER) SQUADRON
Prestwick, Biggin Hill, Gravesend, Acklington

F/O J. Ellis	8 kills, + 1 shared
Sgt R.F. Hamlyn	8 kills, + 1 shared
P/O C.O.J. Pegge	7 kills
P/O S.C. Norris	6 kills, + 1 shared

NO. 611 (WEST LANCASHIRE) SQUADRON
Digby, detachments to Martlesham Heath, Ternhill and North Coates

NO. 615 (COUNTY OF SURREY) SQUADRON
France, Kenley, Manston, Prestwick

F/O Tony Eyre	6 kills, + 2 shared	
F/O L.M. Gaunce	4 kills, + 1 shared	KIA 1941
P/O K.T. Lofts	3 kills, + 2 shared	
	+ 1 kill, + 2 shared with No.249 Sqn	

NO. 616 (SOUTH YORKSHIRE) SQUADRON
Leconfield, Rochford, Kenley, Coltishall, Kirton on Lindsey

F/L D.E. Gillam	8 kills	
Sgt James Hopewell	5 kills	KIFA 1942

No.1 (RCAF) SQUADRON
Middle Wallop, Croydon, Northolt, Scotland

F/L G.R. McGregor	5 kills
S/L E.A. MacNab	4 kills, + 1 shared

No.421 FLIGHT
Gravesend, West Malling, Biggin Hill

No.422 FLIGHT
Shoreham

FIGHTER INTERCEPTION UNIT
Tangmere, Shoreham, Ford

NO. 804 SQUADRON
HMS *Glorious*, Scotland

NO. 808 SQUADRON
Worthy Down

LUFTWAFFE SINGLE-SEAT FIGHTER UNITS AND ACES OF THE BATTLE OF BRITAIN

The standard organisational unit of the Luftwaffe was the Geschwader, which in turn consisted of three Gruppen, each of which would typically be based at a separate aerodrome. Gruppen were numbered using Roman numerals, and themselves consisted of three 12-aircraft Staffelen, which were numbered using conventional Arabic numerals. III./JG 2, for instance was the third Gruppe of Jagdgeschwader 2, while 3./JG 2 was the third Staffel of Jagdgeschwader 2. Each Geschwader thus consisted of nine 12-aircraft squadrons, and this meant that the Luftwaffe effectively out-numbered the RAF in fighter numbers in the operational area. A single Staffel would seldom operate autonomously, with the Gruppe being the normal formation deployed during the Battle of Britain. With elements of nine Bf 109-equipped Jagdgeschwaders deployed for the Battle of Britain (plus three Zerstörergruppen equipped with Bf 110s), the Luftwaffe had more than 90 Staffelen facing No.11 Group's 21 or so squadrons, plus the 14 in No.12 Group, 12 in No.13 Group and nine in No.10 Group (a total of 56 squadrons).

The tallies of individual pilots are given here only when confirmed by study of official unit victory listings during the period of the Battle of Britain itself. Even these totals should be treated with extreme caution, since relatively few claimed kills match up with British losses, and it seems that over-claiming was rife throughout the Jagdwaffe during the Battle of Britain. This was partly as a result of the confusion of air combat, with many pilots claiming the same victim, and was the natural result of a system in which medals, promotion and prestige were all closely linked to a fighter pilot's kill rate. It has sometimes been claimed that the criteria used by the Luftwaffe for confirming kills were exceptionally strict, and ensured some link between ambition and reality, though during the Battle of Britain it seems as though these criteria were largely set aside. It was virtually impossible to confirm a kill through wreckage (most of which fell on Britain or in the Channel) or by ground-based observers, and inevitably some pilots were less rigorous than others in how they interpreted seeing a Spitfire trailing smoke as it left the fight. The lists of pilots with each unit should thus be treated as prominent pilots, rather than Battle of Britain aces, except where a Battle of Britain score is indicated.

JAGDGESCHWADER 2 'RICHTHOFEN'

Beaumont le Roger, Le Havre

Rank/name	Unit	BoB kills	WWII Total
Oberst von Bülow-Bothkamp	JG 2		
Major Wolfgang Schellman	JG 2 & JG 27		
Helmut Wick	I/JG 2		56
Oblt Rudi Pflanz	I/JG 2		52
Siegfried Schnell	II/JG 2		93
Egon Mayer	JG 2		102
Siegfried Lemke	JG 2		96
Werner Machold	I/JG 2		
Kurt Bühligen	JG 2		112
Georg-Peter Eder	JG 2, 1, 26,		78

JAGDGESCHWADER 2 'RICHTHOFEN'

JG 2 was the Luftwaffe's senior fighter unit, and carried on the traditions of the Great War Richthofen Wing. Its pilots wore embroidered 'Richthofen' cuff bands on their uniforms, and most of the unit's aircraft carried the red 'R' on a white shield. By August 1940, JG 2 was based at Beaumont le Roger, apart from Erich Mix's III Gruppe, which was at Le Havre. The Geschwader occupied a sumptuous looking villa, though this was so infested with rats that Assi Hahn slept with a loaded revolver below his pillow! The 'aerodrome', which had previously been standing wheat, was rolled flat to allow operations by the unit's Bf 109s. The last (fifth) victim of Göring's ill-tempered purge of his fighter leaders was JG 2's Commanding Officer, Oberst Harry von Bülow-Bothkamp. The Colonel was a distinguished old fighter pilot, a former commander of Jasta Boelcke in World War One with six kills clocked up in that war. He was replaced by Major Wolfgang Schellman (formerly the Gruppenkommandeur of II./JG 2) on 3 September, though Schellman was himself replaced by Helmut Wick on 20 October. Wick was destined to be shot down himself (by Flt Lt John Dundas, of No.609 Squadron) on 28 November.

JAGDGESCHWADER 3 'UDET'

Wierre au Bois, Grandvilliers, Samer, Desvres, Le Touquet

Rank/name	Unit	BoB kills	WWII Total
Oberst Carl Vieck	JG 3		
Hpt Gunther Lützow	Stab JG 3	8	
Oblt Lothar Keller	1./JG 3	5	
Lt Helmut Meckel	2./JG 3	9	
Oblt Franz von Werra	Stab II./JG 3	4	
Oblt Erwin Neuerburg	7./JG 3	11	
Oblt Willy Stange	8./JG 3	7	
Fw Hans Stechmann	9./JG 3	6+	
Lt Helmut Mertens	9./JG 3	4	
Walter Dahl	JG 3		128

JAGDGESCHWADER 26 'SCHLAGETER'

Audembert, Marquise Est, Caffiers

Rank/name	Unit	BoB kills	WWII Total
Adolf Galland	JG 26 & III./JG 26	36	104
Major Gotthardt Handrick	JG 26		
Oblt Horton	Stab/JG 26	7	
Hptm Rolf Pingel	GK I./JG 26	6	22 + 4 Spain
	KIA 10/7/41		
Oblt Henrici	1./JG 26	5	
Joachim Müncheberg	II./JG 26	13	135
Gerhard Schopfel	III./JG 26	16	
Heinz Ebeling	III./JG 26	13?	18
Gustav Sprick	III./JG 26	12	
Lt Joseph Bürschgen	7./JG 26	8	10
Oblt W. Schneider	SK 6./JG 26	7	

JAGDGESCHWADER 27

Cherbourg West, Plumetôt, Crépon, Arcques

Rank/name	Unit	BoB kills	WWII Total
Oberst Max Ibel	JG 27		
Major Bernhard Woldenga	JG 27 & JG 77		
Major Wolfgang Schellman	JG 2 & JG 27		
Oblt Ludwig Franzisket	1./JG 27	5	
Oblt Erbo Graf von Kageneck	2./JG 27	9	
Hptm Max Dobislav	3./JG 27	7	
Lt Wilhelm Weisinger	Stab II./JG 27	6	
Hptm Wolfgang Lippert	Stab II./JG 27	4	
Oblt Gustav Rödel	4./JG 27	10	
Oblt Ferdinand Vögl	4./JG 27	5	
Oblt Ernst Düllberg	5./JG 27	5	
Fw Schramm	7./JG 27	6	

JAGDGESCHWADER 51

Pas de Calais, Wissant, Pihen, Marquie Ouest, St Omer-Clairmarais

Rank/name	Unit	BoB kills	WWII Total
Oberst Theo Osterkamp	JG 51 & Jafu Kanal		
Ufz Heinz 'Pritzl' Bär	JG 51	13	220
Hermann-Friedrich Joppien	I./JG 51		
Hans Hahn	II./JG 51		
Josef 'Pips' Priller	II./JG 51, JG 26		101
Horst Tietzen	II./JG 51		
Walter Oesau	III./JG 51		123
Arnold Lignitz	III./JG 51	19?	

JAGDGESCHWADER 51

While most of the Jagdwaffe recuperated in Germany following the fall of France, JG 51 moved to Pas de Calais, just a short distance from the RAF, or the 'Lords' as JG 51's leader always referred to them. The Geschwader Stab settled at Wissant, with I Gruppe moving in to Pihen near Calais, II Gruppe (formerly I./JG 71) into Marquise Ouest, and III Gruppe (formerly I./JG 20) to St Omer-Clairmarais. For most of July, JG 51 (also parenting I./JG 77) provided the Luftwaffe bombers engaged in the Kanalkampf with virtually their sole fighter protection, apart from the hopeless Bf 110 'Ironsides'. JG 51's veteran Geschwaderkommodore, Oberst Theo Osterkamp, was replaced by Major Werner Mölders on 23 July 1940, though after Mölders was wounded (by No.74 Squadron's 'Sailor' Malan) on 28 July, Osterkamp continued to lead his unit while his replacement recuperated. Osterkamp escaped Göring's purge of commanders in the fortnight following the failure of Adlertag. JG 52 had some true veterans. Onkel Theo, for example, had been a distinguished fighter pilot during the Great War, having earned the Pour Le Mérite with 32 kills, while rising to command Marinejagdstaffel 2. He scored his sixth kill of the second war on 13 July. I Gruppe played little part in the Battle until mid-August, and III Gruppe was withdrawn to Jever for the whole of September. Only II Gruppe remained in action for the whole of the Battle.

JAGDGESCHWADER 52

Coquelles, Peuplinges, Zerbst (Germany)

Rank/name	Unit	BoB kills	WWII Total
Major Merhart von Bernegg	JG 52		
Major Hans Trübenach	JG 52		

JAGDGESCHWADER 53 'PIK AS'

Cherbourg, Rennes, Guernsey, Dinan, Arcques, near Le Touquet

Rank/name	Unit	BoB kills	WWII Total
Oberstlt von Cramon-Taubadel	JG 53		
Hptm Hans Karl Mayer	1./JG 53	21	30
Lt Schultz	1./JG 53	11	
Lt Zeis	1./JG 53	8	
Uffz Kopperschläger	1./JG 53	6	
Uffz Ghesla	1./JG 53	5	
Uffz Rühl	1./JG 53	5	
Hptm Gunther von Maltzahn	II/JG 53	10	
Oblt Michaelski	II/ JG 53	6	
Olt Schulze-Blanck	4./JG 53	5	
Hptm Heinz Bretnütz	6./JG 53	18	
Hptm Wilhelm Balthasar	Stab III/JG 53	6	
Hptm Harder	III/JG 53		11?
Hptm Hans 'Vader' von Hahn	8./JG 53 & Stab I/JG 2	5	108
Lt Eric Schmidt	9./JG 53	17	
Joseph Würmheller	JG 53, JG 2		102
Herbert Rollwage	JG 53		102
Werner Mölders	JG 53, 51	25?	115

JAGDGESCHWADER 54 'GRÜNHERZ'

Campagne les Guines, Hermelingen, Guines South, Forêt de Guines

Rank/name	Unit	BoB kills	WWII Total
Major Martin Mettig	JG 54		
Major Hannes Trautloft	JG 54		
Hans Philipp	II./JG 54		
Dietrich Hrabak	II./JG 54	16?	
Hans Ekkehard Bob	III./JG 54	19?	

JAGDGESCHWADER 77

Germany, North Sea coast, Scandanavia, Pas de Calais

Rank/name	Unit	BoB kills	WWII Total
Oberst von Manteuffel	JG 77		
Major Bernhard Woldenga	JG 27 & JG 77		
Olt Hahn	2./JG 77	6	
Anton Hackl	JG 77		192

LEHRGESCHWADER 2

Calais-Marck, Böblingen

Rank/name	Unit	BoB kills	WWII Total
Fhr Hans Joachim Marseille	1./LG 2	7	158
Fw Pohland	1./LG 2	4	
Olt Herbert Ihlefeld	2./LG 2	24	130
Ofw Schott	2./LG 2	7	
Ofw Staege	2./LG 2	6	

JAGDGESCHWADER 53 'PIK AS'

JG 53 was an elite unit within the Luftwaffe, packed with an astonishing number of former Condor Legion veterans and aces. The unit began the Battle of Britain headquartered at Cherbourg, with I Gruppe at Rennes and Guernsey, and II Gruppe at Dinan and Guernsey, with III Gruppe (formerly I Gruppe, Jagdgeschwader 1) at Arcques. The Geschwader was transferred to Luftflotte 2 on 25 August and moved further north, closer to Le Touquet. JG 53's original Battle of Britain commander was the aristocratic Oberstleutnant Hans-Jürgen von Cramon-Taubadl. He survived Göring's August reshuffles, but was finally replaced by Major Günther von Maltzahn (former Gruppenkommandeur of II./JG 53) on 30 September. He was removed because he had married a non-Aryan and his commitment to National Socialism was suspect, and von Cramon-Taubadl was the only Battle of Britain Geschwader commander not to be promoted or decorated after relinquishing his command. Herman Göring had earlier ordered the Geschwader to overpaint its distinctive 'Ace of Spades' insignia with a simple red band around the cowling, and this 'punishment' was maintained until the CO's removal. In response, the Gruppenkommandeur of III./JG 53 (Hauptmann Wilcke) ordered the swastika fin badge to be over-painted on the aircraft of his Gruppe. The Geschwader Stab accounted for two of the unit's Battle of Britain kills, I./JG 53 for 98 kills, II./JG 53 for 70 kills, and III./JG 53 for 88 kills

INDEX